PRAISE FOR

Ten Tomatoes That Changed The World

"This spirit of curiosity proves an asset to TEN TOMATOES THAT CHANGED THE WORLD—the writer's reactions and discoveries often seem to be simultaneous with those of the reader. Mr. Alexander holds forth with the goofy charm of a high school math teacher—just swap out the trapezoid jokes for tomato puns—keeping his lessons droll, not dull...I don't know if even the most delicious summer tomato can explain our place on the planet. But knowing more about its improbable history makes every bite that much sweeter."   —*Wall Street Journal*

"William Alexander takes readers on a world tour through history, from the tomato's regional origins in Mexico to its ubiquity in the present day. Alexander's playful sense of humor—perhaps best described as 'dad jokes about vegetables'—makes TEN TOMATOES a delight to read."   —*Bookpage*, starred review

"One of the most delightful history books of the season...By the time you finish his book, you'll marvel at how much [Alexander] managed to squeeze into three hundred pages."   —*Air Mail*

"From the man who grew us *The $64 Tomato*, William Alexander is back in the garden...as well as in pizzerias in Naples (Italy), a ketchup factory, the local Pizza Hut, large-scale tomato farms in Naples (Florida), and the farmers markets where heirloom tomatoes are having their day in the sun, again. TEN TOMATOES THAT CHANGED THE WORLD is a fascinating and funny tell-all tale of how ten tomatoes are shaping our lives in unusual, unexpected, and (in some cases) very delicious directions."
—David Lebovitz, author of
Drinking French and *My Paris Kitchen*

"William Alexander has written an entertaining, broad-ranging history of the tomato, in a conversational, humorous style that uses tomatoes to explore history—from the Aztecs to Italian cuisine and pizza—along with the introduction of fascinating characters, issues such as climate change and hydroponics, heirloom mania, and the search for flavor in a world of GMOs and factory farming."
—Mark Pendergrast, author of *Uncommon Grounds*
and *For God, Country, and Coca-Cola*

"William Alexander is a delightful guide on this whirlwind tour of the tomato's influence on global cuisine and culture. His trademark blend of history, botany, memoir, and travelogue make TEN TOMATOES THAT CHANGED THE WORLD a captivating—and appetizing—read for gardeners and cooks alike."
—Amy Stewart, *New York Times*
bestselling author of *The Drunken Botanist*

"A thrilling history...Alexander's narrative delivers a story that's as informative as it is funny and filled with awe...Food lovers will savor every bit."
—*Publishers Weekly*

"Written in a lighthearted style, this engaging book includes historical photos and illustrations, and is packed with fascinating factoids. This is the type of book where readers will find themselves spouting historical tidbits to everyone in their orbit... A fun book that both instructs and entertains on every page."

—Library Journal

"Culinary history buffs will revel in the myriad anecdotes Alexander unearths here." *—Booklist*

"An engaging look at the humble fruit... Eccentric, informative, and thoroughly enjoyable." *—Kirkus* Reviews

"This witty firsthand narrative transcends its topic, niche, and season while tackling that nagging question we all want answered: Why do winter tomatoes taste so awful?" *—AudioFile Magazine*

"Engaging and immersive." *—Edible Inland Northwest*

"[Readers will] learn lots of history, and the author has a sardonic tone that leavens the tale with a lot of humor." *—Daily Kos*

Also by William Alexander

Flirting with French: How a Language Charmed Me,
Seduced Me, and Nearly Broke My Heart

52 Loaves: A Half-Baked Adventure

The $64 Tomato: How One Man Nearly Lost His Sanity,
Spent a Fortune, and Endured an Existential Crisis in the
Quest for the Perfect Garden

Ten Tomatoes

THAT CHANGED THE WORLD

A History

WILLIAM ALEXANDER

**GRAND
CENTRAL**

NEW YORK   BOSTON

Grand Central Publishing
Hachette Book Group
1290 Avenue of the Americas, New York, NY 10104
grandcentralpublishing.com
twitter.com/grandcentralpub

Originally published in hardcover and ebook by Grand Central Publishing in June 2022.
First Trade Edition: June 2023

Grand Central Publishing is a division of Hachette Book Group, Inc.
The Grand Central Publishing name and logo is a trademark of Hachette Book Group, Inc.

The publisher is not responsible for websites (or their content) that are not owned
by the publisher.

The Hachette Speakers Bureau provides a wide range of authors for speaking events.
To find out more, go to
hachettespeakersbureau.com or email HachetteSpeakers@hbgusa.com.

Grand Central Publishing books may be purchased in bulk for business, educational, or
promotional use. For information, please contact your local bookseller or the Hachette
Book Group Special Markets Department at special.markets@hbgusa.com.

Library of Congress Cataloging-in-Publication Data
Names: Alexander, William, 1953- author.
Title: Ten tomatoes that changed the world : a history / William Alexander.
Description: First edition. | New York : Grand Central Publishing, 2022. | Includes
bibliographical references. | Summary: "The tomato gets no respect. Never has. Lost
in the dustbin of history for centuries, accused of being vile and poisonous, subjected
to being picked hard-green and gassed, even used as a projectile, the poor tomato has
become the avatar for our disaffection with industrial foods - while becoming the
most popular vegetable in America (and, in fact, the world). Each summer, tomato
festivals crop up across the country; the Heinz ketchup bottle, instantly recognizable,
has earned a spot in the Smithsonian; and now the tomato is redefining the very nature
of farming, moving from fields into climate-controlled mega-greenhouses. Supported
by meticulous research and told in a lively, accessible voice, Ten Tomatoes That
Changed the World seamlessly weaves travel, history, humor, and a little adventure
(and misadventure) to follow the tomato's trail through history. A fascinating story
complete with heroes, con artists, conquistadors, and-no surprise-the Mafia, this book
is a mouth-watering, informative, and entertaining guide to the food that has captured
our hearts for generations"— Provided by publisher.
Identifiers: LCCN 2021053701 | ISBN 9781538753323 (hardcover) |
ISBN 9781538753316 (ebook)
Subjects: LCSH: Tomatoes—History. | Cooking (Tomatoes)
Classification: LCC SB349 .A268 2022 | DDC 635/.642—dc23/eng/20220119
LC record available at https://lccn.loc.gov/2021053701

ISBNs: 9781538753330 (trade pbk.), 9781538753316 (ebook)

Printed in the United States of America

LSC-C

Printing 1, 2023

For Anne

CONTENTS

PREFACE: MORE PRECIOUS THAN GOLD

Tenochtitlán, Mexico. July 1, 1520.

The Spanish conquistador Hernando Cortés had miscalculated, badly. Having massacred and connived his way into the Aztec island capital of Tenochtitlán seven months earlier, he and his small army were in desperate straits. Montezuma, both his protector and his prisoner, was dead, struck by a stone hurled by his furious subjects, who now turned their rage on the invaders. Outnumbered, cut off from the mainland, and under siege, the conquistador saw but one hope of saving the lives of his 250 men. Should he fail, the dead soldiers would be the fortunate ones; the unlucky captives could look forward to having their still-beating hearts ripped out of their chests.

Packing up all the stolen treasure they could carry, the Spaniards staged a desperate midnight escape, using portable bridges constructed in secret to span the breached causeways. The heavy load of gold proved unwieldy, however, winding up at the bottom of Lake Texcoco, an incalculable loss of wealth the likes of which the world had never seen. But Cortés would escape, regroup, and reconquer—with a vengeance. Within fourteen months, this once-thriving civilization would be in ruins, having fallen victim to Spanish aggression, germs, and their insatiable lust for silver and gold. But the true treasure of Mexico, one that in the end would have an impact comparable to that of all the precious metals in the New World, would soon find its way on a ship to Europe, to forever change the course of history.

I'm speaking, of course, of the tomato.

Ten Tomatoes

THAT CHANGED
THE WORLD

One

DE' MEDICI'S POMODORO

A Strange Foreign Vegetable Is Given a Name, Then Forgotten

Pisa, Italy. All Hallows' Eve, 1548.

The Grand Duke of Tuscany, Cosimo de' Medici, descended the long staircase of the Palazzo Vecchio after receiving word from his steward that a basket had arrived from the duke's country estate outside of Florence. As the household gathered round to witness the introduction of a strange vegetable from the New World, it would seem that tomatoes were about to be introduced to Italy by the famous and influential Cosimo de' Medici, and really, could you think of a better person? A free-spending patron of the arts and sciences who had just financed Pisa's first botanical garden, the grand duke, in public life since the age of seventeen, was an amateur botanist with a special interest in New World plants, as was apparent from the rows of maize that greeted surprised visitors to Villa di Castello, one of his numerous Tuscan estates. And he had a Spanish wife, Eleonora di Toledo, whose family in Spain had access to the many botanical specimens arriving from the Americas.

Now Cosimo had his hands on tomatoes, destined not only to become almost synonymous with Italy, but on a course to influence the cuisine of the entire world, from American ketchup to Indian tikka masala. Surely an epic moment! What would follow next? The birth of pizza and spaghetti? A dinner invitation to Michelangelo? The dramatic moment is recorded by the steward in reverent, almost biblical tones: "And the basket was opened and they looked at one another with much thoughtfulness."

What they said next was not recorded, but I suspect they looked to the heavens and thought, *What the* fanculo*???*

Given that the following day was All Saints' Day, a traditional feast day, one wonders if the tomatoes might have been intended for that use. But no tomatoes were served for dinner. Not that day, nor the next. Nor the year after, nor the decade after. Nor even the *century* after. In fact, the vegetable that is so closely associated with Italian food that one would be forgiven for assuming (as I confess I once did) that it's a native plant of Italy would not secure its place in Italian cuisine for another *three hundred years*.

Still, the event is historic, as it represents the first documented instance of the tomato's arrival in Italy. And when the steward sends a polite note back to the estate that the basket arrived safely, he gives, for the first time anywhere in Europe, a name to these strange imports from the New World—*pomodoro*.

As for the latest strange New World import to drop in at the Palazzo Vecchio, it's clear that the current occupants can't quite figure out what to make of me either, or why I've come all the way from

America to visit what now serves as a *prefettura*, the government headquarters for the province of Pisa. The palace where dukes and duchesses (and on at least one occasion, tomatoes) once gathered is now an office where you might come to get a fishing license or pay your tax bill. The magnificent baronial chambers of Cosimo de' Medici have been converted into workplaces with metal desks and filing cabinets; the crystal chandeliers have been replaced by harsh fluorescent lighting; and most disappointingly of all, no one here is the least bit aware of the botanical significance of the former palazzo (although they seem cheerfully willing to take my word for it).

Granted, I didn't expect a plaque commemorating tomatoes—perhaps if Cosimo had only *done something* with them—and there are arguably one or two sites of greater historical significance in Pisa, including a certain lopsided tower, but still, I feel a little let down. The secretary who is acting as my guide must notice my crestfallen gaze at the Office Depot decor. "If we kept all the historic buildings as they were," she explains, "we would have no place to live and work. This is Italy."

Fair enough, and I suppose the situation is more than balanced by the fact that Cosimo built Florence's Uffizi, today one of the most magnificent art galleries in the world, as—you'll never guess—*administrative office space*. So, it works both ways. Although that's small comfort at the moment, because after months of working through Italian bureaucracy, a language barrier, and, not least, a global pandemic to arrange this pilgrimage (in retrospect, I should've just said I wanted to do a little fishing in Italy), it seems that I've come four thousand miles to see a roomful of copying machines.

Leaving the dreary offices, the secretary takes me across a courtyard into what she says is an unrestored wing of the palazzo, where the *prefetto*, the regional administrative official, lives on the second and third floors, his staircase guarded by an impressive carved lion's head on the balustrade. I'm led through a doorway, and— *What the* fanculo*???*

We're in Cosimo's old kitchen, dominated by a long wooden table that runs nearly the full length. Indoor plumbing has been added and the appliances have been updated (the *prefetto* has his own residential kitchen upstairs; this one is used for receptions and the like), but, I'm told, the kitchen is mostly unchanged from Cosimo's day. Airy and spacious, it has room for easily a half dozen cooks, but what catches my eye is the stunning blue-and-white sixteenth-century tiled floor that *extends up the walls*, meaning, I note with some envy, that after a messy meal the kitchen could be simply mopped from floor to ceiling.

A pair of windows framed by heavy wooden shutters provide abundant natural light, and the room has direct access to the main road and the Arno river, which is literally across the street. This access is critical, the secretary tells me, because the kitchen is where all palace deliveries, whether by land or sea, would have been received. "Wait, so this would be—" Yes, she confirms, smiling, before I can finish. This is certainly where the de' Medici household would've gathered to greet the mysterious basket of fruits from another civilization.

Just not where they would've cooked them.

What were Cosimo's tomatoes like? His steward maddeningly leaves out any description, but I'm hoping I can get at least an idea by heading across town to the cathedral. This requires passing through the umbra of an almost unnaturally white tower that, to my eye at least, is leaning so precariously that it seems ready to come toppling to the ground like a stack of poker chips should a tour group all stand on the same side after climbing to the top.

You can climb the Leaning Tower of Pisa? I'm shocked—you'd think that this priceless landmark, already around (and listing to the south) for 149 years when Cosimo shrugged off his tomatoes, would be off-limits to anyone not named Quasimodo. And, while we're on the topic, future tower builders take note: *Pisa* is Greek for "marshy land." Maybe next time consider constructing a massive tower in a city whose name means "bedrock."

The tower, although the main attraction of the neighborhood today, was an afterthought, a bell tower built later to accompany the adjacent cathedral, which upon its completion in 1118 was the largest and most magnificent in Europe. The current doors, however, are "recent," cast in 1600 after a fire destroyed the original ones. The three sets of massive, elaborately decorated bronze portals consist of panels of Old and New Testament scenes framed by friezes of both local and exotic flora and fauna: cucumbers, pea pods, apples, nuts, squirrels, turtles. There is even a rhinoceros, which was the emblem of Cosimo's cousin and predecessor as Duke of Florence, Alessandro de' Medici, whose assassination by his best friend in 1537 thrust the teenage Cosimo into power.

And, if you look closely, there, on the lower left side of the far-right door, frozen in time, is what is unmistakably a tomato. Although it's not the kind of tomato typically seen today. It's segmented—ribbed, or furrowed, like an acorn squash, into six sections. The smooth, spherical tomato would not make its debut for another two hundred years, although I've noticed that these ribbed ones are still favored in Pisa markets.

The frieze on the doors of the Pisa Cathedral includes a sixteenth-century tomato. (Photo by the author.)

The cathedral doors were built in the workshop of the Flemish sculptor Giambologna, an inaugural member of the Accademia delle Arti del Disegno, the prestigious art academy founded by Cosimo de' Medici in 1563. Cosimo again! In fact, he knew Giambologna well, although any intriguing notion of a connection between Cosimo's tomatoes and Giambologna's is dashed by the fact that the grand duke predeceased the casting of the doors by a quarter century, dying at the age of fifty-four. Still, the fact that a tomato is represented (two, actually) tells us that the *pomodoro* was alive and well in Italy in 1600. It just wasn't being eaten.

Yet other edible plants brought over from the New World were quickly embraced. Maize was ground into polenta; beans were simmered in soups and stews; all of Europe would soon be smoking up a tobacco-fueled storm; and the potato would even make its way to far-flung Ireland, where it would become, with disastrous consequences, a staple among the peasantry. *All before Italians started eating tomatoes.* What took so long?

I put that question to Giulia Marinelli, a guide at the Museo del Pomodoro, the world's only museum dedicated to the tomato, located a couple of hours north of Pisa, in the Emilia-Romagna region of Italy.

"It was considered for many years a decorative plant," she says, grown as curiosities in botanical gardens. "Although there was a Franciscan who, even in the sixteenth century, understood that the Mexican people ate those fruits, both cooked or turned to sauces, and also raw."

That would be the Spaniard Bernardino de Sahagún, who went to Mexico as a missionary in 1529, on the heels of the Conquest. I don't know how long he'd planned to stay, but probably less than the sixty-one years—the rest of his life—it wound up being. Bernardino was captivated by Aztec culture, even by what remained of Tenochtitlán, a city that Cortés had found "so wondrous it was not to be believed." Before the conquistador left it a smoldering ruin, the island city, crisscrossed by canals filled with small boats and canoes, had been connected to the mainland by five causeways and boasted parks, gardens, plazas, and—well before Europe even had the concept—zoos. Tenochtitlán (the site of present-day Mexico City) was perhaps the largest, cleanest, and most prosperous city in the world, with its jewelers turning out delicate and intricate works that rivaled the artistry of the finest craftsmen of Renaissance Europe.

The sophistication of Aztec civilization extended to its agriculture, much of which took place in *chinampas*, floating farms. Constructed by weaving reeds into stakes planted in a rectangular grid arrangement in shallow lake beds, then filling in the underwater boxes with organic materials (including human waste), these aquaponic farms, totaling 2.3 million acres, grew maize, chile peppers, squash, beans, and a round red or yellow vegetable that the Aztecs called *xitomatl*.

A native of the coastal highlands of Peru and Ecuador, where the pea-sized fruits were apparently neither particularly appreciated nor cultivated, tomatoes had been domesticated in Mexico for at least a thousand years before the Spanish arrived. The Aztecs used them to flavor soups and stews, fried them with peppers, or chopped them up fresh with chiles and herbs to make what the Spanish described as a *salsa* (which simply means "sauce") to accompany meats and fish—as well as the occasional human, as an Aztec victory banquet often featured the flesh of the vanquished. One conquistador reported detecting the disconcerting aroma of bubbling tomatoes from the enemy camp on the eve of battle, speculating that *he* was the missing ingredient, which might be the first recipe of sorts that we have for a Spanish tomato stew.

In Tenochtitlán, Bernardino de Sahagún found an abundance and variety of tomatoes that would put many a twenty-first-century American farmers' market to shame:

The tomato seller sells large tomatoes, small tomatoes, green tomatoes, leaf tomatoes, thin tomatoes, sweet tomatoes, large serpent tomatoes, nipple-shaped tomatoes. Also he sells coyote tomatoes, sand tomatoes, and those which are yellow, very yellow, quite yellow, red, very red, quite ruddy, ruddy, bright red, reddish, rosy dawn colored.

But be careful who you buy from, he warns, because the "bad seller sells spoiled tomatoes, bruised tomatoes, and those which cause diarrhea." (Some things never change.)

The Franciscan has been called "the first anthropologist" because of his original work in pioneering methodical strategies for studying an indigenous culture, including valuing elders and women as sources, learning the native Nahuatl language, and writing history from an indigenous worldview. His work culminated in his twenty-four-hundred-page groundbreaking study of Aztec culture, *General History of the Things of New Spain.*

Bernardino sent periodic drafts of his detailed study of Aztec culture (and diet) back to Spain and the Vatican, continuing his research right up until his death in 1590. His descriptions should've settled any questions about the edibility of tomatoes. "However," Giulia explains, "the manuscript was not published until 1829," having been suppressed by the church for being, let's say, a tad too sympathetic toward the heathens whom Bernardino had been sent over to convert to Western religion and culture— not the other way around. And the last thing the Spanish monarchy wanted published was an account of the Conquest told from the *indigenous* point of view. "So, three hundred years," Giulia says, with a slight sigh.

Yet the book's earlier publication might not have made much of a difference to the tomato's early fortunes. Other Spanish missionaries and naturalists documented the use of tomatoes in Mexico as well, but tomatoes were more challenging than inviting: They're inedible when green, go from ripe to rotten in no time, fall apart when cooked, and have a consistency and flavor that resembled nothing in the European diet. Not to mention the fact that tomatoes had to compete for the public's attention with the dozens of exciting new foods coming over from the Americas almost by the week—some 127 botanical species in all—and, let's face it, tomatoes, much as we love 'em, aren't exactly chocolate.

Just when did tomatoes arrive in Europe? We can pinpoint many events of the Conquest down to the hour, but historians haven't been able to determine even the decade that tomatoes made landfall, because the Castilian tax collectors at the Port of Seville who collected the *quinto real*—the royal fifth—logged every last coin, necklace, and silver plate that came off the galleons, but couldn't have been less interested in plants, never mind seeds. (Future historians of this century will have it easier, being able to study, for example, the May 2018 attempted smuggling of a single slice of tomato into the United States, thanks to the airport sandwich that has resulted in my being flagged by US Homeland Security as an "agricultural violator," I suppose for life. And it was a lousy tomato, besides.)

When the tomato started to circulate throughout Italy, Giulia says, it was so foreign that Italians weren't even sure which part of the plant was meant to be eaten. Some gourmands pronounced it inedible after munching on the leaves. And, Giulia adds, "It was considered poisonous by many." (The leaves, in large quantities, are.) Certainly, being in the nightshade family did the tomato no favors, for its fellow nightshade, belladonna, is one of the most toxic plants on the planet, having killed off more popes, cardinals, and Roman emperors than syphilis. Belladonna's toxicity belies its unthreatening name—"beautiful woman" in Italian—which comes from its former use by Italian women to dilate their pupils to an alluring size, the allure perhaps proving too great for those donna who went from *bella* to blind after repeated use.

Still, one has to wonder why—or even if—the tomato was singled out as being poisonous, while other members of the nightshade family, including some that were obviously more closely related to the tomato than belladonna—eggplant and peppers, for example—had long been part of the Italian diet. In fact, the tomato was sometimes misidentified as a new type of eggplant by sixteenth-century botanists, who therefore certainly knew it wasn't poisonous.

It wasn't until the early 1600s that tomatoes started to be eaten, likely gaining their earliest acceptance in Andalucía, the Spanish province that includes Seville, their port of entry. Records from Seville's Hospital de la Sangre show a purchase of tomatoes during the summer of 1608—but never again, suggesting that its patients weren't clamoring for more. Not surprisingly, Spanish tomatoes were first prepared in the Aztec style, sautéed in oil with chiles. Only in the nineteenth century—three hundred years after their European debut—would the Spanish add tomatoes to the already traditional gazpacho and paella.

In fact, Spain's major sixteenth-century contribution to the tomato, other than "discovering" it, may have been confusing it with the tomatillo. The Aztecs called the tomato *xitomatl* and the (distantly related) tomatillo *miltomatl*, the root for each, *tomatl*, meaning "round fruit," with prefixes to distinguish the different varieties. Unfortunately, Spanish writers of the sixteenth century picked up only the root, calling both *tomate* in Spanish, and that included Francisco Hernández, Spain's most prominent physician and naturalist.

Hernández was sent by King Philip II to Mexico in 1571 to

study the flora and fauna of the New World. Five years later he had compiled sixteen folio volumes detailing the plants and animals he found. Admirable work, although because of his loose nomenclature, his discussion of the tomato was accompanied by an illustration of the wrong *tomate*. Worse, the tomato/tomatillo error followed the vegetables to Italy (and, as you can see, nearly into English), where both vegetables became *pomodoro*, a mistake that bedevils scholars of one or the other to this day.

In Italy, when tomatoes were first consumed, it was by the wealthy, and as an exotic curiosity, much like adventurous eaters today might try fugu, the potentially deadly puffer fish, while visiting Japan. But among the vast majority of Europeans, tomatoes, even after they were recognized as an edible plant, were rarely eaten throughout the Renaissance—the main reason being, in fact, *the Renaissance*.

Oddly enough, the period of unprecedented culture and learning that pulled Europe out of the Dark Ages may have helped usher in the three-hundred-year-long dark age of the tomato. How so? Well, the spark that lit the Renaissance was the rediscovery—and fresh appreciation—of classical antiquity; that is, the culture of ancient Rome and Greece, and everything old was new again, sometimes literally: One of Michelangelo's very earliest commissions, following his teenage years as an apprentice in the court of Lorenzo de' Medici (a half cousin of sorts to our friend Cosimo), was such a convincing replica of an ancient Roman Cupid that it was scuffed up a bit and sold by an unscrupulous dealer as a freshly unearthed artifact. The forgery was soon uncovered (due to flaws in the aging, not in the artistry), but instead of ending Michelangelo's career in scandal before it ever began, his ability to replicate the classical arts established the young artist as a talented sculptor. In fact, the scammed buyer, a Roman cardinal, was so impressed that, even while decrying the forgery, he hired the forger, bringing Michelangelo to Rome. The rest, as they say, is history. The intriguing question of whether Michelangelo launched his career by *knowingly* participating in art forgery is still a matter of debate.

At the other end of his career, Michelangelo was commissioned to redesign the square in front of Rome's Capitoline Hill in order to provide a worthy setting for the only surviving equestrian statue of ancient Rome, a magnificent, larger-than-life bronze of Marcus Aurelius, who ruled the Roman Empire from AD 161 to 180. And, to come full circle, it was Marcus Aurelius' personal physician, Galen of Pergamon, who may well have squashed the Renaissance tomato.

The embrace of classicism that embodied the Renaissance was by no means restricted to art and architecture. Ancient literature, science, and medicine—such as it was—were all unearthed and scoured for clues about how to live a better life. And Renaissance Italians believed there was much to learn from Galen.

Greek by birth, Galen of Pergamon was a juggernaut of a physician: Doctors Spock, Salk, and Oz all rolled into one. After settling in Rome at the age of thirty-three, he quickly rose through the ranks of Top Docs, serving as the personal physician of several emperors and inciting enough professional jealousy among his peers (of which, in fact, he believed he had none) that he lived in constant fear of being poisoned.

Galen was more than just an ambitious self-promoter, however. A physician, scientist, and philosopher, he was the first to demonstrate (by severing the appropriate nerves of a squealing pig) that the larynx generates the voice. He was the first to recognize the differences between arterial and venous blood. He discovered the distinction between sensory and motor nerves and even performed the first successful cataract surgeries.

He wrote books on pharmacology and practiced an early form of what would come to be called "psychoanalysis." His anatomical studies—done with monkeys and pigs because dissection of human cadavers was illegal in ancient Rome—remained the standard reference works in Europe for an astounding fifteen hundred years. Without a doubt Galen possessed one of the finest minds of the Roman era. Perhaps his only flaw (other than his ego) was that he was hopelessly in the thrall of Hippocrates and the ancient Greek physician's theory of humorism, developed back in the fourth century BC.

Humorism is the study, I should note, not of comedy, but of the "humors"—internal substances thought to regulate human health and behavior. Hippocrates had identified them as blood, phlegm, yellow bile, and black bile, writing, "Health is primarily that state in which these constituent substances are in the correct proportion to each other." This doesn't sound particularly revolutionary until you understand that prior to Hippocrates, all illnesses were blamed on the gods, which is one reason why Hippocrates is considered "the father of medicine."

In the second century AD, Galen expanded upon the Hippocratic theories, drawing a connection between specific foods and humors, and between humors and personality types. If you were melancholy, it was because you had too much black bile. The sunny outlook of optimists was due to an abundance of blood. An early proponent of "You are what you eat," Galen, who might qualify as the world's first celebrity diet doctor, believed that by adjusting the diet you could alter both your health and your disposition.

Whether it's the South Beach Diet, the Atkins Diet, or Galen's Diet, dietary theory requires classifying foods, and Galen chose a simple two-way grid: hot or cold crossed with wet or dry. So, while some foods might be, say, hot and dry, others were cold and wet, or cold and dry. A hot-tempered Roman might be advised to eat foods classified as "cold" to correct the imbalance. Runny nose? Eat hot and dry foods to counteract that phlegm. Some foods, given their classification, were best avoided altogether.

During the Renaissance, Galen's fourteen-hundred-year-old writings—based on theories established *another* five hundred years earlier—were being rediscovered and reinterpreted at roughly the same time as the discovery of a cornucopia of unfamiliar New World vegetables, all of which had to then be assigned to Galen's hot/cold/wet/dry/healthy/unhealthy schema.

Tomatoes did not fare well. Relegated to the least favorable Galenic permutation—"cold and wet," like a damp basement—they were, in the opinion of botanists, "dangerous and harmful," with "perhaps the highest degree of coldnesse." A 1585 description granted that "they are cold, but not as cold as the mandrake," giving the new vegetable but a slight nod over a hallucinogenic root. Their chilly, damp nature was thought to hinder digestion, an impression likely reinforced by the tomato's acidity.

The tomato's Galenic classification was unfortunate but spot-on: Tomatoes *are* cold and wet. I'm always amazed at how a ripe tomato, picked from a sunny garden on a warm day, will feel cool—sometimes unpleasantly so—in the mouth. I imagine this stems from its high water content; tomatoes are 95 percent water, among the highest in the fruit and vegetable world.

Additionally, tomatoes were easy to classify as unhealthy because few were eager to eat them. The fruits tasted a bit sour, and the foliage, in the words of several botanists, "stunk." One of

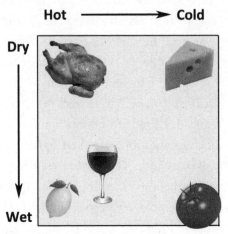

Tomatoes were considered so cold and wet in the Galenic food schema revived during the Renaissance, they're almost falling off the chart. (Illustration by the author.)

the things that has always struck me is how strongly the tomato's foliage smells like its fruits, even as three-inch-tall seedlings. I can't think of any other plant that has this quality, which chefs sometimes take advantage of by throwing a few tomato leaves into a sauce. But while tomatophiles today may cherish the smell as a harbinger of a summer BLT, the strong odor of tomato leaves (thought to be even stronger back then than it is today) seems to have offended Renaissance sensibilities. Flemish herbalist Matthias de l'Obel warned in 1581 that "the strong, stinking smell gives one sufficient notice how unhealthful and evil they are to eat," while the late sixteenth-century English botanist John Gerard thought them "rank and stinking." As late as 1731 the English *Gardeners Dictionary* noted that "the plants emit so strong an effluvium as renders them unfit to stand near an habitation, or any other place that is much frequented."

Contemporary reviews on the tomato's taste aren't much better, although there are not an abundance of them to be found. (After all, people don't write about the tastes of things they don't eat.) A physician from Padua, Giovanni Domenico Sala, writing in 1628 about the revolting consumption of locusts, spiders, and crickets by other cultures, included tomatoes among the "strange and horrible things" that "a few unwise people" were eating. Hernández, for his part, put tomatoes in his chapter on "sour and acid plants," and one "unwise person" who did eat them recommended that cooked tomatoes be sweetened—with sour grapes.

Certainly, the tomatoes of the 1600s were not nearly as pleasant to eat as today's varieties, which have profited from centuries of breeding to make them sweeter and less acidic. The Aztecs themselves preferred tomatillos (which tells you something) and rarely ate tomatoes on their own, generally seasoning them, as mentioned earlier, with chiles, spices, and the occasional bipedal captive.

Unhealthy, smelly, and strange: It's really no mystery why tomatoes were not an easy sell in Renaissance Europe. And we're not done. As if the resurrected Galen hadn't done enough damage, the reputation of this New World vegetable seems to have suffered further from another association with the good doctor, as some believed the tomato to be "Galen's wolf peach," a lost, poisonous fruit described by Galen as possessing strong-smelling yellow juice and a ribbed appearance, which is in fact a pretty accurate description of the yellow tomatoes found in Italy in the 1500s. Although debunked even by some botanists of the day, including Hernández, who pointed out that tomatoes, because they were not even introduced into Italy until the 1500s, could not possibly be Galen's wolf peach, the association stuck, and lives on today in the tomato's scientific, or Latin, name, *Solanum lycopersicum*, with the genus *lycopersicum* meaning "wolf peach."

Both the connection to Galen's wolf peach and the Tuscan Italian name for the tomato, *pomodoro*, suggest that the early tomatoes in Italy weren't always, or even predominantly, red. *Pomodoro* (originally spelled *pomo d'oro*) means "golden apple," or more properly, "golden apple-type fruit." "Golden tree fruit" is an odd name for something that clearly didn't grow on trees, but historian David Gentilcore points out that *pomo d'oro* was widely used at the time to describe all kinds of things: figs and melons, even citrus fruits. And there was a classical, mythical fruit called *pomo d'oro* that shows up in a tale involving Greek nymphs and fantastical golden apples, so rather than add another name to the lexicon, it seems that the Tuscans reached back into antiquity—and remember, there was a lot of reaching into antiquity going on back then—to label this new fruit.

Let's give the Italians some credit for correctly identifying it (at least in name) as a fruit. Admittedly, I've been mostly referring to it thus far as a "vegetable." We'll have to convene the US Supreme Court to resolve this contentious question in the next chapter, but until it gets sorted, I'll mostly call it a vegetable because I eat it in a salad, not on ice cream. But at times I'll also refer to the "fruit" of the plant when that terminology seems appropriate. *Capisci?*

As far as the vast majority of sixteenth-century Italians were concerned, of course, the *pomodoro* was neither a fruit nor a vegetable. It wasn't *food*. And while we've been focusing on Italy, because it was the country that would eventually launch the tomato to stardom, tomatoes weren't any more popular in the rest of Europe, not even arriving in England until the 1590s, when they were initially called love apples or sometimes apples of love. Similarly, the French labeled them *pommes d'amour*. (*Apple* at the time was a generic word for any fruit.)

How the English and the French came to associate tomatoes

with love is a subject of some disagreement, leaving us to choose among the fruit's alleged aphrodisiacal properties, its resemblance to a human heart, and its being put in the same botanical classification as the aforementioned mandrake ("love plant" in Hebrew), which since biblical times has been associated with fertility. Gentilcore believes that the love connection is yet another consequence of that vexing error of the tomato having been conflated with the tomatillo, for as the tomatillo's husk dries, it splits open, revealing the fruit inside, which runs from pale green to purple. The Spanish botanist Francisco Hernández found this "venereal and lascivious" appearance, evocative of a woman's genitals, "horrible and obscene," although to others, less offended, it may have screamed "love apple."

Personally, as one who has such difficulty with foreign languages that I once used my newly acquired French to tell a waiter in a three-star Parisian restaurant, "I'll have the ham in newspaper and my son will have my daughter," I think that the true explanation is much simpler: *Pomodoro* was heard by foreigners as something like *pom' amoro*—"love apple." End of story. Whatever the origin, the "love apple" moniker would stick around until the nineteenth century, when both England and France would lose the love, adopting the Spanish, not the Italian word, leaving us with, respectively, *tomato* and *tomate*, although the masculine *el tomate* transitioned on the way to France, emerging as *la tomate*. Linguistically, the tomato camp remains divided into two worlds: All of Western Europe (outside of Italy) and North Africa use a variation of the Spanish *tomate*, while derivations of *pomodoro* leapfrogged the Adriatic Sea and the Balkans to land in Poland, Russia, Ukraine, and other Eastern European countries.

Whatever you called them, tomatoes remained unpopular, unloved, and uneaten well into the 1600s. Of course, the evidence (including my last two meals here) would suggest that at some point attitudes changed. On the way into the Museum of the Tomato, I'd asked Giulia Marinelli why Italians didn't eat tomatoes for centuries. Now, on my way out, I ask her the converse: "What spurred Italians to start eating them? Was it a cultural change, or had the tomato changed?"

She thinks for a moment. "It was many things. But, you know, in America, in the early nineteenth century, they did, let's say, shows, to let people understand that the fruit was not poisonous."

No, I didn't know.

Two

COLONEL JOHNSON'S BUCKET

An "Odious and Repelling-Smelling Berry" Becomes America's Favorite Vegetable

Things had not been going much better for tomatoes in early America, where, even without the ghosts of Hippocrates and Galen bad-mouthing them, they were believed to be poisonous by some of the population and merely disliked by the rest. The *Horticulturist* labeled them "odious and repelling-smelling" berries. "An arrant humbug," the *Florida Agriculturist* concluded in 1836. *American Farmer* conceded that even though the initial taste may be disagreeable, don't worry, you get used to the unpleasantness as you keep eating the revolting things. Ralph Waldo Emerson spoke for most of his fellow New Englanders when he declared tomatoes an acquired taste, but it was Joseph T. Buckingham, editor of the *Boston Courier*, who got in the last word, in 1834 calling them

the mere fungus of an offensive plant, which one cannot touch without an immediate application of soap and water

with an infusion of *eau de cologne*, to sweeten the hand—
tomatoes, the twin-brothers to soured and putrescent
potato-balls—deliver us, O ye caterers of luxuries, ye gods
and goddesses of the science of cookery! Deliver us from
tomatoes.

Oddly, the diatribe is followed by two tomato recipes.

Despite the colonies' proximity to Mexico, the first tomatoes
likely arrived through a circuitous route involving two transatlantic trips: from Mexico to Spain, and back to America, where they
were grown in the Spanish settlements of what are today Georgia
and the Carolinas. Other tomatoes may have arrived from Spanish
possessions in the Caribbean and in the baggage of English colonists, who still called them love apples. Although, seeing as how
tomatoes were even slower to gain acceptance in England than in
Italy and Spain, remaining quite unpopular well into the 1700s,
one wonders why English settlers would have included, among
their prized possessions on this one-way journey, tomato seeds. In
any event, tomatoes' unpopularity followed them from England
into *New* England, where I've come with my wife, Anne, to see
the object of such derision: the first known representation of a
tomato in American art.

Raphaelle Peale, the eldest son of the famous portraitist Charles
Willson Peale (Raphaelle's brothers, all trained to be painters,
were named Rembrandt, Titian, and Rubens), was one of the
very first still-life artists in America, and so his *Still Life with Fruit
and Vegetables*, hanging without ceremony in a small gallery in the
Wadsworth Atheneum Museum of Art in Hartford, Connecticut,
is one of the earliest still lifes in America. And there, front and
center, is a red, ripe tomato.

Still Life with Fruit and Vegetables, *Raphaelle Peale,*
ca 1795–1810. (Wadsworth Atheneum Museum of Art,
Hartford, Connecticut.)

"Looks like a Brandywine," Anne says.

I'm about to object that this misshapen, bulbous fruit looks like
nothing of the kind when I realize that she means it looks like one
of *my* malformed Brandywine tomatoes. Point taken.

"Or maybe a red pepper," she adds, noting the ribbed, bumpy
shoulders that rise well above the stem. Now we're getting
warmer; some early art scholars have in fact mistaken it for the
wrong nightshade.

But more than anything, it bears a striking resemblance to the
tomato on the frieze framing the cathedral doors in Pisa, meaning that two hundred years after its introduction to Europe, the
tomato is still a ribbed, segmented fruit that looks very little like
the modern version. But that's not all that catches my attention.
What, I ask Erin Monroe, a curator at the museum, is a tomato
doing sharing a canvas with grapes, a peach, and three carrots, all

commonly enjoyed fruits and vegetables? Peale was a Philadel-phian, and thus unlikely to be dining on a tomato in 1795, when the wall text indicates it was painted.

"Now that's interesting," she says, flipping through some notes. "Because since we've had this painting in our collection [1942], it appears we've adjusted the date slightly. In our early findings, it was believed to have been maybe 1810 at the earliest. But I see that one of my predecessors has adjusted that to 1795."

What?! Admittedly, I don't know a Peale from a peel from a peal, but my pulse quickens at the dream of seeing my name added to the painting's wall text ("Redated by William Alexan-der to 1810 or later"). I imagine there was some biographical or other justification for moving the painting into the eighteenth century (although this predates his next surviving still life by almost twenty years), but *botanically* speaking, 1810 is more sound, because any earlier than that, the tomato's most enthusiastic con-sumer in the Northeast was the tomato hornworm.

A truly frightening creature that feasts on both fruits and foliage, this finger-sized caterpillar (one of the largest in North America) sports a menacing horn on its tail and uses its variegated green tone to hide in vegetation until—take it from me—you poke your face in close enough to pluck a tomato. Owing to its terrifying appear-ance, it had acquired a reputation of being dangerous as well. In 1838 Ralph Waldo Emerson described the worm as "an object of much terror, it being currently regarded as poisonous and impart-ing a poisonous quality to the fruit if it should chance to crawl upon it." The worm's toxic reputation continued into the 1860s, with the *Ohio Farmer* reporting that a girl "died in terrible agony" after being stung. The *Syracuse Standard*, meanwhile, wrote that it was "as poisonous as a rattlesnake" and could spew its toxic spittle two feet. In reality, the little critter is as harmless as it is revolting.

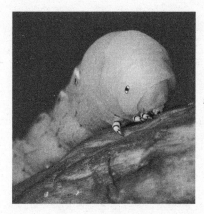

The tomato hornworm: "an object of much terror," in the words of Ralph Waldo Emerson. (Daniel Schwen / CC BY-SA-3.0.)

Southerners, who were familiar with the tomato hornworm's nicotine-addicted cousin, the tobacco hornworm, were no doubt less squeamish, and by the mid-1700s tomatoes could be found throughout the South, reaching Virginia by the early nineteenth century. Thomas Jefferson started growing—and eating—them at Monticello in 1809. The early Southern acceptance of tomatoes is often attributed to the influence of slaves (including household cooks) who'd eaten them while in the slave-trading islands of the Caribbean. Raphaelle Peale was a keen traveler, Erin Monroe tells me, and so he might have eaten tomatoes in the South (or even in Mexico or South America, where he'd also visited), which may explain how they ended up on his canvas alongside carrots and grapes.

But how did tomatoes move from Peale's palette to America's palate, from "odious and repellent" to being cultivated twelve months out of the year? One story (which has apparently made its way to the Museo del Pomodoro) celebrates a single day, September 26, 1820, when the tomato leapt from the flowerpot to the dinner plate. That's when Colonel Robert Gibbon Johnson of Salem, New Jersey, is said to have climbed to the top of the courthouse steps, where, to the horror of the crowd assembled below, he devoured an entire bucket of what I guess we have to call "Jersey tomatoes" to prove to the nation that tomatoes were not only nonpoisonous, but delicious.

To get to the bottom of the bucket—that is, to learn a little more about this courageous colonel—I've driven to Salem on the bicentennial of the courthouse demonstration to meet with members of the Salem Historical Society. We assemble, appropriately enough, at Johnson's crypt in the St. John's Episcopal Church graveyard, a block from the courthouse, in the shadow of an immense church steeple that seems as tall as the town is wide. The towering spire, however, belongs not to this church, but to the adjacent Presbyterian church, where Johnson's portrait hangs. His image suggests a man whose patience seems to be wearing thin, and, when it ran from thin to out in a quarrel with the Episcopalians, he funded the building of a Presbyterian church on adjacent property, offering a bonus of a dollar for every foot that the new Presbyterian spire rose above the Episcopalian steeple.

It would appear he got his money's worth.

Johnson, who inherited wealth and married into more, was a major landowner and avid horticulturist, the founder of the New Jersey Horticultural Society. He was also a slave holder, New Jersey being the last of the Northern states to abolish slavery.

Salem has long celebrated the colonel's exploits on the courthouse steps, inaugurating an annual Robert Gibbon Johnson Day in the 1980s, complete with costumed actors, tomato contests, tomato pies, and T-shirts featuring a tomato-headed Johnson in colonial garb, grinning from stem to stem in front of the courthouse. ABC's *Good Morning America* covered the pageant in 1988, a host ad-libbing the heretofore unknown detail that Johnson was the very first person to eat a tomato in America, which surely would have surprised Jefferson.

The annual festival petered out after a few years, but I'm expecting there might be some kind of bicentennial ceremony today—or at least a couple of tomato aficionados snapping photos. If not, I'm prepared to perform my own reenactment in front of the second-oldest active courthouse in the United States, eating tomatoes with gusto before the startled people of Salem as they climb the steps on their way to court.

Except there are no steps. After reading numerous gripping accounts of Johnson's feat, I had naively envisioned a smaller version of the US Supreme Court staircase, with Johnson standing on the top step as the throng assembled below. In reality the courthouse is but one small step above ground level, bridged by a sloping brick walkway. Moreover, the courthouse is locked, open only a couple of nights a week for parking tickets and leash violations. That means there are no passersby to whom I can proselytize for tomatoes, no one even in sight to witness my homage to Johnson.

No courthouse steps, no spectators, no bicentennial celebration. Was there even a Robert Gibbon Johnson?

There most certainly was, Curt Harker and Ron Magill, current and past presidents, respectively, of the Salem County Historical Society, tell me as we walk from the courthouse to Johnson's former home, which today serves as a Meals on Wheels center. In fact, the colonel was the first vice president of the Historical Society, founded in 1845. Because of Johnson's prominence, we actually know quite a bit about the man. Except when it comes to tomatoes. Johnson and tomatoes don't even appear in the same sentence until fifty-eight years after his death, when William Chew's 1908 *Salem County Handbook* mentions that in 1820, "Col. Robert G. Johnson brought the first tomatoes to Salem... At that time this vegetable was considered unfit for use by the masses."

Robert Gibbon Johnson (1771–1850), whose legend of introducing tomatoes to America has been both embellished and scrutinized. Portrait by George W. Conarroe, ca. 1840s. (From the Collection of the Salem County Historical Society, Salem, New Jersey.)

Then the gilding of the legend began. In a 1937 history of Salem, the town's postmaster and amateur historian, Joseph S. Sickler, repeated Chew's assertion, with the added elaboration that "Johnson patiently educated the natives as to its qualities, showing that it was edible and nutritious."

Three years after that, in his history, *The Delaware,* Harry Emerson Wildes added the courthouse to Sickler's version, writing that not until Johnson "dared to eat a prized tomato publicly on the courthouse steps would cautious South Jersey accept as edible the vegetable that is now its largest crop." (Note that his courthouse, unlike mine, has "steps"—plural.)

Nine years later, Stewart Holbrook enlivened the courthouse scene, writing in *Lost Men of American History*:

> Johnson stood on the courthouse steps in Salem and announced in stentorian tones that he would then and there eat one of the lethal things. This he did with dripping relish, while the gaping crowd waited to see him writhe, then fall frothing to the ground.

Other writers let their imaginations run further amok, adding thousands of jeering spectators, fainting women, and a specific date. Surprisingly, one of these "other writers" is none other than Joseph Sickler, who in 1948 revised his original version to incorporate—and further embellish—the colorful inventions from his protégés, which had been, of course, built from his own original account.

Sickler was by now living in New York, having been booted out of Salem for some shady business involving post office funds, and the ink was barely dry on his revised, now wildly embellished version when he turned up as a paid consultant to the CBS radio program *You Are There* for their January 30, 1949, reenactment of the historic event. We don't know whether he approached CBS or the other way around, but the program was certainly a big break for Sickler, who boasted that it gave him "national acclaim as preserver of the story." *You Are There*, it should be noted, wasn't *Drunk History*. Its broadcasts, later hosted by Walter Cronkite after the program moved to television, were considered reliable historical accounts, often covered in the following day's newspapers, so presumably the production team vetted the material before climbing the courthouse, um, step.

Sickler claimed the original story had been told to him by a man (conveniently deceased) whose grandfather, Charles J. Casper, had witnessed the event. If Sickler was reaching for a credible source, he picked the wrong one, because Casper's own son happens to have been a prominent Salem canner who penned a short history of that industry in which he wrote that "the tomato was brought to Salem, New Jersey, in 1829 by some ladies from Philadelphia." It's hard to believe that Casper would have failed to mention witnessing such a momentous event as Johnson's courthouse coup to his tomato-canning son (but *would* tell the story to the grandson who supposedly related it to Sickler).

This is by no means the last tomato legend we'll be coming across, but it has certainly been one of the most stubborn to snuff out, having appeared in such reliable publications as *Scientific American* and the *New York Times*—even in a 1993 article in the famously meticulous, fact-checking *New Yorker* magazine. Boosted by the world's recent and unprecedented ability to rapidly spread disinformation (aka the internet), the story continues to circulate with, fittingly enough, new embellishments. In one account, a fireman's band playing a funeral dirge has arrived on the scene; in another the courthouse setting has evolved into the poor tomato itself being literally put on trial; the outcome is decided in favor of the tomato only when the colonel... *eats the defendant*!

So, I ask the Salem historians, on the two hundredth anniversary of an event *that never happened*, is there any truth at all to this legend? There are no newspaper accounts of such a demonstration; Johnson's own history of Salem County, published in 1838, does not even mention tomatoes; and while it is true that RGJ sponsored agricultural fairs, records show that tomatoes were not among the crops judged. "Do we know if Johnson grew tomatoes?" I ask. "For that matter, did he even *know* about them?"

As if having anticipated my challenge, Ron Magill gingerly pulls from his briefcase an 1812 book from Johnson's library, *Archives of Useful Knowledge: A Work Devoted to Commerce, Manufacturers, Rural and Domestic Economy, Agriculture, and the Useful Arts*, signed by the colonel on two pages lest a lendee forget from whence it came. Magill opens the book to page 306, where there is a recipe for "TOMATOE, OR LOVE-APPLE CATSUP." The fact that Johnson owned a book with a tomato recipe does suggest that he (and, of course, others) knew that tomatoes were edible. That in and of itself doesn't prove anything, though, unless we also have evidence that he acted out a nineteenth-century version of *Julie & Julia* and made every recipe in the book. Yet both local historians are steadfast in their conviction that Johnson did in fact introduce tomatoes to southern New Jersey, albeit in a much less dramatic fashion, and certainly not in court. Sickler's first version—that Johnson convinced his countrymen that these foul berries were fit for consumption—was accurate, they say, and was likely based on oral histories and/or newspaper accounts. Although if there are newspaper accounts, no one has yet dug them up. But oral histories are not to be discounted, often proving surprisingly reliable.

There is some support for the Johnson legend: There's the initial 1908 account, believable for its simplicity and the fact that the colonel was an avid horticulturist—curious, progressive, and interested in new crops. And there really is no competing story. *Someone* introduced the tomato to Salem County, and Colonel Robert Gibbon Johnson seems as likely as anyone. Certainly, the timing was right, for in the following decades the tomato would rise from obscurity to ubiquity, as tomato recipes filled magazines and cookbooks; tomatoes took over the passions of gardeners and the covers of seed catalogs; and ketchup spilled onto every table in America. And Johnson's Salem County would become the largest tomato farming region in the entire United States.

Legends such as Colonel Johnson's act of derring-do on the Salem courthouse steps often arise to explain the inexplicable. Indeed, how are we otherwise to account for the tomato's startling rise from an "odious and repelling-smelling berry" to the country's most popular vegetable? It's a challenging question without wholly satisfying answers, but it seems that the tomato may owe much of its good fortune to an unlikely confluence of skilled snake oil salesmen, the tomato's sudden reputation as a health food, and a pandemic.

The 1830s were an anxious decade in America, the country having suddenly discovered "health" as well as its opposite. The Popular Health Movement, which took its cue from President Andrew Jackson's anti-elitist views (which included—tell me if this sounds familiar—a mistrust of conventional medicine and science), was in full swing. Weekly newspapers with titles like *Health Journal and Advocate of Physiological Reform* flourished, and a Boston bookstore devoted solely to health literature opened its doors. Health devotees who lived in boardinghouses dedicated to a wholesome lifestyle were fed a diet of fresh fruits and vegetables and required to bathe an unheard-of three times a week.

This sudden interest in healthy living was in part fueled by the cholera pandemic that was sweeping across Europe, having arrived in Russia in 1830, then hitching a ride into Poland and East Prussia in the guts of an invading army sent by Czar

Nicholas I. By 1831, all of Europe was in danger. A year later the sickness had reached American shores. The causes of cholera were not yet understood, nor were means of prevention, but it was sensibly assumed that good nutrition and clean livin' couldn't hurt.

While such prominent voices as Sylvester Graham (of graham cracker fame) and Amos Bronson Alcott (the father of *Little Women* author Louisa May Alcott) were preaching the benefits of vegetarianism, bathing, and abstention from sex and alcohol, an itinerant Ohio physician named John Cook Bennett was making a name for himself with the gospel of tomatoes. Bennett, who was fired from one medical school and failed at an attempt to start another, came to national prominence in 1834 after publishing a lecture he'd given his medical students on the health benefits of tomatoes. Bennett's claims that the still-unpopular vegetable would promote good health and prevent a variety of stomach and intestinal ailments were accepted uncritically by the press (if not by the medical profession) and reprinted in no fewer than two hundred American newspapers. Of particular interest to readers was his assurance that tomatoes, "the most healthy article of the Materia Alimentary," made one "much less liable to an attack of Cholera and . . . would in the majority of cases prevent it."

Thus the tomato, like Coca-Cola a few decades later, first made its way into American diets as a tonic guaranteed to cure all ills. But how was one to eat it? Recognizing that there weren't many tomato recipes in circulation, newspapers, cookbooks, and magazines followed up Bennett's speech with recipes for everything from tomato pickles to sauces and stews. There were recipes for baked tomatoes, stuffed tomatoes, scalloped tomatoes, tomato jam, tomato omelets, tomato paste, tomato pie, even tomato wine. Many of these recipes wouldn't look a bit out of place in last month's issue of *Bon Appétit*. For example, one "Italian-style" tomato sauce recipe calls for tomatoes, onions, thyme, bay leaf, allspice, and—surprising touch here—saffron.

By the end of the 1830s, tomatoes had become not only widely accepted, but de rigueur for any hostess who didn't want to appear hopelessly last-century. A London newspaperman staying at the American Hotel in Madison, Wisconsin, complained that

> tomato was the word—the theme—the song from morning till night...At breakfast we had five or six plates of the scarlet fruit pompously paraded and eagerly devoured, with hearty recommendations, by the guests. Some eat them with milk, others with vinegar and mustard, some with sugar and molasses. I essayed to follow suit, and was very near refunding the rest of my breakfast upon the table.

Imagine his horror if he knew that the grilled tomato would one day become a linchpin of the classic "English breakfast." The tomato tornado, the journalist noted with a mixture of dismay and disbelief, continued at tea and dinner, with tomato pies and patties, sun-dried tomatoes, tomato conserves, and tomatoes preserved in maple sugar.

The 1830s marked the beginning of what food historian Andrew F. Smith calls America's "great tomato mania," but even contemporary observers recognized the vegetable's remarkably rapid rise. In 1858 New York seedsman Thomas Bridgeman wrote,

> In taking retrospect of the past eighteen years, there is no vegetable in the catalogue that has obtained such popularity in so short a period...In 1828-29 it was almost detested; in ten years most every variety of pill and panacea was

extracted as tomato. It now occupies as great a surface of ground as cabbage, and is cultivated the length and breadth of the country.

Every variety of pill? Sure enough, Bennett's health claims and the tomato's rising fortunes had caught the attention of a snake oil salesman (half a century before there was snake oil) named Archibald Miles, a Brunswick, Ohio, merchant who'd been unsuccessfully peddling a product of dubious providence called American Hygiene Pills. This was just one of a number of "cure-all" patent medicines whose advertisements filled the back pages of newspapers, the most popular being calomel, a compound containing mercury and chlorine.

In 1837 Miles had a chance meeting with an unnamed physician—probably Bennett—who suggested he change the name of his medicine. Miles had new labels printed up, and Dr. Miles' Compound Extract of Tomatoes hit the market.

Advertisements crowing that "Tomato Pills Cure Your Ills" claimed that Miles' extract cured "Dyspepsia, Jaundice, Bilious Diseases, Gravel, Rheumatism, Coughs, Colds, Influenza, Catarrh, Nervous Diseases, Acid Stomachs, Glandular Swellings of all kinds, Costiveness, Colic, Headache, &c." Not to mention cholera and syphilis.

The magical ingredient was, Miles said, a concentrated extract "from the *tomato*, which [has] its peculiar effect upon the hepatic or biliary organs"—that is, the liver. In truth, its main "peculiar effect" kicked in a little lower; the pill was essentially a laxative. Marketed as a safer alternative to calomel (which it was; at least it wouldn't give you mercury poisoning), the pill was, Miles said, "undoubtedly one of the most valuable articles ever offered for public trial or inspection."

Before anyone could get around to doing that "public trial or inspection," Miles had lined up distributors from New Orleans to the Canadian border, plus an impressive list of endorsements from physicians and the press. He didn't have the market to himself for long, however. Within a year of its release, Dr. Miles' Compound Extract of Tomatoes was fighting off a contender from Connecticut, Dr. Phelps' Compound Tomato Pills.

Guy Phelps, unlike "Dr." Miles, was actually a physician, having graduated from Harvard Medical School in 1825. Phelps claimed that he had become acquainted with the medicinal properties of the tomato during his studies, but Miles was skeptical, and for good reason: The New York distributor of Dr. Miles' Compound Extract of Tomatoes was none other than the pharmaceutical firm Hoadley, Phelps, and Co., the "Phelps" being Guy's brother, George.

When Miles sent a spy to his New York distributor to buy some of his pills, the agent found that Hoadley, Phelps, and Co. strongly advised against them, telling prospective buyers they were dangerous. Instead, they recommended (surprise!) Dr. Phelps' Compound Tomato Pills. Miles was furious, and more so when, after demanding the return of any unsold pills, received precisely the amount he'd originally supplied—meaning that his New York "distributor" had not sold a single box of his pills in the largest market in the country. The feud soon got uglier than a tomato hornworm, with each side accusing the other of cheating, lying, patent infringement, and endangering the public by producing pills containing calomel or other forms of mercury.

Miles alleged that Phelps had stolen his formula, labeling him a "quack" and a "charlatan." Phelps countered by publishing a letter stating that Miles had "about as much claim to the title of doctor as my horse."

"The most safe and valuable remedy ever discovered," claims this ad for Dr. Phelps' Compound Tomato Pills. *(Burlington Free Press, December 7, 1838. Library of Congress, SN84023127.)*

Both accusations were probably the most accurate claims to ever come out of the mouth of either man. And Miles may have been on to something when he declared that his competitor's product contained no tomatoes whatsoever, noting that Phelps had sold so many pills that "all of the tomato production in Connecticut" would not have been sufficient to manufacture them all. The *Hartford Daily Current*, examining Guy Phelps' invoices in 1839, found orders for licorice, aloe, gum arabic, cinnamon, alcohol, and green and yellow pigments, but hardly any for tomatoes. Phelps in turn had Miles' pills analyzed and claimed that they contained only "aloe, rhubarb, pepper, colocynth [a plant from the gourd family with a robust purgative effect], and some essential oil."

As the mud continued to fly, dirtying both combatants, additional competitors—including Hallock's Tomato Panacea, Dr. Payne's Compound Tomato Pills, and Benjamin Brandreth's Universal Vegetable Pills—were stealing market share. Newspapers benefited handsomely from the melee, publishing tens of thousands of tomato-pill ads during the brief conflict. Brandreth alone claimed to have spent $100,000 annually in advertising, an extraordinary sum at the time.

The tomato-pill market collapsed in early 1840, the public having apparently believed both claims that the other combatant's product was bullshit—which, for all we know, they may have been, literally. The tapering off of the cholera epidemic likely also hastened the pills' demise, as did the Panic of 1837, a financial crisis that hit the northeastern states particularly hard and made health elixirs a luxury that few could afford.

Remarkably, Miles and Phelps not only survived the bruising battle, but continued to prosper afterward. Miles went on to become a successful real estate agent, and snake oil must've been in his DNA, because later in the century a relative would revive the family tradition (and name) with Dr. Miles' Restorative Nervine, using those profits to create the hugely successful Miles Laboratories, which was purchased by the pharmaceutical giant Bayer AG in 1979.

Guy Phelps continued selling various restorative medicines until he stumbled onto an even surer racket than health—death— founding the Connecticut Mutual Life Insurance Company. Phelps himself died in 1869, leaving behind a company with capital in excess of $23 million.

Bogus pills aside, how valid were the health claims for the tomato? They may not cure cholera or dyspepsia, but tomatoes are, in fact, quite healthful. An eight-ounce tomato can satisfy about 60 percent of an adult's daily requirement of vitamin C and 30 percent of your vitamin A. Tomatoes are also rich in vitamin B and iron, as well as lycopene (an antioxidant that gives tomatoes and watermelon their red color), which is thought—apologies to the much-maligned Bennett, Miles, and Phelps—to have some cancer-preventing properties. About the only downside to eating tomatoes is that their acidity can upset some sensitive stomachs, although tomatoes are being bred to be less and less acidic, a trend that began hundreds of years ago.

Even today you will find health claims for tomatoes (mostly based on their lycopene content) that would make Dr. Bennett blush, and many are from legitimate, peer-reviewed research. Tomatoes are said to be helpful in preventing or curing everything from prostate cancer to heart disease to low sperm mobility. As with tomatoes themselves, however, some of this research is best taken with a grain of salt because many of these studies use—get ready for it—concentrated tomato *extracts*, the concentrations of tomato material so high in some cases that to ingest the equivalent amounts you'd have to eat up to six tomatoes or half a can of tomato paste each and every day. Or take a pill.

Tomato pills may have fallen from grace by 1840, but the tomato—now firmly in the public's consciousness, thanks in no small part to Bennett, Miles, and Phelps—continued to win over America's hearts and stomachs. Yet it would take more than a health fad to propel the once-scorned vegetable to the top of the vegetable world. America was changing, transitioning from an agrarian society to an industrial power; from a labor force of skilled craftsmen to one of assembly-line workers, and the tomato was destined to be at the center of it. In the coming decades, tomatoes would roll onto some of the first assembly lines; be among the first foods preserved in cans and jars; introduce the concept of food branding; become processed almost beyond recognition; and go to war. The tomato would, in other words, be the story of nineteenth-century America.

Tomato production continued to soar throughout the 1800s. New Jersey, led by Salem County with its rich soil, the climate-moderating effect of the Atlantic Ocean, and its proximity to three large markets (New York, Philadelphia, and Wilmington), became the leading producer of tomatoes in the country. So many tomatoes were grown in the Northeast and the Mid-Atlantic that in August, when the crops were at their peak, market prices would fall precipitously. Edmund Morris, who began tomato farming on ten acres in Salem County in 1855, noted that while his earliest tomatoes fetched $2 a basket, the price fell to 25 cents a bushel by midsummer, a level at which farmers would leave tomatoes to rot in the fields, the costs to pick and transport them being more than the tomatoes were worth.

Thus the incentive to grow early tomatoes was substantial. Several strategies were employed, including hothouses heated with steaming manure to give the plants a head start, adding fields in the warmer states of Maryland and Virginia, and saving the seeds of tomatoes that ripened early. But farmers needed a way to profit from their midseason glut of tomatoes.

Salvation came, indirectly, in the unlikely person of Napoléon Bonaparte. In 1800 Napoléon, who is credited with famously saying that an army marches on its stomach, had put his money where his soldiers' mouths were, offering a 12,000-franc prize for an improved method of food preservation. The prize was won not by a scientist, but by a Parisian chef, Nicolas Appert, who at an 1806 exposition demonstrated his method of preservation, packing meats, fruits, vegetables—and his pièce de résistance, a whole goat—into glass bottles sealed with cork and wax, which were then dunked into simmering water, a method not wholly unfamiliar to home canners today. By the late 1820s, tomatoes were among the first foods to be bottled commercially in America, a testament not only to their growing popularity, but also to the fact that their high acidity made them less prone to spoilage.

Within ten years, an Englishman, Peter Durand, had improved upon Appert's invention, replacing fragile glass bottles with iron cans lined with tin (to reduce rusting), which was found in abundance in southwest England. Durand, however, neglected to invent one other critical accessory—the can *opener*—so, unsurprisingly, the tin can didn't catch on until 1855, when another Englishman, Robert Yates, invented the means to get into the blasted things.

That was just in time for the Civil War. During the world's first "canned" war, the Union army's canned food stores allowed it to travel with at least some of its food, rather than having to stop and commandeer supplies from the local unfriendlies. For Confederate soldiers, who had to scour the countryside for provisions other than dried goods like flour, a successful battle was often followed by a pantry raid on Union stores, after which the poorly fed Confederates eagerly supped on Northern canned meat and vegetables.

Many soldiers from both sides got their first taste of canned tomatoes during the war and, having developed a taste for them, sought them out after they'd returned home. The war proved to be a boon to both the tomato and the nascent canning industry. By 1870, a hundred canneries were producing thirty million cans of tomatoes a year, a sixfold increase over prewar figures. As impressive as that sounds, though, it amounted to less than one can per person annually, a paltry amount reflective of the limits of manufacturing.

Canning was a deliberate, dexterous process, beginning with the construction of the cans, each of which needed to be cut, rolled, and soldered by hand. Grower Edmund Morris picked up the process from there, describing a tomato cannery in southern New Jersey:

At one end of the room [are] three large boilers; and adjoining is another large boiler, in which the scalding is done. The tomatoes are first thrown into this scalder, and after remaining there a sufficient time, are thrown upon a long table, on each side of which are ten or twelve young women, who rapidly divest them of their leathery hides. The peeled tomatoes are then thrown into the boilers, where they remain until they are raised to a boiling heat, when they are rapidly poured into the cans, and these are carried to the tinmen, who with dexterity truly marvelous, place the caps upon them and solder them down.

The cans were then submerged in boiling water for four to six hours to kill off bacteria and other microorganisms. They were not airtight, however; a small hole, to be sealed later, was left in the top to vent steam, lest the cans burst. With all the sealing being done by hand, spoilage was always a risk, as was ingesting traces of the tin-lead solder.

But help was on the way for this laborious process. The widespread adaption of steam power following the Civil War, coupled with the ability of American innovators to automate seemingly any repetitive process, spurred exponential growth in tomato canning. Inventors designed belt-driven can fillers that could fill forty to sixty cans a minute and tomato scalders that loosened the skins with steam and water, facilitating peeling.

The drive to automate the canning process was motivated not only by the need to increase volume, but also the difficulty and expense in hiring and keeping skilled labor in the years following the Civil War. Cappers—the "tinmen" Morris referred to who soldered the tops onto the filled cans—were in particularly short supply, and they knew it, so cannery owners always faced the threat of strikes by cappers well aware that scabs were unlikely to be procured.

However, it was the processors—those who handled the critical step of submerging the sealed cans in boiling water to sterilize the food within—who both garnered the biggest salaries and represented the greatest barrier to expansion. In the decades following the war, processing was still a bit of a mystical art, practiced by a limited number of men who held their secrets as tightly as magicians, and who sold their services to the highest bidder. Processing required a delicate balance between cooking the food long enough to safely preserve it, but not so long as to degrade it. A mistake in one direction would lose customers; a mistake in the other would kill them; and a seasoned processor knew how to balance the two.

The processors' hold over the canning industry began to wane in the late 1870s following Andrew Shriver's invention of the steam kettle. This forerunner of the modern pressure cooker utilized pressurized steam rather than boiling water to process canned foods, taking the informed guesswork—and skill—out of the critical processing step.

The cappers were next to fall to the relentless march of automation after a Bridgeton, New Jersey, mechanic named J. D. Cox introduced a device in 1887 that could cap and solder six cans at once, eliminating, in the words of his blunt sales brochure, "the Capper who, having received his pay, required more time to sober up than his boss thought necessary." Fighting to protect their livelihoods, the workers resorted to arson and bloodshed, prompting owners, who faced death threats on almost a daily basis, to carry revolvers and hire factory guards.

Eventually, it goes without saying, technology won the day. In the last years of the century, a can with rolled seams was introduced, and the modern can was pretty much in place, although automation of the final step in canning—attaching the label—remained a surprisingly difficult challenge until the 1893 invention of the Knapp automated labeler. Labeling was a low-wage job performed mainly by women, and the automatic labeler was adopted with less resistance than the automatic capper.

These innovations transformed the canning industry, but

perhaps the most significant and enduring innovation of the era, one whose impact would be felt in virtually every factory, was the introduction of the "automatic line" that moved vegetables through the various stages of a cannery—decades before Henry Ford "invented" the assembly line for automobile manufacturing. One such system, the Triumph Platform Conveyor Peeling Table, streamlined the still largely manual task of peeling tomatoes.

*The Triumph Platform Conveyor Peeling Table introduced the assembly line to tomato processing. (*Sprague General Catalog of Canning Machinery and Supplies, *1913. Smithsonian Libraries and Archives. Image provided by John Hoenig.)*

As automation assumed more and more of the job of preserving fresh food, one might have expected that this trend would have presaged the corporate takeover of canning; yet the opposite happened, because the equipment required to go into the canning business was relatively inexpensive and widely available. And with each innovation, less skilled labor was required. Thus canning—in particular, tomato canning—became one of the great cottage industries in America, as entrepreneurs opened small seasonal and regional canneries near (or sometimes in) tomato fields. In fact, many farmers operated their own canneries as a way to dispose of their glut of tomatoes at the peak of summer.

By 1900, the number of canneries in the United States, just one hundred in 1870, had reached at least eighteen hundred, with corn, oysters, and condensed milk joining tomatoes as popular canned goods. Perhaps contributing to the legend, Colonel Johnson's own Salem County, already a bellwether in fresh tomatoes, led the nation in canned production. Charles Casper wrote in his history of canning that "1892 seems to have been the banner year for canning in Salem County," with thirty-one canneries turning out twelve million cans. The tomato industry had encouraged innovation, and innovation had transformed the tomato industry. But now another change, as American as technical ingenuity, was poised to take place from *within* the can.

Shortly after the Civil War, fifty-year-old Joseph Campbell left his job as a purchasing agent for a Philadelphia fruit and vegetable company to become a partner in a New Jersey canning firm. Located in Camden (just forty miles from Salem), the company was owned by a former tinsmith named Abraham Anderson. Campbell—yet another Jersey boy—had grown up on a fruit farm in nearby Bridgeton, the town that also produced the capping inventor J. D. Cox. In 1877 Campbell bought out his partner, retaining the copyright to one of their signature products: a "beefsteak" tomato (a term Anderson invented) so large, ads boasted, that a single one filled a can. It was just a tomato in a can, no different (other than its size) than any of the hundreds of other brands of canned tomatoes available, but with branding and heavy advertisement, Campbell marketed his Celebrated Beef-steak Tomato (as well as his Strictly Fancy Small Peas, and Fancy Asparagus) as unique products unavailable elsewhere.

The name-brand tomato had been born.

The public was unconvinced, however, and Campbell's was oozing money when Joseph sold control of the company to businessman Arthur Dorrance in 1893. Arthur's nephew, John Dorrance, who carried degrees from MIT and the University of Göttingen, joined the company four years later, and immediately picked up the tomato that Campbell had dropped, looking for a way to make Campbell's canned goods truly unique products available nowhere else.

The answer he came up with was tomato soup, *condensed* tomato soup, to be precise. The nomenclature is a bit misleading, as condensed soup is not made by "condensing"—that is, removing water from the soup; rather, the additional water is never added to begin with. Regardless, selling concentrated soup had a number of advantages: Smaller cans cost less to manufacture, label, and ship; and they took up less shelf space, both at the grocery store and in the cupboard. Within a year of the soup's release (accom-panied by condensed consommé, vegetable, chicken, and oxtail varieties), Campbell's was profitable again.

A new product needed a new label. The company had been working on a redesign of its orange-and-black label whose sub-liminal message was less "M'm! M'm! Good!" than "Trick or Treat!" when Penn hosted Cornell for the 1897 Thanksgiving Day football game. Among the fans in attendance was a Camp-bell's employee and future treasurer, Herberton Williams, who was struck by the bold red-and-white visiting Cornell uniforms. Back in the office, he suggested that the colors would be ideal for the new label. His bosses agreed, and the redesign was wrapping its way around cans within two months. It has barely changed since.

The Campbell's Soup label was elevated from the familiar to the iconic in 1962 when Andy Warhol exhibited a series of thirty-two silk-screened canvases of Campbell's Soup cans (one of each variety). The artist, I suspect, was being a bit coy when asked why he chose his subject, saying, "I used to drink it. I used to have the same lunch every day, for twenty years." Which does sound like a very Warholian thing to do. But having been an advertisement illustrator before he quit his day job, Andy would surely have been drawn to the aesthetics of the label as well: a clean, uncluttered design that lets the soup speak for itself while subtly suggesting simplicity and wholesomeness.

"M'm! M'm! Good!" The attractive, bold, and compact Campbell's Soup can. (Image used with permission of Campbell Soup Company and its subsidiaries.)

In truth, the simple label belies the industrial complexity behind the soup, including a process that Campbell scientists developed to capture the volatile gases escaping the vats of simmering soup—those volatiles are what gives foods their aroma—and return them back into the soup.

Condensed soup transformed the tomato from a preserved vegetable to a complete meal; from a minimally processed food to a highly processed one. It was, in fact, an early and hugely successful example of what would come to be called a *convenience food*. A busy mother (or artist) could open a can, add water, break out some saltines, and have lunch on the table in ten minutes, a ritual as simple and comforting today as it was then.

The advent of highly processed convenience foods, made possible by the advances in industrialization and automation that had transformed the canning industry, would have wide-ranging consequences for American diets and society, including allowing women to more easily enter the workforce by freeing them from time-consuming food-preparation duties. Many of these convenience foods, such as spaghetti sauce and frozen pizza, would include tomatoes.

The popularity of tomato soup was another jewel in the crown for the tomato, which by the late 1800s had become America's most popular fresh vegetable and (with corn) one of the two best-selling canned vegetables. Although there were those who insisted it wasn't a *vegetable* at all, insisting all the way to the highest court in the land. This controversy would land the tomato back at a courthouse again—but this time for real, in front of the nine robed justices of the United States Supreme Court.

The one with steps.

The Civil War, while popularizing canned tomatoes, had a disruptive impact on fresh tomatoes, as Northern sellers, who had been shipping early tomatoes from fields in Virginia and other Southern states before the war, turned to Bermuda and the Bahamas for their off-season produce. As the postwar South rebuilt, Southern farmers, in a bid to get their business back, successfully lobbied for the inclusion of a 10 percent duty on imported vegetables in the Tariff of 1883. The tax applied to imported "vegetables in their natural state, or in salt or brine," with an exclusion for "fruits, green, ripe, or dried."

Three years later, John Nix, whose New York company was one of the largest fruit and vegetable importers in the United States, professed to be shocked when Edward Hedden, the collector of the Port of New York, informed him that under the Tariff Act, he would have to pay the duty on a shipment of tomatoes. Nix paid under protest, claiming that since, botanically, the tomato was a fruit and not a vegetable, it should not be subject to the tariff. A year later he followed up with a lawsuit against the collector to recover all back duties.

In 1893, *Nix v. Hedden* reached the US Supreme Court, which found itself in the position of having to rule whether the tomato was a fruit or a vegetable. This was only one of the two Supreme Court cases during that term in which Hedden was a defendant (the other being a similar case whose outcome hung on the definition of "finished" furniture), suggesting that the job of being a customs collector was a fraught business back then.

The oral arguments turned into a battle of dictionaries, with Nix's counsel reading into evidence definitions of the words *fruit*, *vegetable*, and *tomato* from *Webster's* and other dictionaries.

Hedden's counsel countered with *Webster's* definitions of the words *pea*, *eggplant*, *cucumber*, *squash*, and *pepper*, arguing that if the court were to rule that the tomato was a fruit, it would also have to put all these other time-honored vegetables into the same basket. He had a point: *Webster's* 1888 dictionary defines *pea* as "a plant and its fruit, much cultivated as food" and *eggplant* as "a plant allied to the tomato, and bearing a large smooth fruit, shaped somewhat like an egg."

Nix's counsel then rebutted with the dictionary definitions of the common vegetables *potato, turnip, parsnip, cauliflower, cabbage* ("a leafy plant commonly eaten as a vegetable"), *carrot,* and *bean* to demonstrate how dissimilar the tomato was to its alleged brethren. Then, to the relief of all, both sides rested. Not exactly as scintillating as the court's 1964 attempt to define "hard-core pornography."

The court unanimously decided in favor of the duty collector, who, having died in February, was unable to savor the victory (nor lament losing the furniture case, whose ruling was delivered on the same day). Justice Horace Gray's clearheaded decision stated that

> botanically speaking, tomatoes are the fruits of a vine, just as are cucumbers, squashes, beans, and peas. But in the common language of the people, whether sellers or consumers of provisions, all these are vegetables, which are grown in kitchen gardens, and which, whether eaten cooked or raw, are, like potatoes, carrots, parsnips, turnips, beets, cauliflower, cabbage, celery and lettuce, usually served at dinner in, with or after the soup, fish or meats which constitute the principal part of the repast, and not, like fruits generally, as dessert.

The reason that tomatoes, cucumbers, peas, and the rest are botanically fruits is that the definition of a fruit is (quoting, in the spirit of the trial, *Webster's*) "the usually edible reproductive body of a seed plant." Apples, oranges, tomatoes, and cucumbers are all reproductive vessels; carrots and celery are not. Another way to think of this is that fruits are fleshy and contain seeds, while vegetables consist of roots, stems, and leaves.

Or, in other words, the diet of a panda, which (again, in the spirit of the trial) brings us to the dictionary one last time: A panda enters a bar, eats a sandwich, fires a gunshot into the air, and walks out. "What was *that?*" the customers ask, baffled. To explain, the bartender wearily produces a sloppily punctuated dictionary and reads the entry for *panda*: "Mammal, native to China. Eats, shoots, and leaves."

Three

THE MIRACLE OF SAN MARZANO

A Tomato Defines a Country—and Its Cuisine

On the twenty-fourth of August in the year 79, Pliny the Elder, the great naturalist and chronicler of the Roman Empire, was relaxing after lunch at a friend's villa on the Bay of Naples when he observed a plume of smoke from the supposedly extinct volcano across the bay. With thousands of terrified people fleeing on land and by sea, Pliny, not about to miss out on the most important natural event of his lifetime, hopped aboard a small boat and sailed toward the source.

He would never return.

Within an hour of the eruption, day had turned to night. For eighteen hours the sky rained a deadly mixture of gray-white ash, pumice, and, most distressingly of all, sizzling boulders, all at the unfathomable rate of forty thousand cubic meters a second, while the earth trembled from below, leaving the rich and poor alike an agonizing choice—whether to take shelter from the falling debris or flee.

Shortly after midnight, the village of Herculaneum disappeared under a wall of volcanic mud. Six hours later, as the sun rose cloaked in smoke and dust, a smothering cloud of fiery volcanic gas and debris rolled down the slopes of Vesuvius and swallowed the city of Pompeii whole, the 750-degree plasma of magma and gas killing its victims instantly, contracting their muscles and leaving their bodies frozen in the haunting fetal positions preserved in the ash to this day.

The eruption, while a disaster for the twenty thousand residents of Pompeii and Herculaneum (although not as much of one as is generally believed; some 90 percent of the population escaped), was an environmental blessing, as the planet, in literally turning itself inside out, refreshed the land. This left—after centuries of weathering, regeneration, and pasturing—a landscape ideal for growing, among other things, one particular variety of tomato whose impact, two millennia after Vesuvius, would spread farther than the volcano's towering plume of smoke.

By the mid-1600s, the pall that had been cast over the tomato was starting to lift. The Renaissance had given way to the Enlightenment, and by the next century such modern thinkers as Newton and Linnaeus had displaced Galen and Hippocrates. The two-thousand-year-old theory of bodily humors was finally put to rest, and with it the "cold and wet" stigma that had dragged tomatoes down. Attitudes toward foods in general changed, not only in Italy, but throughout Europe. A new word, *gastronomia*, the art of eating well, of actually *enjoying* food, entered the Italian lexicon.

Still, it wasn't until 1694—a century and a half after their introduction to Italy—that tomatoes first appeared in an Italian cookbook, *Lo scalco alla moderna*, or *The Modern Steward: The Art of Preparing Banquets Well* (as the tomato's luck would have it, a book better remembered for giving the world the first published recipe for sorbet). The author, Antonio Latini, an orphaned street urchin whose first restaurant job was washing dishes, had worked his way up the culinary ladder and down the Italian Peninsula until, at the age of forty-one, he was offered the prestigious post of house steward for a Spanish regent who owned a villa on the slopes of Vesuvius (this being while the Kingdom of Naples was under Spanish rule). It was possibly through this Spanish influence that Latini first dabbled—tentatively, it seems—in tomatoes. Of the three tomato recipes in Latini's two-volume work, only one features them as the main ingredient, a salsa that consists of charred tomatoes, minced onions, chiles, thyme, salt, oil, and vinegar. Which happens to be *exactly* how salsa is made today in the Mexican state of Chihuahua.

Latini suggests that his salsa be served over boiled meats "or anything else." Even though there was little that sounds "Italian" about his use of the tomato, which was still being treated as a Mesoamerican condiment, the fact that Latini was cooking with tomatoes at all indicates some degree of acceptance in Italy by the end of the seventeenth century, at least in the south. Then the trail goes cold, as *The Modern Steward* was the last Italian cookbook to be published for the next eighty years. With that kind of a gap in the historical record, how can we know how (or even if) Italians were using tomatoes for almost a century?

God bless the monks and nuns, who, if they didn't invent record keeping, elevated it to a high art. In monasteries they wrote down *everything*, especially how they spent every precious lira. We know, for example, that in the mid-1700s the Jesuits of the Casa Professa in Rome were eating tomatoes in a frittata every Friday during July. The Celestine nuns of Trani had tomato soup on exactly twenty occasions in 1751. Benedictine nuns in Sicily were eating tomatoes and herbs in a pastry they called *mortaretto*.

Finally, with the 1773 publication of *Il cuoco galante*, or *The Gallant Cook*, we're able to get a fuller picture of how tomatoes were being adopted in eighteenth-century Italy. The author, Vincenzo Corrado, was a Celestine Benedictine monk in Naples who traveled widely, visiting other Benedictine orders, so his book provides a nice sampling of the different uses of the tomato throughout Italy. And Corrado finds tomatoes on anything that walks, swims, or flies: cooked and strained atop turtledoves and fish, stuffed with veal or rice, pummeled into soup, baked with anchovies and bread crumbs, and minced with cheese, eggs, and spices to make rather delicious-sounding croquettes. Clearly, Italians were starting to put their own stamp on the tomato. No longer content to merely chop it up into salsa, they were now using the vegetable with traditional ingredients, creating dishes that resemble modern Italian cuisine.

These are the recipes of the privileged class, however, and belie the fact that tomatoes were having their greatest impact not in dressing turtledoves, but as a staple of the poor in southern Italy and Sicily, where the peasantry subsisted on a largely vegetarian diet. Meat of any sort was a rare luxury, as suggested by an Italian proverb: "When a peasant eats a chicken, either the peasant is ill or the chicken is." Tomatoes became an important part of that vegetarian diet, and with good reason: They could be grown in abundance, were reasonably nutritious, and added a splash of bright color to an otherwise drab diet.

By the early 1800s, southern Italy was tomato country, with

vines stretching from Naples to Sicily. However, the problem with tomatoes, as any home gardener knows, is that they possess a pair of complementary and challenging traits: a short growing season, but one during which they come on like gangbusters. Impoverished Italians, who subsisted on vegetables, had to find a way to eat tomatoes year-round, to preserve the bounty of August for the paucity of March.

The earliest and simplest way of doing this was to yank some plants out of the ground while the tomatoes were still green, and hang them upside down in a cool place, where they could be plucked off and eaten throughout the winter.

The fruits could also be pickled—that is, salted and stored in a jar of vinegar or brine, a method of preserving food in use since ancient Greece. This, for the poor, carried the disadvantage of requiring a substantial investment in ceramics (and space). But no expenditure was required for the next innovation, something still popular today, although less with the peasantry than with the Sunday brunch crowd: the sun-dried tomato. The climate of southern Italy, with its warm Mediterranean sun, steady breezes, and low humidity, is ideal for drying tomatoes. And it couldn't be easier: Slice the tomatoes in half, salt lightly to draw out moisture, and lay them out on your terra-cotta roof. Within a week or so, the tomatoes will lose around 90 percent of their weight to evaporation, leaving a shelf-stable product.

Before you start climbing a ladder, however, note that if you don't have a terra-cotta roof, chances are you also don't have a climate suitable for sun-drying tomatoes. I've tried drying them outdoors on wire screens on several occasions, but the late-summer humidity in the Northeast prevents them from fully dehydrating, and they eventually wind up looking like a third grader's science experiment gone to mold.

Pickling and sun-drying were a means of providing a year-round substitute for the fresh variety. But the next adaptation would transform the very use of the vegetable, making the preserved tomato a food unto itself, with an identity and a role distinct from the fresh tomato.

Tomato paste.

Southern Italian housewives had found they could preserve tomatoes by reducing them to a thick paste, one far drier and stiffer than the tomato paste sold in cans and tubes today. Ripe tomatoes were simmered down into a thick sauce in large outdoor vats, then strained to remove the seeds and skins. The remaining thick mush would then be spread thinly onto boards to dry in the sun for a few days. Once the paste had reached the consistency of the dried apricot leather you find in supermarkets today, the translucent sheets, called *conserva nera* (black preserve), were rolled up in oiled paper or formed into loaves. Used to enhance soups, stews, and sauces, this nutritious *conserva* was so concentrated that a mere teaspoon was sufficient to flavor a large pot of soup. A recipe from the town of La Spezia that appeared in an American newspaper in 1850 stated that a *conserva* roll would "keep for years."

Conserva preparation, with its days of simmering, straining, and drying, may sound like sheer drudgery, but judging from this 1881 description by French archaeologist François Lenormant, it was more of a festival:

In every Calabrian house, tomato preserve is made for use during the rest of the year. It is a solemn occasion in the popular life of these· lands, a kind of festive celebration, an excuse for get-togethers and gatherings...Neighbors, and especially the neighborhood women, get together in

different houses one after the other for the making of con-
serv di pomi d'or, a procedure that culminates with a large
meal; and they gossip as much as they can while crushing
and cooking the tomatoes. It is here that for several months
the locale's chronicle of scandal is identified and commented
on; it is here that those old rustic songs, which are today so
avidly collected by scholars keen on folklore, are repeated
from generation to generation.

Other observers were more impressed by the flies that,
attracted to the sweet paste, arrived in swarms of biblical pro-
portions and had to be constantly shooed away. Nonetheless, the
communal making of *conserva* became such a cherished tradition
that it continued into the twentieth century, well after the availability of commercial canned tomato paste made all that work
quite unnecessary.

The canning industry in Italy proceeded roughly in paral-
lel with its American counterpart, although tomatoes were not
among the first foods preserved, because meats, fruits, and more
exotic vegetables such as asparagus and peas were more profitable.
In fact, the man whose name would become synonymous with
canned tomatoes in Italy initially canned everything *but* tomatoes.

Francesco Cirio (pronounced "cheerio") opened his first food
preservation factory in Turin, in northern Italy, in 1856 when
he was only twenty, achieving early success with canned peas,
an extremely short-season crop much in demand. Soon after, he
expanded into pears, asparagus, artichokes, peaches, and, eventually, tomatoes.

The area around Parma, in the fertile Po Valley of Emilia-
Romagna, would become an important tomato processing
region, although tomatoes were introduced here later than in the

south, and almost as an afterthought, according to the Museum of the Tomato's Giulia Marinelli. She explained that agronomy science and social conscience reached Italy simultaneously in the middle of the nineteenth century. "There were people very concerned about the quality of life of the peasants," Giulia said. "And so, they started to go and teach the peasants what to do," including introducing the new science of crop rotation. And one of the crops rotated was tomatoes. To this day, she says, "cereals, tomatoes, and hay—this is basically their rotation now, in the Parma region."

It was tomato paste—*conserva*—not whole tomatoes, that Cirio initially canned, for several reasons, one being that the first canned tomato products simply replaced homemade *conserva*. Additionally, the tomatoes common in Cirio's northern Italy, with their high water content, gloppy gel, and tendency to collapse when peeled, were not well suited to being canned whole. Even if they had been, there was another disadvantage: They were round. And spherical items are impossible to pack tightly (see how many tennis balls you can fit into an empty tomato can), so you end up with as much filler as tomato.

The tomatoes in the North were still of the large, round, and deeply furrowed varieties that had briefly graced Cosimo de' Medici's kitchen, but growers farther south, around Naples, had long favored small pear- or egg-shaped tomatoes, such as the Fiaschella and the Re ("King") Umberto. These varieties, with their higher ratio of flesh to gel and smaller core, not only made better cooking tomatoes, but they were more suited to canning, as their elongated shapes allowed them to be packed tightly, like sardines. So by the late 1800s, when Francesco Cirio expanded his business south to Campania, the agricultural region that runs from Naples and Vesuvius down the Amalfi Coast, there was already a thriving tomato farming and processing business underway.

Around the turn of the century, representatives of Cirio, then the largest canning company in Italy, arrived at the farm of Michele Ruggiero with some new tomato seeds that they wanted to try growing in Campania. According to the oral tradition of the Ruggiero family, still prominent in the region, Michele was chosen because he was highly respected, known as the *guardiano delle terre*—guardian of the land—a title that recognized his role as a kind of de facto sheriff in this rough-and-tumble part of Italy, settling landowner disputes and keeping bandits at bay.

Michele's life reads like an Italian opera, so . . . cue the overture!

ACT I: The curtain rises on the early years of the twentieth century. Preceded by his flamboyant handlebar mustache, Michele appears onstage with a cardboard suitcase and a little savings, fresh off the boat after two years spent chasing his fortune in America. Having returned to his homeland of Campania, he falls in love with a beautiful orphan, the adoptee of a neighboring family. But, alas, the fifteen-year-old Nunziatina is betrothed to another man. The lovers, nevertheless, carry on their affair in secret.

ACT II: Risking everything, the star-crossed couple flee, only to be caught and returned home by the disgraced families, who, putting their mutual acrimony aside, agree that at this point, with the tarnished Nunziatina's engagement most definitely off, the best of their bad options is to legitimize this mess with a shotgun marriage. It will turn out to be a happy (and productive) union, as Nunziatina, afforded an early start, will bear Michele ten children over the next twenty-five years. Michele, meanwhile, makes a decent living from farming while earning his reputation as the guardian of the land.

ACT III: The year is 1935. Tragedy strikes as Michele walks along the banks of the Sarno River, returning from the long journey to Cirio's offices, payment for the season's harvest tucked away under his jacket. Exhausted, he falls asleep, awaking to find that his wallet, with the entire 45,000 lira he was carrying—a good part of his annual income—has been stolen. The guardian of the land, the keeper of the peace, robbed—cruel irony! Desperate to feed his large family, Michele mortgages his house to a local wealthy landowner for 40,000 lira, but falls into a deep depression as a result of his misfortune. Finding himself unable to work, leave his room, or even speak, he cannot pay when the mortgage comes due, losing the house.

Bring on the fat lady for a final aria. Michele, now *truly* despondent, falls ill, to never recover, a broken man who, once respected by all, dies pitied by all. But his memory will live on, not only in the ten children he fathered, who will continue to farm—and protect—the Sarno for generations, but in those experimental tomatoes from Cirio that had already changed the landscape and Italy's fortunes in ways that no one could have predicted.

The seeds that Cirio had given Michele were of a new type of canning tomato, a cross between three southern varieties: the Fiascone and the Re Umberto, both widely grown in Campania; and the Fiaschella, a favorite of Puglia (the heel and ankle of Italy's boot) that grew prolifically in large clusters of small fruits. (Fiascone and Re Umberto are often referred to as being the same tomato today; however, 120 years ago these were likely two separate varieties whose identities and DNA have since blurred.)

This new canning tomato seemed to have the best qualities of each of its progenitors. Its slim profile, more elongated than pear-shaped, was ideal for canning; it had few seeds, a very small core, a thin skin that could be easily removed, and it held its shape, not collapsing into mush after peeling and processing. (Italian plum tomatoes are nearly always canned *pelati*, or "peeled.") But most importantly, the tomato tasted great out of the can, noticeably sweeter and less acidic than its contemporaries.

Cirio rightly thought this variety was a winner, and the company distributed samples of these seeds throughout the Italian Peninsula to see in which regions they grew best. And where they grew best was in the rich volcanic soils below Vesuvius. Soon the tomato took the name of the town in which Michele Ruggiero's farm was located: San Marzano.

Vesuvius—still very much an active volcano that last erupted in 1944 when it buried two villages and nearly a hundred Allied B-25 bombers under a swath of molten lava a half mile wide— is considered the most dangerous volcano on earth, given that it looms over a dense metropolis of three million people. Yet if the current population is concerned, they don't show it.

"*La terra felice*—we call this the happy land," Michele's great-grandson, Paolo Ruggiero, tells me as I keep one wary eye on the volcano. The fourth generation of Ruggieros in Campania, Paolo is in his own way the guardian of the land, working to keep the traditions, quality, and reputation of the San Marzano tomato alive with DANIcoop, the tomato cooperative founded by his father, Edoardo. The co-op purchases and cans tomatoes from seventy or so small farms in the valley, selling the tomatoes worldwide under the Gustarosso brand. A trim, balding forty-year-old dressed in jeans and a T-shirt, Paolo disappointingly has not inherited Michele's sweeping mustache—although it has landed on the Gustarosso label. Yet from what I've heard about

Michele, I think that I can see a bit of the founder in the pride and intensity emanating from within Paolo's dark eyes. The hint of worry that crosses his face suggests that this is not an easy business.

"The happy land" seems an incongruous name for a place whose fieldstones literally *fell from the sky*, but in fact the epithet predates the AD 79 eruption, and I'm about to see one of the sources of that happiness. Surprisingly, it is *not* the famous volcanic soil that is almost always mentioned in the same breath as San Marzano tomatoes.

"Where are we going?" I ask Nancy Gaudiello, Paolo's assistant and translator. I'd thought we were headed to a tomato farm where the harvest was in full swing, but Paolo, whose English is only slightly better than my Italian, is driving through the narrow, winding streets of the ancient town of Sarno, settled centuries before nearby Pompeii.

"To see the source."

"The source of what?"

"The source—the *three* sources—of the Sarno River," Nancy says with a reverence that suggests she's speaking of the Holy Trinity. We arrive at the first, a stone-lined watercourse, maybe four feet wide and lined with potted plants, that suggests a Roman bath. Emerging from under a building at the foot of the steep mountain, the stream, so clear that you could read a book placed on the bottom, runs under our feet before disappearing beneath the town.

"The source," Paolo declares solemnly in English before driving us to the remaining two sources, his pride in the water as clear as the stream itself. In this he is not alone. Not only will Sarno's minister of culture insist on showing me the sources again the next morning, but archaeologists have discovered evidence of a water cult (which, from what I'm seeing, remains very much alive today) from 3500 BC that worshipped the "holy sources." The ancient Etruscans even named the town after them; *Sarno* means "river from many sources."

Italians have long had a thing for water; ancient Rome had hundreds of public baths and swimming pools open to all citizens, and the remnants of aqueducts still dot the European continent today. Clear, clean water was especially prized and protected, for obvious reasons, with prohibitions against urinating or romance at water sources. Thus the ancient Romans might not have been pleased at what we see at the last of the three sources of the Sarno: people and dogs splashing in the cold stream, enjoying this "happy land" on a 90-degree day, while a hundred yards upstream, a man rolls up his trousers and wades in to fill a dozen liter bottles to take home.

Despite the language barrier—and my impatience to see some tomatoes—Paulo's message gradually sinks in: Before you see the tomatoes, before you can *understand* the tomatoes, you have to see their lifeblood: the water. For without the Sarno River, there would be no San Marzanos, volcanic soils or not.

No one mentions this, but I've learned that the Sarno serves another, less lofty purpose: It is the valley's industrial sewer. Clean enough to bottle and take home at the source, by the time it reaches the sea, this river, although a mere fifteen miles long, has the distinction of being the most polluted in Europe, running reddish-brown with waste from the tomato processing plants, tanneries, and other factories strategically located along its route. Although reclamation plans have been on the books since 1973, cleaning up the river remains more of an ambition than a work in progress, in part because of the thousands of jobs dependent upon the polluting factories that line its route to the Bay of Naples.

Finally, we head into the countryside, arriving a few minutes later at the farm of Vincenzo Zio, a third-generation farmer, and his wife, Porzia. And the first thing Vincenzo wants to show me is...the water. Sarno water gushes through his property—even in mid-August, near the end of the dry season—and Vincenzo bends over to pull up a wire trap teeming with large, very excited crayfish that seem to sense they're tonight's dinner and a couple of small, mellow catfish that don't.

Of course, the stream's main purpose is irrigation, and after Vincenzo turns on a pump—the only piece of machinery visible on the farm—water fills a trough while Vincenzo, using a battered hoe, directs the flow first down one irrigation ditch, then another, closing the first sluice with the hoe, then with a few efficient strokes opening another. This guy seems to be about my age, and I recently started collecting Social Security. I point to my back. "Hard, no?"

He laughs, nodding, rolling his eyes and grabbing his back. Vincenzo, it turns out, is not my age. He is seventy-seven. "He has been giving us tomatoes for fifty-seven years," says Paolo. "His grandfather gave my grandfather tomatoes. Three generations." Tapping his chest, he adds, "But I, four generations," the message, in a place where family and tradition matter, being, "My family has been here longer than his."

Vincenzo's advanced age is not unusual for a San Marzano farmer. Edoardo, on the adjoining farm, is ninety. I ask Paolo if, given the age of the farmers, he has concerns about the future of San Marzano tomatoes.

"No," he says. "We have also some younger farmers."

"How young?"

"Fifty to sixty years old."

Paolo must see my eyes widen. "Farmers' sons," he explains, "don't want to work in the fields. Our mission is to involve young people to work in the field and to explain the importance of this work, showing them the love that our farmers have for their land. We have to teach young people to come back to the field if they want to be sure about what they eat." The challenge is, even those young people with a strong back and a willingness to work hard lack what Vincenzo and the other geriatric farmers have: a government pension, which critically supplements what little they make on their small farms.

The sprightly Vincenzo, after six decades of labor, is the very picture of an Italian farmer, his friendly face tanned and weathered by sun and wind, but quick to flash a smile, his eyes narrowed into a permanent squint from years of working in the brilliant sunlight, but still bright and lively. I can't shake the feeling that I've seen him somewhere, but that seems quite unlikely. It must be the stereotype that's familiar.

"Other than being clean and plentiful," I ask Nancy, "is there anything special about the Sarno water?"

"Oh, yes!" she says, surprised at my ignorance. "It is very rich in minerals. Especially calcium. It is very important to the tomatoes." Indeed, calcium deficiency is thought to be a cause of blossom end rot, which is why American tomato gardeners have been known to bury eggshells and even a few Tums alongside their plants.

Having exhausted (I hope) the topic of water, we all head out into the field, which is shockingly small. "This can't be more than two acres. Does Vincenzo have another field?"

"No, no, this is it." Paolo points across a low fence. "Edoardo." He points in the other direction. "Gino." Both fields are similar in size to Vincenzo's, as are, he says, the other farms in the region. Sensing my confusion, he explains, "San Marzano tomatoes make up less than one percent of all the tomatoes grown in Italy," just

370 acres in total, an area so small it could wither unnoticed on any commercial tomato farm in Italy or the US.

Paolo scoops up a handful of soil. "Vesuvio," he says, no other explanation needed as he spreads the soil out in his hand for me to examine. To me it looks like plain old dirt, and some that could use a little organic matter at that, but what do I know?

That debris from a volcanic eruption—which evokes images of lava flows, sizzling rocks, and ash—is highly fertile does not feel at all intuitive, although one look at Hawaii, with its lush vegetation and forests rimmed by black volcanic sand, tells you that it must be. The pyroclastic material is not immediately arable, of course, but becomes so after centuries of weathering break down the volcanic basalt and feldspar, releasing iron, calcium, magnesium, sodium, potassium, phosphorus, sulfur, silicon, and other important trace elements. And there is something else in this soil that Paolo wants to show me. He searches for the English word.

"Clay." A foot or two beneath the soil lies a substrate of clay. Through Nancy, Paolo explains its significance: "Even when the soil on top is dry, the clay holds water, so the roots of the plants are able to get moisture and nutrients out of the soil. Very important."

No argument there; I can unhesitatingly vouch for the importance of keeping tomato roots consistently moist, having found that the cycles of drenching and dryness resulting from my own criminally lazy watering habits (successive days of forgetting to water followed by guilty overcompensation) are a sure way to ruin your tomato crop.

The ability of the soil to hold moisture also means that the tomatoes need less irrigation, which makes for a less watery and thus tastier tomato. With all the water flowing down from the mountains, the region is blessed with a high water table, so that even farms that, unlike Vincenzo's, don't have a tributary of the

Sarno passing through can easily reach the same rich aquifer with a shallow well.

As if the Vesuvian soil and Sarno water aren't enough to explain the singularity of the San Marzano tomatoes grown here, Nancy points out the last of the three (hmm... there's that sacred number again) factors that define the distinctive *terroir*—a term originated by French winemakers to describe the unique, sometimes intangible aspects of a locale that make its wine irreproducible elsewhere—of the Sarnese-Nocerino region: the sea.

The Mediterranean is but a half dozen miles from here. In fact, Pompeii had a port before Vesuvius drove down waterfront property values by laying a mile of fresh land between it and the Tyrrhenian Sea, and the moisture and saltiness of the maritime air are claimed to be part of the San Marzano magic as well. Additionally, the sea moderates temperatures, so it's never too hot or too cold for the tomatoes.

Finally... *tomatoes*. At long last, there they are: rows of surprisingly tall plants tied to gnarly wooden posts cut from tree limbs, making me feel like I've been transported onto the set of the Italian film *The Tree of Wooden Clogs*, especially when Vincenzo steps into the frame. Speaking of movies, I have to confess this does all feel like a bit of theater—the fiery volcano, the sacred water, the old man bent over his hoe—but at the same time it *is* awfully hard not to want to be an extra in this appealing pastoral, so I tuck away my cynicism as we head into the field.

I've timed my visit to see the harvest, which I'd read was done mostly by African and Eastern European migrant laborers who work long hours for low wages, yet there is no one in sight.

"Nancy, where are the harvesters?"

"Right here!" she says as if I were blind, motioning to the seventy-seven-year-old Vincenzo and his wife. "Most farmers get their children to come help for the harvest, but their children live far away, in Rome." *No accident*, I think to myself.

It's just these two grandparents harvesting the entire crop of tomatoes? I feel like I should be pitching in, but with noon approaching, they're done picking for the day. After Vincenzo takes his morning's harvest to the cannery, he and Porzia will spend the afternoon doing other chores on the farm, which explains the full kitchen back by the stream. During the farming season, Vincenzo and Porzia are here from dawn to dusk, not even going home for lunch. Even the end of harvest brings no rest; once the San Marzanos are all off the vine, Vincenzo and Porzia will be clearing the fields for late-season beans, peppers, and squash.

Nancy swears that this literal mom-and-pop operation is typical, and I'm sure, from what I've read in other accounts, that it's not *atypical*, but many of these farms do rely on migrant labor, although not to the extent, nor as scandalously, as the factory farms in Puglia that produce the vast bulk of Italian processing tomatoes today. When I ask about labor on those farms, Paolo's face darkens and he just mutters, "Mafia," choosing, perhaps sensibly, not to elaborate. Instead, he plucks a ripe tomato from the vine, showing me its characteristic shape. Slimmer than conventional plum tomatoes, San Marzanos taper down to a point, with a distinctive little nipple at the tip. We slice one open to examine the interior, which reveals another aspect that made the San Marzano revolutionary. Cut a typical slicing tomato across the equator, and you'll likely see five or more distinct segments—locules—filled with a gelatinous material and seeds. A San Marzano has only two, with almost no gel and remarkably few seeds, giving it a higher ratio of edible flesh to disposable gel. It also has a small core, critical for a tomato that is going to be canned whole.

Those qualities, combined with its narrow shape, easily removed skin, firmer flesh, and intense flavor when cooked (often described as the ideal balance of sweetness and acidity), made the San Marzano far superior to anything that had come before. Introduced in the 1910s, it quickly took over the fields of Campania, where it became known as "red gold." By the late 1920s the San Marzano had generated jobs for sixty thousand Italians who worked in some six hundred canneries. Tomato exports rose a hundredfold in the first few decades of the century, the largest exporter being Cirio, whose labels displayed a field of crimson San Marzanos with a smoking Mount Vesuvius looming across the Bay of Naples. (The artist's perspective would seem to be from the vicinity of Pliny's guest villa.) Nearly a quarter of these exports went to tomato-mad England, in effect returning the English tin in which they were canned to the source. And a good many went across the Atlantic as well, as they were preferred by the Italian immigrants who were then arriving in North and South American cities by the millions.

Cirio ad featuring San Marzano tomatoes and a smoldering Vesuvius, ca. 1930. (Courtesy of Conserve Italia soc. coop. agricola.)

Coming out of the First World War, which left Italy in shambles, the young agrarian nation had few major industries. The explosion in tomato processing and exporting gave a huge boost not only to this poor farming region and the poverty-stricken city of Naples, but also to the economy of Italy as a whole.

Because we tend to associate modern Italy with high-end fashion, thousand-dollar shoes, and Lamborghinis, it takes some effort to grasp just how poor Italy was through much of the twentieth century, so poor that by 1920 an astounding one-quarter of the population had emigrated to escape the poverty. Even as recently as 1958, when the iceman was virtually extinct in America, he still cometh in Italy, where only one Italian household in eight had a refrigerator. *A decade before men would walk on the moon, 87 percent of Italians did not own a refrigerator.*

The San Marzano tomato, horticultural writer Amy Goldman noted, provided canneries with a "sturdy, flawless subject, and breeders with genes they'd be raiding for decades" (including, as we'll see, for the tomato that supplanted it), making it, in her words, "the most important industrial tomato of the twentieth century." Even though it accounts for only a tiny fraction of Italy's tomato harvest today, one could say it's done its job, having helped transform that country into the world's largest exporter of canned tomatoes, a position it still easily holds. Even with growing global competition (including from China, which leads the world in tomato production, most of it going into paste), Italian fields are the source of four out of every five cans of imported whole tomatoes consumed anywhere globally.

Yet as great as the San Marzano's economic impact has been, its cultural influence has been far greater. Canned tomatoes, rightly or wrongly, have come to define Italian cuisine for the rest of the world, while becoming the foundation for two of the most popular foods on earth: pizza and spaghetti. And San Marzano tomatoes in particular have achieved a kind of exalted status rarely seen in the food world. Watch the Food Network for a month and you'll likely never see a host specify a variety of asparagus or dried beans. But if a can of tomatoes is opened, you can bet that they will be San Marzano, and don't be surprised to hear them spoken of with the reverence given a fine wine.

This, as we'll see, is no accident.

Vincenzo Zio drives his morning's harvest of ripe tomatoes into town, his diminutive three-wheeled pickup, not much larger than a golf cart, looking like a toy duck bobbing in a roiling ocean of tractor trailers loaded with pallets of canned tomatoes, with trucks coming, going, backing up, beeping, pulling out—organized, noisy chaos.

The fact that Vincenzo's tomatoes are going to a cooperative does not mean that they will be "cooperating" with those from other farms. In fact, quite the opposite; each farmer's tomatoes are processed in a separate run the same day they are picked. Every can is stamped with a code representing the farm, the date of canning, and the expiration date (three years hence), all requirements of (deep breath) the Consortium for the Protection of the San Marzano Tomato of the Agro Sarnese-Nocerino, the official body that regulates and monitors every—and I mean every—phase of San Marzano tomato production, from seed to label.

The Consortium is a reminder not only of the San Marzano's success, but also of its failure, the group having been founded in 1996 in an attempt to save a tomato whose fortunes had fallen as quickly as they had risen. Because of accidental crossbreeding that resulted from the lack of technical skills in the region, coupled with the intentional introduction of other, hardier varieties, by the 1950s the San Marzano "brand" had been diluted. Then, in the 1960s a devastating tomato disease (thought to be the cucumber mosaic virus) swept through the Sarno, wiping out entire farms and threatening the very survival of the San Marzano varietal. In the meantime, the small farmers in the region found themselves competing with vastly larger corporate farms in Puglia and Parma that were growing a heartier, more disease-resistant hybrid from America.

The Roma tomato was, as the name suggests, developed near a nation's capital, but not the one it's named after. In the 1950s, plant breeders at the USDA's Plant Industry Station in Beltsville, Maryland, a Beltway town just a tomato's throw from Washington, DC, crossed San Marzano with Pan America and Red Top varieties, the result being a plant that bore larger fruits, was more resistant to disease, and—most appealing of all—was determinate.

Tomato plants are divided into two distinct types, determinate and indeterminate. Determinate plants stop growing and setting new flowers when they reach a height of about three to four feet, while indeterminate varieties such as San Marzano will, if conditions allow, continue growing, sometimes to ten or twenty feet or more, flowering and producing fruit until something stops them, whether pruning, disease, or frost, although for practical reasons the San Marzanos are topped at a reachable six to seven feet.

Roma tomatoes, with their three-foot height, bushy habit, and stronger stems, don't have to be pruned or staked like San Marzanos, which is a huge labor savings. And because the blossoms tend to all form within a short period of time, the tomatoes also ripen at more or less the same time, meaning you can send your pickers out into the fields to harvest everything at once and then dismiss them for the season.

The shrewdly named "Roma" (presumably a tomato named the "Beltway" wouldn't have been as marketable) was exported to Italy, where it was embraced by Italian growers and canners, replacing its parent San Marzano as "the" Italian plum tomato, dominating Italian fields for several decades and returning to America in cans.

Let's pause for a moment to consider the journey of the peripatetic tomato up to this point: Originally from the Americas, the tomato has traveled across the Atlantic to Europe, come back to America as the San Marzano, returned to Italy as the Roma, and sailed back to America in cans, having crossed the Atlantic more times than a bandleader on the *QE2*. If you can come up with a more truly Italian American food, I can't imagine what it would be.

Meanwhile, by the 1990s the San Marzano, a victim of disease and genetic weakening, was hanging on by a thread, as were its farmers. The Slow Food movement, founded in Italy just a few years earlier, had heightened awareness of the need to preserve traditional farms and foods, and local Sarno farmers, assisted by agronomists at Cirio, set out to rescue—and protect—this historic and important tomato. But with all the crossbreeding that had taken place, no one was really sure what the genuine article was anymore. Old seeds, if they had any, weren't of any use, because unlike, say, date palm seeds from Pliny's lifetime that have been found and successfully germinated, tomato seeds lose their viability in just a decade.

So, agronomists from the Cirio Research Center went out to the remaining farms and fields in the Sarno in search of the

original San Marzano. Identifying twenty-seven possible cultivars, they grew tomatoes in test fields for two years before anoint-
ing not one, but two "official" San Marzano varieties that they
christened San Marzano 2 and Kiros, the latter an improved cultivar with superior disease resistance that became the new San
Marzano of choice.

Now they had the tomatoes and the farmers eager to raise them
again, but faced the question of how to market them. That is, how
to distinguish these "true" San Marzanos—grown by hand in
Vesuvian soil, Sarno water, and Tyrrhenian Sea air—from all the
other canned tomatoes produced in Italy, including San Marzano
varieties grown outside Campania. And, more to the point, with
the advent of large farms growing more productive varieties and
the increasing use of automation, how could these Sarno farmers
possibly earn enough from their "small-batch" tomatoes to preserve their traditional ways of farming?

The same way that cheese makers in Parma protected the reputation and price of their Parmigiano Reggiano cheese after half
the world started imitating it: with a DOP designation. Similar
to the concept of French AOC appellations for wine and cheese,
a Denominazione di Origine Protetta (Protected Designation
of Origin) certification confers status as an authentic, usually
premium product, and the designation not only helps to guard
against impostors, but often fetches a higher price. The San Marzano farmers and processors—Michele Ruggiero's grandson,
Edoardo, among them—got together and formed a consortium
to work with the Italian Ministry of Agricultural, Food and For-
estry Policies to come up with a DOP application for Pomodoro
San Marzano dell'Agro Sarnese-Nocerino (San Marzano Tomatoes from the Sarnese-Nocerino region).

The resulting regulations, although filling just seven pages, leave little to the imagination, covering every conceivable aspect of San Marzano tomato production, stopping just short of how to open the can. This rule book, after a preamble that describes (stop me if you've heard this one before) the volcanic soil, spring water, and coastal climate that make this region unique, begins with the land itself, listing three dozen municipalities within the Agro Sarnese-Nocerino region where the tomatoes can be grown, specifying the dates during which the seedlings can be transplanted and harvested; permitted methods of support (staking) and harvest (by hand); the maximum density of planting; even the loaded weight (less than 250 kilograms) and composition (plastic) of the containers used to transport the tomatoes from farm to cannery.

The can is regulated as well, with specifications for the font (Gill Sans MT Condensed) and the four-color-process (or CMYK) printing designation for each of the eight colors (e.g., cyan: 24; magenta: 99; yellow: 97; black: 0) that can be used in the printing of the San Marzano seal, which must contain in "strong primary colors the red of the tomato, the green of the leaves, and the surrounding white band that recall the colors of the national flag," as well as the blue Tyrrhenian Sea and Mount Vesuvius in the background. All this in a graphic a half inch across. I literally had to use a magnifying glass to see that my Gustarosso can ticked all the boxes.

But most of the document deals with the tomatoes themselves, specifying the permissible length (60–80 millimeters, or about 2⅜ to 3 inches), pH, sugar content, proportion of skin by weight, ratio of tomato width to length, and a few fuzzy qualitative requirements ("red color typical of the variety"), plus an innocent-sounding sentence whose significance is easy to miss: "The yield of product transformed must not be more than 70%."

What that means is that no more than 70 percent of the tomatoes that arrive at the processor are allowed into a can. As low—even arbitrary—as this seems, in practice it's even lower; during one recent season, just 66 percent of the San Marzano tomatoes received at Consortium packers made the cut. The idea is to ensure quality, but knocking out a third of all the tomatoes harvested, not even counting those left on the vine because of their obvious flaws, makes Vincenzo's small farm seem even smaller.

The best of the rejects are used to make the juice or puree that the tomatoes are packed in, but still, that high percentage of waste has got to include a fair number of what you and I would consider perfectly good tomatoes. Yet no one seems to complain, given that the primary selling point of a DOP status is a guarantee of quality.

It's up to the Consortium to enforce the DOP regulations, and it takes its responsibility seriously, doing everything from supplying the seeds to testing the soil. In short, everything about DOP San Marzano tomatoes is regulated to the hilt. And if it occurs to you that these are the kind of regulations that invite a court battle, well, stay tuned.

"I don't understand something," I say to Nancy back at the cooperative. "Even if there are a thousand farms here the size of Vincenzo's," which there aren't, "I'll bet I can buy more San Marzano tomatoes in New York alone than you can grow in all the Sarno. What am I missing?"

"You have a problem in the United States."

"No kidding."

"No, I mean with tomatoes. Most of your San Marzanos are fake."

"Most" was quantified in 2011 by Edoardo Ruggiero as meaning *95 percent.* How, I ask, does this happen?

"A lot of the factories here, they mix tomatoes. For export they may put in 15 percent San Marzano and the rest Roma from Puglia and label them 'San Marzano.' And the Consortium cannot control abroad."

"That's why I only buy those marked 'DOP,'" I say, trying to distinguish myself as an educated consumer.

"Those are mostly fake too."

"What?" I sputter with the shock and indignation of someone who has just found out the Rolex he bought on the street for fifty bucks isn't genuine. "Are you telling me that even some cans marked 'DOP San Marzano' are fake?"

"Not some, *most.* The DOP designation is only enforceable in the European Union. So, in Europe it is difficult to find a fake. But in the US, they cannot stop it." The Italian police do their best—in 2010 they seized one thousand tons of counterfeit San Marzanos destined for the United States—but seeing as how knockoffs of luxury Italian handbags, watches, foodstuffs, clothing, perfumes, and cosmetics cost the economy $30 billion in lost sales annually, a thousand tons of fake Marzanos is small tomatoes.

"Well, then, how can I be sure I'm getting the real thing?"

She grabs a can off the shelf and places it in front of me, and that's when I realize where I've seen Vincenzo: on every single can of Gustarosso tomatoes, that familiar face pensively gazing down at the soil while his tired frame, dwarfed by tall tomato plants on either side, leans heavily on that battered hoe.

"There are two seals," Nancy explains, pointing to the DOP

seal and then to that Consortium seal, which is described in excruciating CMYK detail in the regulations. She flips the can over. "And here on the bottom you will find a certification number, with a unique stamp with the date and time the tomatoes were canned, and the farm they came from."

Okay: two seals and a stamp. Sounds easy. Except that more than half of the Sarno-grown San Marzanos sold in the US are neither outright fraudulent nor Consortium-approved DOP tomatoes. These are the cans sold by Cento, a New Jersey importer of everything from tomatoes to tuna. A familiar sight in supermarkets, their bright yellow cans bear the words, in large type, "Certified San Marzano tomatoes." I ask Nancy where they fit in.

"Fake. They are fake tomatoes," she says flatly, with a hint of anger. "*Certified*?" She makes a face and gives the classic Italian shrug. "What does that mean? In Italy, that law doesn't exist. The only certification the law recognizes is the DOP, so if you are not DOP, you cannot say you are certified San Marzano."

In fact, Cento *was* selling DOP San Marzanos until 2008, when they withdrew from the Consortium, forfeiting the DOP designation and going their own way, which explains the bitterness I can sense hanging in the air.

Now, we've already covered a lot of ground here, so let me say that normally I wouldn't waste my time—or yours—on what is apparently some kind of DOP(ey) turf war, except that Cento isn't just another unscrupulous little company slapping fake San Marzano labels on Roma tomatoes in an unmarked warehouse in the Bronx. They sell more Sarno Valley San Marzano tomatoes in the US than *all other companies combined*; Cento is often the only Italian San Marzano tomato brand on your supermarket shelf. And the dispute gets to the very heart of the question, an existential one for San Marzano farmers: *What is an authentic San Marzano tomato?*

A few days after returning from the Sarno, I email Cento requesting an interview about why they left the Consortium. Usually this is the first step of a weeks- or monthslong process to try to get anyone—even blood relatives—to talk to me about anything, so I'm shocked when, thirty minutes later, my phone rings and the vice president of Cento is on the other end. Maurice Christino is more than willing to give me Cento's side of the story.

"The dispute is over labeling, not tomatoes," he says.

"Labeling? You forfeited DOP status over a *label*?"

Indeed. Even stranger, the dispute was over the label's use of the prohibited words—you'll never guess—*San Marzano*.

In the early 2000s, Christino explains, the resurrected San Marzano tomato was becoming all the rage in America. It was featured on the Food Network, hyped in cooking magazines, and praised by top chefs everywhere. Cento, to "take advantage of the free publicity," as Christino puts it, replaced the Consortium-approved (and trademarked) term *S. Marzano* on their labels with *San Marzano*, which is what everyone called them.

The American shoot-first-and-ask-questions-later strategy didn't sit well with the Consortium, which demanded that Cento change the wording back to "S. Marzano" on all labels and marketing material. Cento, with millions already invested in the San Marzano name—and convinced that reverting to the shortened name was going to harm sales—tried to convince the Consortium that "San" was really the smarter way to go with the American public, who might not know that in Italian, *S.* is an abbreviation for *San*.

"They didn't want to budge," recalls Christino, despite the fact that the use of *S.* was an accident. The original DOP application was actually for San Marzano dell'Agro Sarnese-Nocerino, but at some point along the way, as the paperwork got shuffled from

Campania to the Italian Ministry of Agriculture to the EU, some paper pusher, probably as sick of writing out "San Marzano" as I've become in this chapter, casually substituted S. for San, the equivalent in English of writing "St." for "Saint." Unfortunately, that's how the designation and the trademark were subsequently recorded in Brussels. The difference may not be a big deal if you're referring to jolly old "San Nick," but it is if you're registering a trademark with the EU.

So S. Marzano it was and, unable to get the Consortium to over-look the American label, Cento decided to strike out on its own, continuing to adhere (with some tweaks), says Christino, to the DOP guidelines, and hiring their own third-party agency, Agri-Cert, to "certify" that Cento's product met Cento's own guide-lines. By offering a better crop price to the growers, they also took a good portion of the Sarno Valley farmers with them (although some grow for both Cento and Consortium canners). It was noth-ing short of a juicy coup that left the Consortium stewing.

The Consortium fought back, initiating two class-action law-suits in US Federal Court against Cento, ostensibly on behalf of US consumers who'd been tricked into their purchases by "false and misleading" labeling and advertising. Cento, the plaintiffs argued, could not possibly be selling "certified San Marzano" tomatoes because "the Consortium is the only entity which can certify and approve a San Marzano tomato." More damning, the suits also claimed that not all of Cento's tomatoes are grown in the official Sarnese-Nocerino region and that they do not meet San Marzano quality standards (assertions that Cento flatly denies).

"I'm not trying to play mediator," I say to Christino, sounding every bit like one, "but it seems to me that this schism isn't good for anyone. This is a tiny niche industry to begin with, and now you each have half the influence you had before."

He doesn't disagree, adding ruefully, "It didn't have to be this way." That seems especially true in light of the fact that the Consortium has come around to Cento's thinking on the name, having filed an amendment with the EU in 2019 to change the trademark to—wait for it—*San Marzano*! In other words, this long-running Hatfield-Macaroni feud (which began back when Paolo's father, Edoardo, was DANIcoop's president, making it, like all good Italian feuds, a truly generational affair) is over an issue that no longer exists.

"So, with *San* back in good graces, is there a chance you might go back to the Consortium and the DOP?" I ask Christino. If I spoke Italian, I'd offer to patch things up myself and get these two kids, so obviously meant for each other, back together.

"Maybe...you know, I don't want to say *never*," but I can tell from his voice that it is clearly not a priority. And who knows, maybe there are other reasons for Cento's departure from the Consortium, but the fact is, Cento has little incentive to rejoin at this point. In 2020, according to Cento, they shipped a record 1.5 million cases—31.5 million pounds—of their "certified San Marzano" product to America, which is more than the entire Consortium canned. They can do this because they know that the average American consumer likely doesn't know a DOP from an SOB. But the consumer has probably heard of the San Marzano tomato. They also can do it because, even though San Marzanos are generally more expensive, Cento's cans sell in Trader Joe's and Walmart stores for about the same price as other imported plum tomatoes.

Having been put on the defensive, the company has gone out of its way to legitimize its product to American consumers, even encouraging them, via an app on their website, to type in the code stamped on the can and see on Google Earth the actual farm that grew their San Marzanos.

The first of the two federal lawsuits brought by the Consortium was dismissed in 2020 without a trial by a Long Island, New York, judge who, not sympathetic to EU traditions and regulations, ruled, in effect, "Who died and made the Consortium king?" Not swallowing the plaintiff's contention that only the Consortium could certify San Marzanos, the judge icily wrote that the court "need not devote time to Plaintiff's claims regarding the minute differences allegedly found between Consortium tomatoes and the [Cento] product."

The second lawsuit, filed in California, ended in a confidential settlement, which most certainly did not include removing the words "Certified San Marzano" from the label. Cento may have dodged the long arm of the law, but not the vitriol of the Consortium members, who remain furious at the American bully who stomped home with its half of the game board when the opponent—some of whose families go back three and four generations—wouldn't agree to change the rules midgame.

Cento claims that they are equally committed guardians of the land, supplying only the highest-quality seed to their growers and certifying every step of the process with the zeal of the Consortium. Maybe that's true; I'm in no position to judge. But shifting that responsibility from the independent oversight of the Consortium, whose members have farmed the land for a century, to a New Jersey canned food importer certainly gives one pause.

As for the Consortium, it is not exactly blameless either. If its members hadn't gotten their backs up against this New World interloper, perhaps they could've admitted that a mistake had been made in the original filing instead of waiting eleven years to change the trademark, and the whole dispute could've been resolved.

I just hope that the schism doesn't represent the next puff of smoke from Vesuvius, threatening the San Marzano heritage once again. I'm not naive; I suspect that a bit of a Potemkin village was constructed in the Sarno for my benefit (and for that of actor Stanley Tucci, who just two weeks earlier was brought to Vincenzo's farm for a television series on Italian food), and that I was shown the picture-perfect S. Marzano farm with the even more picture-perfect S. Marzano farmer—so perfect his face graces a million labels. I also know that not all the farms in the Sarno are nearly as cinematic as Vincenzo's. All that being said, it's hard not to root for those that are, and for those farmers working a few small acres with a hoe and spring water to keep alive the heritage of the tomato that first put Italy on the world culinary map.

Yet Beatrice Ughi, the Italian-born founder of Gustiamo, a New York importer of high-end Italian foods (including San Marzano tomatoes), told me that, for all the controversy with Cento, there is a far more dangerous threat looming. "The San Marzano farmers are decreasing because they are *dying*," she says. "You were there; you saw how old they were. And the children do not want to continue because this job does not pay." In other words, it's not Cento that's stealing the farmers from the San Marzano fields; it's the Grim Reaper. And he doesn't care *what* the label says.

Four

THE QUEEN, THE WRITER, HIS WIFE, AND THEIR PIZZA

TOMATOES MEET FLATBREAD AND CHEESE, GIVING THE WORLD ITS FIRST GLOBAL FOOD

Approaching Naples, Italy, on the E45 Autostrada, 10:00 a.m.

I am jerked awake by the sudden, startling swerve of our rental car, hurtling down the Autostrada in heavy traffic at 120 kilometers an hour. *Oh my god, what is happening?! Is Anne about to get us into an accident?*

Unlikely, I realize with a start. I'm driving.

One hour earlier

Trying to stay awake in the passenger seat, with my role as navigator not requiring much attention for the next hundred kilometers, I start playing with the touch screen on the dashboard and notice that the car's lane-departure assist—the feature that steers you back into your lane should you wander across the line—has been switched off. I tap the screen to turn it back on. Can't be too careful. Neither of us slept on the overnight flight from New York, and as far as our bodies are concerned it's not nine o'clock in the morning, but 3:00 a.m.

"Why don't you pull over at the next rest stop," I tell Anne. "You look tired. I'll drive."

Two hours earlier

"I have a nice Toyota Corolla for you," the young, cocky auto rental agent—the word *Europunk* comes to mind—at the Rome airport says through a vaguely malicious grin.

"I reserved a Mercedes A-Class."

"Or"—he makes air quotes—" 'similar.' "

I actually have no idea what a Mercedes A-Class is, having never driven a Mercedes of *any* class, but I know it's not a Toyota Corolla, and I let the agent know that it is certainly not—air quotes—"similar."

"Do you have much luggage? I can give you a Fiat 500."

I fear that if I keep arguing we'll end up on a *Vespa con sidecar*, but I also know that the Fiat is less a serious offer than an opening gambit to set me up for the next play, one he's been anticipating since I walked in the door, an easy mark—that is, a tourist. I decline the diminutive Fiat, and now Europunk shows his hand. You know it's coming, because it *always* comes, whether you're in Rome, Italy, or Rome, New York: the dreaded upgrade pitch. And sure enough, in the next breath: "For another 60 euros a day, I can give you a Volvo S60."

Sixty euros a day! But after I conspicuously start craning my

neck in the direction of other rental counters—all empty of customers at this ungodly early hour—it turns out he can also give
me a Volvo S60 for just another *15* euros a day, so we drive away
in the Volvo. Still, I'm not happy at being upsold, treated like a
rube from America, asleep, you might say, at the wheel.

Of course, I'll be whistling a different tune in a few hours.

One hundred seventy years earlier

Naples in 1850 was the filthiest, poorest, and most crowded city
in Europe. Hemmed in by the sea on one side and low mountains
on three others, its four hundred thousand residents lived literally
on top of one another in crowded apartment buildings a perilous
five and six stories high, barely separated by narrow, dark alley-
ways, and often bridged by a shared laundry line. Sunlight was for
most an unaffordable luxury.

A visitor to the city found the chaotic streets

> steep, narrow, dirty, and bordered at every story with over-
> hanging balconies; a mass of petty shops, open stalls, men
> and women buying, selling, gossiping, gesticulating and
> elbowing each other...a labyrinth of paved tortuous lanes
> buried in dust and strewn with orange peel, melon-rinds,
> fragments of vegetables, and other refuse...All is bustling,
> eating, drinking, and bad odors; it reminds one of rats in a
> rat-trap.

The threat of fire hung continually in the smoky air, made
smokier by the presence of the nearly one hundred pizza ovens
that dotted the city, their wood fires burning, smoldering, glowing from dawn past dusk. But the oven was cold the morning of

A Neapolitan street, ca. 1897. (J. F. Jarvis, Publisher. Library of Congress LC-USZ62-73726.)

May 4 at the pizzeria of nineteen-year-old Luigi Mattozzi, for it was the annual date on which all the city's apartment leases expired, and so once again Luigi—whose seven siblings would be born at seven different addresses, all in the same Porto neighborhood—was in the street with his family, pushing a hand-cart containing all their possessions as they slowly wove their way through a traffic jam of thousands of other Neapolitans on a similar journey in this increasingly unaffordable city.

Pizza had been a staple in Naples since the mid-1700s, although the eighteenth-century version hadn't yet been codified into the tomato and mozzarella combination that we know today. But you would certainly have recognized these early incarnations, round flatbreads with a raised rim, topped with various ingredients, including cheese, anchovies, vegetables, and tomatoes.

While nitpicking academics like to argue that baked or grid-dled flatbreads are about as old as grain and a hot stone, what we think of as contemporary pizza—a flat, yeasted bread covered with tomatoes and/or cheese and baked in an oven—was unques-tionably born in Naples. From published accounts, we know that by the late 1880s tomatoes, whether whole, sliced, or crushed, had become a common, if not yet obligatory, component of pizza.

Pizza was *the* staple food of the Neapolitan poor. Often con-sumed multiple times a day, it was cheap, easy to eat on the run, and when topped with vegetables and small fish, could even be nutritious. Not everyone was a fan, however. Pinocchio, for one, hated it. Or rather his creator, the Italian writer Carlo Collodi did, characterizing pizza in an 1886 novel as an unappetizing "patchwork of greasy filth that harmonizes perfectly with the appearance of the person selling it." As early as 1831, American Samuel Morse, inventor of the telegraph, thought it "a species of most nauseating cake...Covered over with slices of tomatoes, and sprinkled with little fish and black pepper and I know not what other ingredients, it altogether looks like a piece of bread that had been taken reeking from the sewer." Some suspected it played a role in the transmission of cholera.

The first *pizzaioli* plied their craft from storefronts and street carts, using *lazzaroni*—homeless street urchins, often barefoot and dressed in rags—to run through town with slices, meaning that pizza *began* as a take-out and delivery food. Over time, some of the more successful vendors moved indoors and added a few tables (which, over *more* time, Domino's would come along and take out), and by the middle of the eighteenth century the modern pizzeria had taken shape.

The origin of the word *pizza* is more difficult to tease out, hav-ing, in the words of one Italian scholar, "poisoned etymologists and tormented food historians" for years, partly because there are a number of similar words in Arabic, Greek, and Latin that suggest a connection, although some seem an unnecessary stretch. Now, I'm no historian—I'm barely a writer—but this all seems like self-induced torment to me, because if you drive a short distance out of Naples you bump into the magnificent Greek temples still standing in Paestum, a reminder that this area was settled by the Greeks. And *they* happen to have long had a flatbread they call *pitta* (or *pita*), a connection that seems too obvious for anyone but a scholar to ignore, especially as *pizza*, like *grazie*, is pronounced as if it has a soft *t* in it.

To me, the more interesting question is, Why did pizza originate in, of all places, Naples? The food's very ingredients provide a clue, for just on the other side of looming Vesuvius lay some of the world's finest tomato fields, even before they were planted with San Marzanos; buffalo-milk mozzarella originated in and is still a prized specialty of the region; and wheat has been milled locally since Roman times. Anchovies, a favorite topping, came daily from the Bay of Naples, and the olive trees of the Sorrento Peninsula, which forms the southern end of the bay, supplied oil. In other words, pizza was the original locavore food two hundred years before the word existed.

The Mattozzi family's new home provides another clue about why, you might say, pizza chose Naples. As is typical for the time, among the Mattozzi apartment's missing amenities were running water and a kitchen. Very few of Naples' lower classes lived in quarters with any cooking facilities, their accommodations more resembling college dormitories than apartments. And we know how popular pizza is in dorm rooms. Luigi's apartment would likely not have had a private bathroom, either, and if the building had a toilet at all, it would be nothing more than a filthy hole in a tile floor, shared by all the tenants. Sorry to say, I have more than a passing familiarity with this style of—and I use the word loosely—toilet, having had to use them the last time I was in Naples, in the 1970s, just after an outbreak of cholera (which I'd assumed had disappeared from Europe along with the steam engine) left seven Neapolitans dead and one young American tourist very wary of antiquated public restrooms.

Cholera is what brought the king of Italy, Umberto I, to Naples in 1884. Formerly the capital of what was called the Kingdom of the Two Sicilies (the "other" Sicily being Naples—don't ask*), Naples had been part of a unified Italy since only 1861, after King Victor Emmanuel II and his swashbuckling general, Giuseppe Garibaldi, expelled the last of the Austrian, French, Spanish, and local rulers who'd controlled various portions of the Italian Peninsula for centuries.

The "liberation" of the Two Sicilies from the Spanish Bourbon dynasty by a northern, Piedmontese king had been as about as popular with the local citizenry as the liberation of Atlanta from the Confederacy by General Sherman. Thus Umberto, who at the time of his visit to Naples had been king for only six years, had his work cut out for him. It is, after all, one thing to conquer, but quite another to govern. Or, as one statesman aptly put it,

---

* If you must know, both the Naples region and the island of Sicily were sometimes called the Kingdom of Sicily by their dueling rulers before being united under a single king who, not wanting to play favorites, anointed the new territory "Kingdom of the Two Sicilies."

"We have made Italy; now we have to make Italians." So, when Umberto heard about the deadly cholera outbreak in the largest city of Italy, he threw caution to the wind and came down both to observe the conditions for himself and to be seen by his new subjects—one of whom had tried to assassinate him during his only previous visit.

Umberto was aghast at the medieval sanitary conditions, although "medieval" is a misnomer, because much of the plumbing far predated medieval times, with some portions going back to the reign of the emperor Caligula. While touring the city, Umberto, seeing the wretched living conditions and alarmed at how the municipal systems barely distinguished between drinking water and wastewater, uttered the famous declaration that has been repeated countless times since, in a myriad of contexts, including by this writer: "Naples must be disemboweled!" Plans were laid for the city's reconstruction, the *Risanamento* (literally "making healthy again"), which lasted into the Second World War, when Allied bombers would express their own ideas about how to disembowel the city.

Umberto's visit, during which he visited cholera victims in a hospital, was a huge success. His bravery was touted in the press and cheered by onlookers, and five years later he returned for the official inauguration of the Risanamento, this time bringing his wife, the queen of Savoy. During their monthlong visit, the queen (so the story goes), tired of the heavy French cuisine served at court, and looking to curry some favor with her subjects, requested to dine on local fare, and no cuisine was more local than pizza.

A celebrated *pizzaiolo*, Raffaele Esposito, was summoned to the Palace of Capodimonte to make pizza for the queen. Esposito made three pies: the first with olive oil, cheese, and basil; the second with anchovies; and a third with tomatoes, mozzarella, and basil to represent the red, white, and green of the new Italian flag.

That the queen would even eat a pizza—the humblest dish of the poorest city in Italy, often prepared by grimy peasant hands in unsanitary conditions—was a hugely symbolic (and calculated) act that the British historian John Dickie likens to the moment a hundred years later when Princess Diana embraced a patient with AIDS. And when the queen declared the red, white, and green pie of Italy to be her favorite, the meal took on even more significance.

Esposito returned the compliment by naming the flag-colored pizza after the queen, and behold, the Margherita pizza was born!

Relegated to a historical footnote, the tomato used on the queen's pizza, a small egg-shaped variety we met earlier, had already been named for the queen's husband, Re Umberto, and, in true royal fashion, this egg would in time hatch another king, the king of tomatoes: the San Marzano.

It's a nice story, and by now a well-trod one that usually ends with the tired debate about whether Raffaele Esposito invented the tomato, cheese, and basil pizza in June 1889 or simply named an existing combo after the lucky queen. But before we regurgitate that mozzarella ball, let's take a closer look at this fellow who is said to have launched a gazillion pizzas and united a nation.

Raffaele Esposito married into a pizza family, his father-in-law being a successful *pizzaiolo* named Giovanni Brandi, and purchased an already venerable pizzeria in a favorable location in the city. He seems to have continued the Brandi family success, but still, in a city with a hundred *pizzaioli*, one wonders how Raffaele Esposito came to be the one summoned to make the queen's pizza. Why not, say, Luigi Mattozzi, or any of his six brothers (out of six) who themselves had become *pizzaioli*, beginning a family tradition that continues to this day?

That's what Italian historian Antonio Mattozzi (a descendant of the *pizzaiolo* dynasty) wanted to know, and while digging through the city archives, he found an intriguing request by Esposito to rename his newly purchased restaurant Pizzeria della Regina d'Italia (Pizzeria of the Queen of Italy)—*in 1883, six years before making the queen's eponymous pizza!* So, either Esposito was a clairvoyant, or he had been conspiring to make his royal mark long before the queen's visit, which invites speculation as to what else he might've done to worm his way into the palace. We simply don't know, but it's a safe bet that more than good fortune was at play.

What we *do* know is that this enterprising young *pizzaiolo* was not the first to make what was already known as *pizza alla mozzarella*, there being multiple earlier references to such pizzas, including an 1853 essay by Emanuele Rocco that unambiguously describes a pizza made with "*basilico, muzzarella e pomodoro*," the three canonical ingredients of the pizza Esposito "invented" thirty-six years later. That fact, however, does not diminish Esposito's political astuteness in selecting this topping for the queen, let alone naming it for her.

If, in fact, any of this happened at all. With Esposito looking more and more the rascal, I wonder, Did he even make pizza for the queen, or is that Pinocchio's nose I feel poking me in the ribs? It's time for both a little investigative journalism and lunch, and fortunately Esposito's old red-sauce-and-mozzarella joint, Pizzeria Brandi, is still firing up the ovens at the same location 130 years later. Although now that Anne, the Volvo, and I have made it here alive I can't decide whether I want to investigate, eat, or take a nap.

Since the menu, the walls, marble plaques—pretty much everything but the toilets (modern, thank God)—are still shamelessly milking their royal cash cow, I can do the first two tasks at the same time, ordering her pizza while investigating the story. And the restaurant does have an impressive letter, complete with a royal stamp. Translated into English, it reads:

Household of Her Majesty

Capodimonte
11 June 1889

Most esteemed Mr Raffaele Esposito Brandi
  I confirm to you that the three kinds of Pizza you prepared for Her Majesty were found to be delicious.

Your most devoted servant
Galli Camillo
Head of Table Services to the Royal Household

A little detail about the pies and Her Majesty's preferences for the tricolor one would've been nice, and the perfunctory nature of the note suggests that it might've been obligatorily jotted off at Esposito's request, but I'm satisfied that at the very least the core of the story seems to be true. Besides, I have another mission to fulfill here.

"I'll be back before the pizza arrives," I tell Anne.

"Where are you going?" she asks, looking alarmed.

"To make the pizza."

I didn't come all this way just to *eat*. Pizza is one of my passions, which explains the bulky flamethrowing, hot-as-the-surface-of-Venus pizza oven on my patio. But because my passion doesn't always translate to quality, I want to see how these *pizzaioli* do it. I talk my way into the kitchen—or rather let Google Translate do the talking—in the hope of grabbing a quick lesson in making a Margherita pizza at the very birthplace of the Margherita pizza. And it will be "quick" because they turn out a pizza in less time than you can translate "*Sono uno scrittore Americano.*"

Even though the finished pizza materializes so quickly that I have to repeatedly watch the video I record to absorb what I've witnessed, the pace seems so unhurried that I'm later amazed to find that the *pizzaiolo* (with an apprentice tending the oven) turned out our two pizzas—the Margherita plus one with several toppings (which takes extra time to prepare)—from a ball of dough to a dinner plate in 2 minutes and 15 seconds flat. While carrying on a conversation during which he spoke nonstop while I nodded nonstop like the manic bobblehead doll I become when confronted with a foreign language.

The first step, transforming a ball of dough taken from a tray into a precisely even thin crust, takes the *pizzaiolo* just 15 seconds, the final form taking shape with a magician's sleight of hand when he flips the flattened dough between his hands—left, right, left, right—three times, a process called *chiaffo* ("slap"), which stretches out the center until it's translucent, while keeping some heft to the edge, which when subjected to the 900-degree heat of the oven will blossom like a time-lapse movie of an opening flower into the two-inch tall puffy rim—the *cornicione* (literally "cornice" in English)—characteristic of a Neapolitan pizza. The Margherita pie spends just 62 seconds in the oven before being extracted, bubbling, with just a suggestion of charring here and there, like a leopard's spots.

They don't toss and spin the dough in the air here, a showy technique frowned upon by serious Neapolitan *pizzaioli* that was developed to attract passersby. No such theater is needed to convince locals to eat pizza in Naples, where you can't swing a dead *gatto* without hitting a pizzeria. Pizza is more popular in Naples than anywhere else on earth; consider that on the first day that the city's pizzerias were allowed to reopen for takeout following the 2020 COVID-19 lockdown, some *sixty thousand* pies were ordered.

And yet American tourists often return from this pizza shrine feeling a little underwhelmed by their culinary experience. Food writer and Serious Eats founder Ed Levine went on a pizza binge for his book *Pizza: A Slice of Heaven*, visiting fifteen of Naples' top pizzerias in search of the city's best pizza. He ruled it a fifteen-way tie, finding them all "eerily similar," the pureed canned tomatoes neither drained nor cooked down, making for "wet pizzas that occasionally bordered on swampy."

Levine was raised on New York pizza, which we'll get to in a bit, and it's tempting to dismiss Americans' lackluster reviews of Neapolitan pizza as a natural preference for what we're familiar with. And that certainly is a factor. But the real problem with Neapolitan pizza is that it's frozen in time, intentionally.

Levine's contest ended up in an all-contestant tie for first (and last) place because Naples' storied pizzerias all make the same *verace pizza Napoletana* (authentic Neapolitan pizza), following the rules specified by the Associazione Verace Pizza Napoletana, a group founded in 1984 to safeguard the legacy of Neapolitan pizza.

This traditional pizza that each *pizzaiolo* is trying to outdo the others at (whether or not the pizzeria seeks certification from the AVPN) must conform to a set of standards that make those for DOP San Marzano tomatoes seem downright lax. Everything, including the chemical properties of the flour (protein and ash content, moisture absorption rate, and more); the type of yeast (brewers); tomatoes (either San Marzano or Roma); and cheese (buffalo or cow's milk mozzarella); the temperature of the oven (800–900 degrees Fahrenheit, wood-burning only); how the sauce is spooned on (using a spiraling motion from the center); even how the finished product must be eaten (on-site, hot enough to separate the epidermis from the roof of your mouth) is laid out in almost comical detail.

This does not allow for a lot of creativity, to say the least.

So, what exactly is this Neapolitan pizza, this sacred relic that the city's pizza fathers are working so hard to preserve? It is what we might call an individual "artisan pizza," the size of a dinner plate, with a tall, airy rim that tapers to a wafer-thin (no more than 1/10 inch), wet center. The sauce is simply crushed or pureed canned tomatoes topped with a parsimonious scattering of mozzarella chunks, three or four basil leaves, and a swirl of olive oil, the finished product resembling a red sea punctuated with scattered white islands of cheese, around which sail boats of green basil.

The idea behind the AVPN's minimalist pizza, as with the Consortium for the Protection of the San Marzano Tomato, is to preserve an important heritage (and protect a brand). In that regard they seem to have succeeded. Not satisfied with obtaining DOP status in 1997, the group also sought and won recognition from the United Nations for *pizzaiuolo*, the art of traditional pizza making, joining Azerbaijani carpet weaving and the Armenian performance of *Daredevils of Sassoun* on UNESCO's "Lists of Intangible Cultural Heritage of Humanity." (So I never made it past the *A*'s; sue me.)

No one would argue that maintaining one's cultural and culinary heritage isn't important, but the flip side of the pie is that Naples, in its determination to preserve some version of the past, has made itself into a living fossil of pizza, to the extent that the AVPN recognizes only two varieties: the cheeseless marinara, with only tomato sauce and oregano, which made its debut in 1734; and the Margherita, around since at least 1853. This strikes me as particularly odd because the original Neapolitan pizzas were topped with everything from the catch of the day to the slightly overripe harvest of yesterday. Even Queen Margherita had two other varieties to choose from.

Returning to the queen and 1889, the embrace of pizza by the royal family may have been a public relations coup for the monarchy, but it did surprisingly little for pizza, which, like the tomato itself three centuries earlier, would labor in Italian obscurity for decades to come. As late as World War II, pizza was still virtually unknown outside Campania.

The omnipresence of pizza around the world today suggests that pizza must have been a preordained success, but the truth is, there was nothing inevitable about it. The number of pizzerias in Naples, about fifty at the beginning of the nineteenth century, was only a hundred by the end of the century, despite major population growth. Municipal records show how often new pizzerias failed, and being a *pizzaiolo* was demanding, dangerous work that barely provided a living for the practitioners of this fiery art. The one known nineteenth-century attempt to "export" pizza—all of 130 miles to Rome—failed miserably.

In fact, the trail to pizza's world domination would be blazed not in Italy, but on the other side of the Atlantic.

They came as single men and as entire families, some with a little savings and some penniless. From 1880 to 1920, thirteen million

Italians migrated out of Italy, the largest voluntary emigration in the history of the world.

Four million of them, largely from southern Italy, the poorest region of the country, arrived in the United States, most coming in the years between 1900 and 1914, settling mainly along what is today the I-95 corridor that runs from Philadelphia through eastern New Jersey and New York City, before continuing north through New Haven to Boston. Of course, like all immigrants, they did not abandon their customs and diets from the old country, and for those Italians from Naples and the surrounding Campania region, that included their beloved pizza. Everywhere Neapolitans settled, pizza followed, first sold in bakeries, then in dedicated pizzerias.

Pizza historians have long credited the first pizzeria in the United States to a precocious nineteen-year-old, Gennaro Lombardi, who, it was believed, opened Lombardi's in 1905 at 53½ Spring Street, in New York's Little Italy. Lombardi's became a New York institution, in business continuously (with the exception of a decade in the 1980s, after which it reopened a few storefronts away, at 32 Spring Street) into the twenty-first century, a record of longevity perhaps not impressive by Neapolitan standards, but downright Methuselahian for New York, where restaurants have the average life span of a butterfly.

The fact that Gennaro Lombardi introduced pizza to the New World was accepted as fact for decades, repeated in countless books and articles on pizza. However, most of the pizza histories ever written were invalidated in 2019 when a professional accountant and amateur pizza sleuth from Chicago named Peter Regas discovered an inconvenient detail while researching the history of New York pizza: In 1905 the pizzeria at 53½ Spring Street was registered not to Lombardi, but to one Filippo Milone, a name not familiar to pizza historians. And that address wasn't Milone's first pizzeria in the city. The emigrant from Sorrento, just south of Naples, had previously made pizza in Brooklyn back in 1898. Even that wasn't the first pizzeria in America, having been predated by others that tax records and restaurant licenses prove had sprung up in New York as early as 1895.

So not only was Lombardi's not the first pizzeria in New York, but Gennaro Lombardi wasn't even the first owner of Lombardi's. Furthermore, Regas discovered, the heretofore unknown Milone also founded what would become the *second*-most-famous pizzeria in New York, the future John's of Bleecker Street, which Milone sold to John Sasso, a Lombardi alumnus (and future Milone in-law) in 1929.

Said *New York Times* restaurant critic Pete Wells of Regas' discovery, "It was like as if we found out some other dude wrote The Federalist Papers and The Declaration of Independence and then, like, gave them to Madison and Jefferson and we never knew it. It was some guy named Tony all along."

Or, I suppose, as if we found out that Queen Margherita had nothing to do with the Margherita pizza.

Even though Lombardi did not introduce pizza to America, he certainly deserves the credit for refining and popularizing what would become known as New York–style pizza, and for training a generation of *pizzaioli* who fanned out to start their own pizzerias, all making pies in the Lombardi style. A direct descendant of Neapolitan pizza, the *verace* New York version differs from its *babbo* in several important aspects, its most distinguishing characteristic being that it is baked in a coal-, not a wood-fired, oven. This likely came about because in New York coal was more readily available (already being delivered for the home furnace), cheaper, and slower to burn, while taking up less space to store.

Like hardwood, coal burns at around 1500 degrees Fahrenheit and lends a pleasant, charred flavor, the searing heat being essential to the development of a tender, tasty crust.

Because the first pizzerias opened in insular Italian neighborhoods, most of America remained unfamiliar with pizza through World War II, as is apparent from a 1939 *New York Herald Tribune* article that warned, "If someone suggests a 'pizza pie' after the theater, don't think it is going to be a wedge of apple. It is going to be the surprise of your life," adding, helpfully, that it was pronounced "peet-za."

A decade later the *New York Times* was still explaining pizza to Americans—even New Yorkers—in 1948, writing, "A round of dough is baked with tomatoes and anchovies and cheese atop, cut into wedges, then eaten with the fingers between gulps of wine," predicting with great prescience, "The pizza could be as popular a snack as the hamburger if Americans only knew more about it."

Some pizza histories claim that GIs returning from southern Italy after World War II were mainly responsible for popularizing pizza in America (and in some versions in the rest of Italy as well, requesting it wherever they were posted), and while there may be a kernel of truth to the theory, it's hard to imagine that there were enough GIs who'd cycled through southern Italy to have such an impact. As for Italy itself, the proliferation of pizza up the peninsula was due not to hungry American soldiers, but to the postwar migration of southern Italians to the more prosperous north, that country's version of America's Great Migration.

Back in America, whatever role veterans returning from the Italian theater had in popularizing pizza was dwarfed by two other consequences of the war: the GI Bill and the postwar housing boom, which, together, allowed many Italian Americans returning from the war to move out of their Italian enclaves into suburbs and smaller cities, bringing pizza with them. Even that would likely not have been enough to ignite the pizza explosion about to happen were it not for two strictly American inventions: the Hobart commercial mixer and the gas-fired pizza oven.

Prior to those innovations, the life of a pizzeria owner—before gas ovens, electric mixers, or refrigeration—was not much different from that of a nineteenth-century Neapolitan *pizzaiolo*, as described by pizza historian Evelyne Slomon:

> The daily pizza making was not for the meek or weak, it was a physically demanding operation. The day would begin early in the morning when the dough would be mixed by hand and kneaded on a giant table by four or five men with arms so muscled that they could barely bend them. After fermentation, the dough was shaped and stored in wooden boxes, ready to be turned into pizza. The ovens had to be cleaned and stoked by shoveling a pile of coal into the chamber. If a local source of mozzarella cheese was not available, the *pizzaiolo* would frequently have to go through the chore of working fresh curd in 180-degree water... There was no mixer to mix the dough, no distributor to call for shredded mozzarella, no flick of the switch for the oven to heat up, and no refrigeration to hold the ingredients.

The Hobart mixer, that big floor-standing model with a dough hook that you've seen if you've ever peeked into the back of a bakery or pizzeria, became popular in the 1940s, relieving the chore of kneading the tight, glutinous dough by hand. But the real game changer was the gas-fired oven.

The brick coal-burning pizza ovens in use at the time were massive, filthy, and demanding structures as large as twelve feet square, with heavy foundations designed to retain heat. They took forever to heat up and required frequent cleaning, maintenance, and feeding. Installing a multiton brick oven was a risky commitment; you weren't moving your operation down the street if the landlord chose to raise the rent, which of course gave the landlord great incentive to raise the rent. But the availability of inexpensive, clean-burning gas ovens—the familiar stainless-steel deck ovens you see in nearly every pizzeria today—substantially lowered the bar for getting into the pizza business.

Like the first pizzeria, the gas-fired pizza oven has competing origin stories. Most sources credit Ira Nevin, a New York brick-oven builder and World War II veteran who'd served in Italy (although as a third-generation oven mason he was certainly familiar with pizza before the war) and who built his first gas oven in 1945 at the request of a local pizzeria. Having neglected to patent his invention, Nevin almost lost his business when imitations sprang up, but he persevered, building his Bakers Pride company into one of the leading manufacturers of deck ovens today.

However, in 2016, an industry newsletter, *PMQ Pizza Magazine*, credited a forgotten Italian immigrant named Frank Mastro with inventing the gas-fired pizza oven almost a decade before Nevin, claiming that he sold three thousand of them between 1938 and 1953. Mastro also pioneered the turnkey pizzeria concept, supplying everything an aspiring *pizzaiolo* might need to start a business, from financing to ovens to canned tomatoes— even frozen dough.

The Mastro family legacy ended suddenly and tragically, with Frank dying of cancer at age sixty and his son, Vinnie, who had taken over the business, following just seven years later. Vinnie died of heart failure at the age of just thirty-three during the great Northeast blackout of 1965. That same night, under the cover of blackout and chaos that affected thirty million people, thieves broke into the company's offices in the Bowery and, in what was either a case of corporate espionage or Mafia strong-arming, made off with contracts, client lists, and other critical documents, plus a large sum of cash. Whomever the culprit and whatever the motivation, the family never recovered, and Frank Mastro passed into obscurity.

The Mafia doesn't enter the narrative lightly; with their common southern Italian roots, the Mafia and pizza were as natural a combination as tomatoes and mozzarella. From 1975 to 1984, the mob distributed heroin valued at $1.6 billion through New York pizzerias (one wonders if there was a code word for a topping of smack), culminating in the sensational 1985 Pizza Connection trial. Lasting a record seventeen months, the trial featured twenty-two Sicilian-born defendants, the murder of a defendant-turned-witness, the attempted murder of a second witness, enough new inductees into the Federal Witness Protection Program to form a soccer team, and, last but not least, the testimony of everyone's favorite undercover agent, Johnny Depp—rather, Donnie Brasco, who was memorably portrayed by Depp in the nail-biting 1997 eponymous film.

Regardless of who invented the modern pizza oven, the slogan "Now you're cooking with gas!" never took on as much import as with pizza, because gas ovens allowed pizzerias (or "pizza parlors" as they were sometimes quaintly called) to proliferate on every city street corner; in every town in America; in every strip mall in the suburbs. *Newsday* reported in 1958 that new pizzerias were opening across America at the rate of one hundred per week.

These gleaming steel ovens also severed the last connection that American pizza had with its Neapolitan brethren. Not able to achieve the searing heat of a wood- or coal-fired oven, the pizzas were cooked at lower temperatures and by less-skilled *piz-zaioli*, and what we think of as "New York pizza" was gradually transformed from the Lombardi-style charred version into what it is today: a Fiat-tire-sized pie characterized by a thin, flexible crust covered with a sauce made from pureed canned tomatoes, with a thick layer of gooey mozzarella running from edge to edge, topped by a copious pour of oil (probably not olive) that drips down your forearm as you eat. Not as thin or sloppy as a *verace* Neapolitan pie, a New York slice is thick enough to hold its shape and thin enough to be eaten in the traditional New York manner: pinched in half, bringing the two base points of the triangle together at the rim—a fine pizza when it's made well, with good ingredients, but by no stretch up to the standards of the brick-oven original.

Which is why, in a twist that few early twentieth-century *piz-zaioli* would have seen coming, the wood-fired brick oven is back in vogue, having risen from the ashes to become the hallmark of artisan or Neapolitan-style pizza. There are probably more wood-fired pizza ovens—some of them in backyards—in the US today than when the first gas ovens were introduced.

The gas-fired ovens also led to another what's-old-is-new-again phenomenon: pizza by the slice. Although pizza was originally purchased by the slice in Naples, early New York pizzas were sold only as whole pies, as is still the case today in New York's few surviving coal-fired pizzerias. But with deck ovens, pizzas could be cooked in advance, put out in display cases, and, when ordered, a slice popped onto the deck for a quick reheating.

Finally, the affordable, portable gas oven that allowed the spread of pizzerias from cities into suburbs also sparked another phenomenon: the take-out pizza, which would become home delivery. Of course, to take a pizza home, you need something to take it home *in*. Evidence is sketchy, but the descendants of uncredited gas-oven pioneer Frank Mastro claim that he was also robbed of credit for inventing the pizza box, which has proved as seminal to the growth of take-out pizza as the automobile. Before the cardboard box, take-out pizzas were rolled up, wrapped in white craft paper, and tied with string, not unlike a salmon from your fishmonger.

Whoever thought of it first, there was now a way to carry the pizza home without ruining either your trousers or the upholstery in your car. The deck oven, the Hobart mixer, the pizza box, the automobile, and a booming postwar economy: By the late 1950s, nearly all the ingredients were in place to launch pizza to unprecedented heights. One more innovation was needed, and this would come not from Italy or from New York, but, of all places, Kansas.

Pizza originated in Naples in part because that's where the tomatoes were. *Chain* pizza originated in Kansas in part because that's where the students were. In 1958, brothers Frank and Dan Carney, both students at Wichita State University, borrowed six hundred dollars from their mother and opened up a place they called Pizza Hut near the Wichita, Kansas, campus. Although they knew even less about pizza than about running a business, the cheap snack was such a hit with their fellow students that within six months they'd opened a second location. Within a year they had six and had started franchising, adding four thousand locations over the next twenty years before selling the chain to PepsiCo for over $300 million, a nice return on the six C-notes they'd borrowed from Mom.

Meanwhile, in 1960 a couple of other Midwestern brothers, Tom and James Monaghan, bought a location of a local chain called DomiNick's on a corner in Ypsilanti, Michigan, best known as the home of Eastern Michigan University. Eight months later, James, needing some wheels, traded his half of the struggling business to Tom for the Volkswagen Beetle they'd been using for deliveries. As business picked up, Tom started his own franchise under the name Domino's.

Despite the fact that Pizza Hut was founded by undergraduates, it was Domino's that more aggressively targeted the college and youth market, focusing on delivery, *very fast* delivery. Monaghan installed ovens that baked pizzas on what looked like little revolving Ferris wheels, accommodating more pies and faster handling, and even invented a corrugated pizza box, an improvement over the original paperboard variety that got soggy and often leaked through. Beginning in 1984, Domino's ran an ad campaign promising "30-minute delivery or it's free," spurring bad publicity and even boycotts by consumer groups alarmed at reports of Domino's cars running traffic lights and racing down residential streets as bike-riding kids scurried for their lives.

In reality, the greater risk was to the drivers themselves: A 1989 study by the National Safe Workplace Institute found that Domino's employees had a death rate of 50 per 100,000, on a par with coal miners and *twice as hazardous as being a roofer*. The emphasis on fast delivery was finally dropped in 1993 after a pair of lawsuits awarded tens of millions of dollars to plaintiffs who'd been maimed or killed by Domino's delivery drivers.

The 30-minutes-or-it's-free fiasco was not Domino's only advertising flub. In 1986 the company ran an ad campaign featuring a diabolical red-suited, bucktoothed, rabbit-eared character called "the Noid." This annoyed another Noid, a paranoid schizophrenic from Georgia named Kenneth Lamar Noid, who, believing the mascot was modeled after himself, entered a Chamblee, Georgia, Domino's with a .357 Magnum and held two Domino's employees hostage. Luckily, the employees escaped while K. L. Noid ate a pizza he'd forced them to make at gunpoint. Domino's subsequently discontinued that ad campaign as well, but not until after Kenneth Lamar Noid, freed from an asylum but reportedly still feeling persecuted by Domino's, committed suicide in 1995.

In 1998 Tom sold the company, now with eight thousand locations, to the investment firm Bain Capital for a cool *$1 billion*. Brother James should've at least held out for, I don't know, a Volvo.

A billion dollars is a lot of pizza, and Americans *were* obviously eating a lot of pizza—one hundred acres a day—and it showed in our waistlines. On the surface, pizza should be a healthful snack, and in fact the version sold in Naples—bread, tomatoes, olive oil, and just a scattering of mozzarella—has the elements of a Mediterranean diet. However, American pizza has morphed into something else entirely: a 400-calorie slice with a day's or a week's worth of saturated fat and salt. And the chains keep finding new ways to make pizza even unhealthier, stuffing yet more cheese *inside* the crust and piling four types of fatty, salty meat on top.

You might think there isn't much a pizza chain can do to the sauce, and, of course, you'd be wrong. Traditionally just canned tomatoes, either pureed or smashed, pizza sauce has "evolved" into a brew of (to quote from Domino's website): "Tomatoes, Tomato Puree (Water, Tomato Paste), Onions, Sugar, Romano and Parmesan Cheese (Cultured Milk, Salt, Enzymes), Carrot

Puree, Salt, Celery Puree, Garlic, Spices, Butter, Olive Oil, Citric Acid, Sunflower Oil, Natural Flavor, and Xanthan Gum."

With little to distinguish between them from a culinary stand-point (although each company has its devoted fans), Domino's and Pizza Hut have chosen to compete on rapid delivery, deal pro-motions (e.g., offering three pies at a price that would put a local pizzeria out of business), or sheer gimmickry (Pizza Hut's hot dog bites pizza, with cocktail franks embedded in the *cornicione*—if I dare use that word here—comes to mind) to garner media cover-age and customers with iron stomachs.

Whether buying from a chain or the local pizzeria, busy par-ents, like Neapolitan peasants a century earlier, found that pizza was an easy, filling, and cheap family dinner. A 2014 study found that between an astounding one-quarter to one-third of Ameri-cans' caloric, saturated fat, and sodium intake was coming from pizza. The situation is particularly alarming for our nation's chil-dren, partly because pizza made a friend in school: namely, the cafeteria, which in many schools offered pizza as a lunch option every single school day of the year. A 2015 study published in the medical journal *Pediatrics* concluded that the extra calories *from pizza alone* could well make the difference between a healthy ado-lescent and an obese one.

School lunch reform, then, ought to have been a no-brainer, but when Michelle Obama launched her healthy school lunch initiative, which, among other things, strove to get *daily* frozen pizza and French fries off school menus, the response from the Republican-controlled Congress was to pass legislation classify-ing pizza *as a vegetable*. It would be funny if it weren't tragic.

As if there aren't enough health concerns with American pizza, the very carton that it's delivered in has also come under scrutiny.

In 2016 the FDA banned three substances commonly used as oil and moisture repellents in pizza boxes. The compounds are all in a class of chemicals called *perfluoroalkyl and polyfluoroalkyl substances*, or PFAS. Also found in microwave popcorn bags, countless cosmetics, and firefighting foams, PFAS poses a host of health risks, including cancer, weight gain, and, scariest of all, childhood development issues. And you didn't have to eat the box to ingest the chemicals; researchers found that adults and children who ate take-out pizza frequently showed elevated levels of PFAS in their bloodstreams. It seems that take-out pizza is determined to take *you* out one way or another.

And not just Americans. The massive assault by pizza giants on the diets and wallets of our citizens was but a dress rehearsal for the main battle, like the Germans testing their blitzkrieg strategy in Poland before moving on to the real goal: world domination.

Here's a drinking game you can safely play with your kids: Google "pizza" plus the name of any town or city in the world you can think of ("pizza Kampala") and knock back a shot if you don't get a hit. Trust me, you will all stay quite sober. Pizza is the most popular food on the planet, found in every corner of the globe, from Siberia to Cape Horn, accounting for a not insignificant portion of the forty million tons of processed tomatoes produced worldwide every year. Truly the world's first global food, pizza is one of the very few to be known by the same word in every language.

It is often said that Italy gave pizza to America, and America gave pizza to the world. You don't need an MBA to understand how this happened: one chain location at a time. Domino's has 1,200 stores—*in India*. Worldwide, the chain has 15,000 locations in 84 countries, which puts them second only to Pizza Hut, with more than 18,000 restaurants, many of them easily recognizable from that horrendous red-hat roof. A Pizza Hut advertisement seen in Poland perfectly captures pizza's multinational status: The poster features an Indian woman and Polish text selling an Italian food owned by an American chain.

A $230 billion global market, which, to give some perspective, is more than double the global entertainment market, pizza consumption is soaring at an annual rate of more than 10 percent, driven by growing urban population, increasing youth population, and frozen pizza, which dwarfs in-store sales. How to account for pizza's extraordinary popularity? Both psychological and biochemical explanations have been offered, ranging from the obvious (it tastes good and it's cheap) to the unconvincing (its round shape appeals to everyone).

While it's true that one of pizza's strengths is its versatility, the crust presenting a blank canvas that easily accepts cultural adaptations (such as toppings of smoked salmon in Russia or squid in Japan), the world's most popular variety of pizza is not far removed from the classic Margherita, starting with a base of tomatoes and cheese. The sweetness (often enhanced with sugar or corn syrup) of the sauce, the saltiness and fattiness of the cheese, and the savory appeal of the crust—not to mention the appealing contrast of textures, from chewy to crunchy in a single bite—combine to make pizza a food that simultaneously lights up all of our brains' pleasure centers like few other foods.

While tomatoes are a major reason for the popularity of pizza, the relationship between the two is a symbiotic one. Without tomatoes, pizza might well have continued to be a niche food, a local Neapolitan specialty. But without pizza, tomatoes would not so easily have achieved their own conquest of the globe. I daresay there are people around the world whose only contact with a tomato *ever* is on a pizza.

One place the chains have not yet conquered is Italy. But they are getting ready to cross the Rubicon: In early 2020, Domino's announced plans to expand its Italian branches from just the 28 locations it has today (mainly in the metropolises of Rome and Milan) to over 900. Now, that takes some pair of meatballs in a country that, with less than a fifth of America's population, has nearly as many pizzerias, some 60,000, and where half of all new pizzerias fail within five years.

One's feelings about *verace pizza Napoletana* aside, the best pizza in the world is still to be found in Italy, some of it in and around Rome and Tuscany, where it is often sold as *pizza al metro*, pizza by the meter. It comes out of the oven as a long rectangle, you indicate how much you want, and the server cuts it off and throws it on a scale. The crust tends to be crispier than the Neapolitan version, and you'll find more variety among the toppings, such as a white pizza with overlapping thin slices of potato sprinkled with sea salt, rosemary, and olive oil.

If Domino's is going to compete with Italian pizza, they'll have to do so not on quality, but on delivery service or the desire among the youth to (shudder) emulate young Americans, which can't be discounted. But this is the country that started the Slow Food movement in response to a McDonald's opening at the foot of Rome's Spanish Steps. Italians don't like to have their cherished traditions messed with, and Domino's Noid—welcomed back to the fold in 2021—may well meet a similarly chilly reception. Time will tell. Italian pizza has been through worse (cholera, wars, and a bad review from Pinocchio), so I'd like to think it will survive Domino's.

☙

I'm still awash in the glow of having watched a Margherita pizza made at the historic birthplace of Margherita pizza (admittedly, I'm the kind of sucker who gets a chill from standing on historic ground, marveling, "This is where Pickett's Charge began!" or apparently, "This is where de' Medici first saw tomatoes!") when, just two days later, my Neapolitan mission completed, I stumble across a scholarly paper that leaves me gagging. That letter at Pizzeria Brandi from the queen's chamberlain that I'd examined—okay, glanced at—and figured it looked pretty legit? Well, a Harvard historian named Zachary Nowak took a closer look. A *much* closer look, not only at the letter, but at the entire Margherita story, publishing his findings in the March 2014 issue of a scholarly journal called *Food, Culture & Society.*

So beloved and so accepted is the Margherita ur-myth that "a Neapolitan friend of mine advised me not to publish it," Nowak tells me over the phone as I'm still digesting my visit to Brandi. "He said people are going to want to break my leg," referring presumably not to the Camorra, Naples' infamous mob, but to the countless scholars and authors who've swallowed the legend hook, line, and mozzarella over the decades, arguing over the queen's motives, interpreting the significance of the event, even, as we've seen, comparing the queen to Princess Diana.

Not that all the scholars were sold on every detail of the story, but even the most skeptical have argued only that the Savoy house might have fabricated or embellished the story to burnish their populist chops. Well, you may have noticed by now that the tomato and pizza worlds have had more than their share of legends, liars, and charlatans, from pill peddlers through the

Lombardi legend and fake San Marzano tomatoes. What if it turned out that for almost a century everyone—authors, scholars, and Brandi customers—had been the victim of the biggest con of them all, an audacious twentieth-century marketing hoax?

That's exactly what Nowak claims.

"What raised your suspicions?" I ask. "It's such a good story."

"That's exactly it. It's *too* good. *Too* neat. With a little red, white, and green bow on top. I mean, it really *is* a great story, how the queen meets the commoner and reunites Italy with this pizza with the red, white, and green of the flag. It's just too perfect."

And it's not even original, he adds, but a recycling of a tale of one of the Bourbon kings dressing up as a commoner and walking the streets of Naples unrecognized to satisfy a pizza craving. In fact, a version featuring Queen Margherita even appeared in a newspaper nine years earlier—but with father-in-law Brandi playing the part of the *pizzaiolo*!

Well, it's one thing to be skeptical. Where's the proof? I ask. What about that thank-you note from the royal chamberlain, the Turin shroud of Margherita pizza? I saw it with my own eyes.

"It's a forgery," Nowak says bluntly. "I'm 100 percent certain. Not even 99 percent. A hundred percent."

Nowak finds several problems with the letter. First, there is no record of it in the logs of the royal household's official correspondence, which is highly unusual. Next, the official seal is stamped, not preprinted on stationery, as was the custom. But perhaps most convincing is the fact that the florid handwriting in the note does not remotely resemble any other known samples from the chamberlain.

My pilgrimage to the shrine of pizza starting to feel as wobbly as the center of a Neapolitan pie, I ask Nowak if a lot of this couldn't be plausibly explained away: The traveling royal party didn't have any official stationery with them; the busy chamberlain had a junior clerk write the note for him; and he simply neglected to make a log entry for a letter he didn't want to write (or wasn't authorized to write) in the first place.

Nowak knocks down my arguments like shooting toy ducks at a country fair. No stationery? Every other document from the royal household during the queen's visit to Naples (which did in fact take place in June 1889) is printed on stationery with the official seal preprinted. The stamp used in place of the seal doesn't match any known seals, and as for my theory that the chamberlain could have had an assistant write the note for him, Nowak says that there is no instance in the archives of any of Camillo Galli's correspondence being written by anyone but Galli himself. Because, Nowak says, Galli *was* a secretary. His job included writing notes, and Nowak finds it incredulous that "the secretary would have a secretary." (Nowak clearly doesn't work in corporate America.)

Pressed, the historian concedes that, while you *could* come up with some convoluted "Rube Goldberg machine" to manage your way around all the discrepancies, the far easier explanation is that the letter is a forgery. Well, then, by whom?

Esposito, who, remember, had named his pizzeria "Queen of Italy" six years before Margherita's visit, would seem the most likely suspect, but for one detail: Galli's letter is oddly addressed to "Raffaele Esposito Brandi," and, as Nowak notes with some understatement, "Italian men, in the nineteenth century as now, did not take their wives' surnames." Not only is this apparent slipup more evidence of a forgery, but it also removes suspicion from Esposito, who would not have miswritten his own name. Who does that leave? Who would gain by changing the *pizzaiolo*'s surname to "Brandi"?

Someone named Brandi. In 1927 the pizzeria was passed down to two nephews of Esposito's wife, Maria Brandi, leading Nowak to conjecture in his paper:

> The Brandi brothers, in the midst of the Great Depression, desperate to raise their pizzeria's visibility, decide to bend a "family myth" to their advantage. They somehow find the name of Camillo Galli, decide on a plausible date, and have a believable (though not terribly accurate) facsimile of the royal seal made in rubber. Some old paper and a pen (an error here too in not using a fountain pen), exaggeratedly elegant script, and a forgery is made.

If Nowak is right, this must be one of the most successful, enduring, and profitable forgeries of all time. Even Michelangelo's fake Cupid was sniffed out before the little fellow could break any hearts, but this little thank-you note has put Pizzeria Brandi, one of only three nineteenth-century Neapolitan pizzerias to survive into the twenty-first, into every guidebook on Naples and every written history of pizza for the past hundred years, bringing in millions of (I admit) gullible tourists who think they are eating a slice of history, not to mention gullible historians wasting untold academic hours arguing over the Savoy queen's motives on that June evening.

Of course, it's possible that *both* things are true: that Esposito did in fact make pizza for the queen and that the nephews forged the letter fifty years later in order to bolster the family legend and scare up some business. But you'll never convince Nowak of that.

Happily for Zachary Nowak, it turns out that no one wanted to break his leg after all, because his paper received surprisingly little attention. He tells me, "Funny thing is, you're, like, the first scholar"—I let the almost hilarious inflation of my credentials pass—"who's taken any notice of it at all." I suspect a good many did notice but chose to ignore it. The Italians have a saying: "It may be too good to be true, but even if it's not, it's such a good story!"

Five

ANTICIPATION

A Penniless Pickle Peddler from Pittsburgh Purifies Ketchup

We've all been there: You're in a restaurant, perhaps with a date, and the waiter has just put a bottle of ketchup on the table for your hamburger or fries. And the damn stuff just won't come out of the bottle. You tap it, you shake it, you make a mess by plunging your knife deep into the bottle's narrow neck, but *still* no ketchup, and you know, you just *know*, this isn't going to end well, for you or your date. As your food grows cold and the frustration mounts, you might just find yourself wondering why this has to be so hard.

Turns out, there's a reason. And his name is likely on the bottle.

Americans have long had a not-so-savory reputation abroad as vulgar cowboys who slather ketchup onto everything, in the manner of Thomas Wolfe's Depression-era truck drivers who "poured great gobs and gluts of thick tomato ketchup on their hamburgers" in *You Can't Go Home Again*. But even they can't hold a candle to Supreme Court justice Brett Kavanaugh, who, it was revealed during his confirmation hearing (apparently to burnish his all-American image following sordid allegations of sexual assault), pours even greater gobs of ketchup on his spaghetti.

Yet while ketchup is as American as apple pie and the Supreme Court, it is, like Worcestershire sauce and the Puritans, an early British import. The British, in turn, adapted both the condiment and the name from Southeast Asian fish sauces, which made their way to England on the ships of seventeenth-century English and Dutch merchants. In the Hokkien language of coastal southern China, these proto-ketchups are variously translated as *kê-tsiap*, *kôechiap*, or *ke-tchup*.

The first English ketchups (or "catsup," as it was also spelled—the twin spellings go back three centuries) were made from mushrooms, walnuts, or fish well before Brits were eating tomatoes. Mushroom and fish ketchups aren't hard to fathom. After all, ketchup's kissin' cousin, Worcestershire sauce, gets its kick from anchovies. But how one coaxes ketchup out of walnuts is not immediately obvious. That's because the tomato ketchups of today are far thicker than those early versions, which were essentially the brine left over after pickling mushrooms, fish, and nuts for months. Walnuts were steeped in vinegar for up to a year.

Tomatoes, still considered ornamental plants in the 1600s, wouldn't come to ketchup until ketchup came to America, in what *New Yorker* writer Malcolm Gladwell calls "the union of the English tradition of fruit and vegetable sauces and the growing American infatuation with the tomato." The first recipes for tomato ketchup do not appear until the early 1800s (you'll recall that Colonel Robert Gibbon Johnson owned a recipe for "love-apple catsup"), and commercial ketchups would not be common until after the Civil War, a direct outgrowth of the new popularity of canned tomatoes. Canners of whole tomatoes routinely rejected diseased, insect-ridden, underripe, and rotten fruit, tossing it to the floor to later be swept up or hosed into a gutter and disposed of. But tomato ketchup gave canners a convenient—and profitable—way to clean the floor of what they referred to as trimming, waste, or slop. The resulting concoction, after being fermented, boiled down, skimmed off, and spiced up, was an unappetizing shade of brown, so artificial colorings, notably coal-tar dyes (originally developed for the textile industry), were used to give ketchup its bright red color.

As the popularity of canned tomatoes soared in the late nineteenth century, so did its by-product (or waste product), ketchup. There were, as noted earlier, some eighteen hundred canneries in America, and it must have seemed like every one of them was making a little ketchup on the side. If you've ever found yourself paralyzed at the supermarket when having to decide between Heinz, Hunt's, Del Monte, and the generic store brand, pity the Connecticut shopper who in 1897 had no less than ninety-four brands of ketchup to choose from. Some eight hundred unique ketchup brands sold in the United States before 1915 have been identified, with the true number likely several times higher. Facing such stiff competition, some manufacturers tried to make their products stand out with a catchy name, giving us Best Yet, Home Comfort, Mother's Kind, Mother's Sharp, Time O' Day, and four distinct ketchup brands named Climax.

Ketchup was in such demand that some manufacturers even had to buy fresh tomatoes to supplement the cannery scraps, and many also contained apples, pumpkin, squash, turnip, or other fillers. In 1896 the *New York Herald Tribune* anointed ketchup the national condiment, reporting that it was found on "every table in the land"—and the ketchup most often found on American tables was a brand called Heinz.

Henry J. Heinz was born to German immigrants in 1844 on the South Side of Pittsburgh and raised in nearby Sharpsville, five miles up the Allegheny River. His paternal grandmother, Charlotte Louisa Trump, was a second cousin to Friedrich Trump, grandfather to the forty-fifth president of the United States, who, true to his Heinz bloodline, is reported to have a predilection for smothering his well-done steaks in ketchup.

Unlike his second cousin twice removed, Henry Heinz was a self-made man who got his start in business at the age of eight, peddling excess produce from his mother's vegetable garden to the neighbors. When demand outstripped the family garden, his parents gave him three-quarters of an acre of his own, which had grown to nearly four acres by the time Henry had reached twelve. The precocious lad bought a horse and buggy with his profits, having figured out that being a wholesaler—unloading his produce to grocers and hotels—was a heck of a lot easier than going door-to-door for nickel sales. He also found that he could extend his business beyond the end of summer by adding preserved foods such as horseradish and sauerkraut to his product line.

Horseradish was a particularly strong seller among the Germans and Brits who'd settled in large numbers in western Pennsylvania. Useful for masking slightly overripe meat and seafood, horseradish is time-consuming and inconvenient to make at home. The gnarly roots need to be scrubbed, peeled, and grated, often resulting in scraped knuckles, stinging eyes, and burning sinuses. Henry had helped his mother with horseradish since he could walk, and now the teenager enlisted his two sisters to assist with preparing and bottling the pungent root with salt and vinegar.

Although imported British condiments were available in the nineteenth century (the well-known brand Crosse & Blackwell was founded in 1706), most American condiments were produced by small, regional companies, often with low standards and lower scruples. If you bought a bottle of any condiment in the nineteenth century, you could assume it was (at best) contaminated with stones, weeds, or stems, or (at worst) adulterated in some way or other, either with additions of sawdust or grated turnips for filler, or with potentially dangerous preservatives to prevent spoilage. Henry, betting that housewives would pay more for a premium product, marketed his horseradish on a guarantee of purity, packaging it in expensive clear bottles, rather than the standard opaque brown or green bottles that hid a multitude of sins. The strategy paid off handsomely, with the seventeen-year-old Heinz selling (in today's dollars, as all figures in this chapter will be) $56,000 of horseradish in a single year, while also taking some night courses in business and serving as bookkeeper for his father's brickyard business.

In 1869, Heinz, now a twenty-five-year-old newlywed, joined up with friend L. Clarence Noble to form Heinz & Noble (renamed Heinz, Noble & Company after Noble's brother joined the firm in 1872). Beginning with just three-quarters of an acre and two employees bottling horseradish in a tiny kitchen, their rise was astronomical; within a few years the company, one of the fastest-growing in Pittsburgh, was cultivating 160 acres and employing a seasonal staff of 150, having added celery sauce (a popular condiment believed to be a brain food), sauerkraut, vinegar, ketchup (from Henry's mother's recipe), and their signature product, the one that would both make the company and bring it down: pickles.

Pickled cucumbers were immensely popular in the 1800s, when fresh salads were still rare, and nearly all were imported from England. Thus Heinz and Noble found a ready market for their product, which they sold from spotless, tricked-out wagons adorned with colorful advertising and drawn by meticulously groomed jet-black horses that would've made the Budweiser Clydesdales look like nags. Demand for their pickles was so great that in 1875, amid an unsteady economy, Noble recklessly contracted with a large Illinois farm to take their entire crop of cucumbers at a guaranteed price of 60 cents a bushel.

Heinz delivery wagons, such as this 1900 model, doubled as ornate advertisements. (H. J. Heinz Company Photograph, Detre Library & Archives Division, Senator John Heinz History Center, Pittsburgh, Pennsylvania.)

Noble and Heinz got more than they bargained for. That year produced the bumper crop of bumper crops. The cukes rolled into Pittsburgh like a tsunami. Their numbers would've tested the company's capacity for pickling in any year, but the Panic of 1873, which had begun two years earlier in New York and closed the Stock Exchange for a week, reached Pittsburgh at about the same time as the cucumbers, shutting down the iron forges, steel mills, and factories that were the lifeblood of that city. Unemployment soared to 40 percent, the bottom fell out of the pickle market, and Noble's cucumbers, arriving at the staggering rate of two thousand bushels a day, had no place to go.

The company was already overextended from an ambitious nationwide expansion and Noble's profligate spending even before the historic financial crisis—the nation's worst until the Great Depression—and with little capital, not only were Heinz and Noble unable to pay for the cucumbers, they couldn't even afford to pay for their disposal. Cucumbers and debt piled up. Creditors started calling in loans, the company couldn't meet payroll, and on December 17, 1875, Heinz, Noble & Company became one of thirteen companies to file for bankruptcy in Allegheny County in a single week.

Heinz' detractors and competitors took schadenfreudian delight in the upstarts' downfall, the *Pittsburgh Leader* crowing, "Trio in a Pickle." Heinz was broke, flat broke, not even able to afford a Christmas present for his wife. Neighbors who'd invested in the company showed up angry at his door. Even his in-laws turned on him, as did his former partner and best friend Clarence Noble, who publicly blamed Heinz, not his own cucumber conundrum, for the company's downfall. For Henry, a devout Lutheran and Sunday school teacher, the worst blow was the shame and guilt he bore over having stiffed his creditors in the bankruptcy, all of whom he resolved to repay. Some creditors he recompensed by noncash means; Abraham Anderson, Joseph Campbell's partner in his canning empire, agreed to take Heinz' white stallion as payment, and delighted in parading around Camden on Heinz' horse.

Like San Marzano tomato farmer Michele Ruggiero after he'd lost everything, Heinz fell into depression and illness over his misfortune. But unlike Michele, Henry pulled himself out of it after the new year. With the support of his family, who sold whatever they could to scrape together start-up money, a new company was formed. Heinz moved back into the Sharpsville homestead kitchen to return to, you might say, his roots, once again grating horseradish.

Humbled but not defeated, Henry put in long days, walking the fields in the morning and making sales calls in the afternoon. Finding himself in desperate need of a horse, the man whose gleaming teams of matched stallions were once the pride of Pittsburgh noted in his diary that he had finally been able to buy "a cheap $16 horse to help us out," adding simply, "He is blind."

Pittsburgh may have been recovering from an economic depression, but people still needed horseradish. Heinz reconnected with his former customers, some of whom had been buying from him since he was in short pants, and business picked up throughout the first summer. Henry received a chillier reception from bankers and potential creditors, who refused to lend him the capital he needed to get back into the lucrative pickle business, which required vinegar generators and boilers. With no chance of receiving fresh credit on the heels of a bankruptcy, Heinz turned to a highly profitable product that he could quickly manufacture and sell without a heavy initial investment: tomato ketchup.

All that is required to get into the ketchup business is a few tomato canners looking to get rid of slop, plus some vats. Unlike horseradish, you don't even need to grow anything. Ketchup had been the last product added to the Heinz, Noble & Company line before the company went belly-up, but now Henry jumped in with both feet, entering the market with three different offerings, a kind of *good, better, best.* His premium ketchup, the one with the most tomatoes, sold for a substantial six to seven dollars a bottle, about twice the price of the competitors' ketchups (and his own low-end variety). Heinz knew from experience that if making horseradish in the home kitchen was laborious, ketchup was worse. Tomatoes had to be peeled, cut, seeded, mashed into pulp, and boiled down for hours, and Pittsburgh was decidedly not southern Italy, where housewives turned the making of *conserva* into a weeklong block party. A Heinz employee writing in the company newsletter in 1901 told his younger colleagues how fortunate they were "to have been born a generation or so late, and to have escaped the miseries of…the boiling of jellies and the parboiling of his face and hands as he stirred, stirred and constantly stirred the catsup to keep it from burning."

The stirring and scalding was still fresh in the thirty-two-year-old Heinz' memory. Hoping to reproduce his success with horseradish by selling convenience and quality, he advertised his ketchup as "blessed relief for Mother and all the women in the household." As with horseradish, Heinz sold his ketchup in clear glass bottles. His hunch that quality and transparency were the keys to success once again paid off handsomely. The company sold over a million dollars' worth of ketchup in its very first year, allowing Heinz to repay every last penny to his Heinz, Noble & Company creditors, even though the bankruptcy filing had absolved him of that obligation.

Over the next quarter century, Heinz not only duplicated but exceeded by a wide margin the success of his first company, selling more than five dozen products, from relishes and other condiments to soups and beans, and, of course, pickles. As the twentieth century began, the largest-growing company in Pittsburgh wasn't U.S. Steel, or Westinghouse, or a Carnegie company; it was H. J. Heinz, which, on the back of pickles and ketchup, was well on its way to becoming America's largest international firm, not to mention its most visible. Heinz, like Campbell's Arthur Dorrance, believed in heavy consumer advertising, and he literally outshone the competition, erecting New York City's first large electric sign, six stories high, its twelve hundred bulbs flashing "Heinz Tomato Ketchup" in rotation with pickles and other products at Fifth Avenue and Twenty-Third Street (the busy intersection where the Flatiron Building stands today). A "Heinz 57" sign nearly seventy feet long topped the banks of the Rhine River in Germany.

The "Heinz 57 varieties" slogan, adopted in 1896 (he already had exceeded that number, but liked the ring of "57"), had become so well-known that the nation's passenger railroad tracks and prominent hillsides from New York to San Francisco were peppered with huge signs that simply read "57." No one had to ask, "Fifty-seven *what*?" Heinz was a master of public relations. He even constructed a pier into the ocean at Atlantic City that led, after an exhilarating walk over the waves, to the Heinz 57 pavilion. Its cooking demonstrations, free tastings, souvenir pickle pins, and a large painting of Custer's last stand made it one of the boardwalk's most popular tourist attractions.

Heinz was an innovator in the workplace as well. In what sounds like a prototype for Silicon Valley, his factories provided employees (many of them recent immigrants) with a swimming pool, gymnasium, showers, lunch, lectures featuring the prominent speakers of the day, free on-site health care, lounges, rooftop

The Heinz ocean pier and pavilion at Atlantic City attracted tourists with ocean breezes, a mural of Custer's last stand, and free merchandise. (H. J. Heinz Company Photograph, Detre Library & Archives Division, Senator John Heinz History Center, Pittsburgh, Pennsylvania.)

garden spaces, and a fifteen-hundred-seat theater built solely for the benefit of the employees. The company even employed its own music director.

Henry Heinz believed in the adage of "doing well by doing good," and as the Gilded Age was drawing to a close, he was doing *very* well, fabulously wealthy and as famous as Carnegie and Rockefeller. Yet an existential threat to his empire was looming, not from his wealthy and powerful peers, but from a former professor of classical languages in a white lab coat.

❀

Harvey Washington Wiley was born in a log cabin in Indiana in 1844, the son of a farmer and itinerate preacher. After serving as a conductor on the Underground Railroad and fighting in the Civil War, he earned an MD from Indiana Medical College but never practiced medicine, instead preferring to teach chemistry, Greek, and Latin, before leaving for Harvard, where he earned a bachelor's degree in science in a single semester. In 1878, while Henry Heinz' newly rebooted company was pumping out ketchup, Wiley had been in Germany studying with the world's top chemists. Each man was unknown to the other, yet their paths were on a direct collision course that was destined to fundamentally change the nature of the country's most popular condiment.

When Wiley was appointed the chief of the Bureau of Chemistry in the US Department of Agriculture in 1882, there were no federal laws whatsoever governing food safety, labeling, or additives, a direct consequence of the Popular Health Movement of the 1830s through the 1850s. Far from ensuring "popular health," the Jacksonian anti-elitist movement (the same one that helped fuel the tomato-pill craze), in favoring individual judgment over science, succeeded in preventing virtually any government regulation of health care. As a result, even a half century later, anything could go into a jar of baby food or a can of peas—and it did, usually without the consumer's knowledge. Plaster whitened and thickened milk, while formaldehyde preserved it. Arsenic gave chocolate its gloss, and lead provided color to the hard candies favored by children. Patent medicines had evolved since the relatively innocent days of tomato extract and calomel into sometimes dangerous concoctions containing cocaine, heroin, morphine, alcohol, and cannabis. Most famously, cocaine was the "Coca" in Coca-Cola. Then there were the chemical preservatives found in ketchup and other foods.

Tomato ketchup was one of the earliest foods to introduce artificial preservatives because crushed tomatoes begin to ferment in short order, giving ketchup a shelf life of just a few days. Ketchup's role as a condiment meant that it was used in small amounts over a period of time (think about how long that bottle of ketchup has been in your refrigerator—or maybe *don't*), and consumers of ketchup made from walnuts, mushrooms, or anchovies demanded a similar shelf life from the tomato version.

Those pre-tomato ketchups (which were sold by Heinz and others into the twentieth century) owed their long shelf lives to the natural preservative properties of salt and vinegar, as well as to the fact that many were boiled down to obtain added thickness, in the process killing spoilage-causing bacteria. Anchovy and mushroom ketchups were typically good for up to a year, and walnut ketchup even longer.

Not surprisingly, ketchup made from the detritus of tomato canning factories did not come close to that kind of longevity. Ketchup that used fresh tomatoes fared better, but still started fermenting well before the bottle was empty. And "bottle" is key. Canned tomatoes were submerged in boiling water for hours after being sealed in their cans, killing bacteria, but ketchup, like other condiments, was traditionally sold in glass bottles that would often shatter when subjected to high temperature. Thus, the ketchup had to be heated to kill bacteria *before* bottling, allowing airborne contaminants to enter the bottles during the filling process (as well as after, around the cork top). Without a chemical preservative, bottles would spoil on grocers' shelves, and once opened by the consumer, even the most diligently made ketchups lasted no more than a week. So manufacturers added preservatives such as boric acid, salicylic acid, and benzoates to retard spoilage.

Heinz' ketchup, as far back as the Heinz, Noble & Company

days, had always relied on preservatives, the first being willow bark, which contains salicylic acid, a natural preservative (and relative of aspirin) that German scientists learned how to synthesize in 1874. Heinz switched to boric acid after huge deposits of borax (which also found use as the popular household cleanser, 20 Mule Team Borax) were discovered in California, and finally to sodium benzoate (the salt of benzoic acid) after German chemists devised the means to extract it from coal tars, meaning that Heinz ketchup had not one but *two* ingredients derived from coal: preservative and dye.

The liberal and unregulated use of preservatives in ketchup and other processed foods drew the attention of the nation's chief chemist, Harvey Wiley. Were these additives safe? In what quantities? No one knew, because no one had ever tested them. To answer these questions, in 1902 Wiley created what the press dubbed a "poison squad," consisting of twelve (formerly) healthy men enlisted to establish safe limits of food additives. Cheerfully adopting the motto "Only the brave dare eat the fare," the men were sequestered in a dormitory/laboratory where Wiley fed them three squares a day, the meals spiked with increasing levels of such common food additives as benzoates, borax, and formaldehyde, until the men became too ill to leave their beds.

Only three of the volunteers managed to persevere to the end of the ten-day benzoate trial, which left the men with enflamed throats and esophagi, stomachaches, dizziness, and weight loss. Although the escalating amounts of sodium benzoate were far higher than those used in ketchup, Wiley concluded that benzoates, the most commonly used ketchup preservative, were (to borrow a phrase from a future consumer protection pioneer) unsafe at any speed. The scientist, described by his biographer as "a holy roller kind of chemist," began to vigorously campaign for a total ban on benzoates just as Congress was formulating the nation's first food legislation, the Pure Food and Drug Act. Thus began the great benzoate battle, with Harvey Wiley on one side, Henry Heinz on the other.

Ketchup was the leading condiment in the United States; Heinz was the leading ketchup manufacturer; and ketchup was its best-selling product, having helped make Henry J. Heinz a multimillionaire, one of Edith Wharton's "Lords of Pittsburgh" alongside Andrew Carnegie, Henry Clay Frick, George Westinghouse, and Andrew Mellon. Heinz could envision a couple of possible outcomes from the war on benzoates, neither good: The government could ban the preservative, effectively banning ketchup; or another company might somehow figure out a way to make preservative-free ketchup first, ruining him overnight.

The stakes for Heinz, now churning out four million bottles of ketchup a year, were enormous. But, he realized, so was the opportunity.

Attitudes toward the nation's health had changed since the laissez-faire years of the Popular Health Movement. Beginning in the 1870s, a grassroots coalition of medical societies, women's clubs, temperance organizations, and civic organizations known collectively as the Pure Food Movement had been campaigning for federal food safety regulations. With little to show for their decades-long efforts, the movement's leaders brought reform proponents, senior officials from processed-food companies, and Harvey Wiley together in St. Louis for several days of discussion and debate at what they called the Pure Food Congress of 1904.

After hearing Wiley and others warn of the dangers of preservatives, Heinz research manager G. F. Mason took the stage and explained how his food chemists had spent years trying unsuccessfully to produce a ketchup free of additives. "Every possible means of preserving with none but natural agents were used, without satisfactory results," Mason told the conference, reporting that invariably within just sixty hours the ketchup spoiled from fermentation. It was, he said, virtually impossible to make a preservative-free ketchup.

The response from Harvey Wiley was that perhaps ketchup "would be a product we ought to do without." Even as those words caught in the throats of ketchup bottles across America, North and South Dakota had already limited benzoic acid to one-tenth of 1 percent, a level too low to be effective—essentially outlawing commercial ketchup—and other states were not far behind. Several countries in Europe, where Heinz had more operations than any other American food company, had imposed stringent regulations on the importation of American processed foods because of safety concerns. In Washington, the pressure on Congress to enact some form of food safety legislation was building, with Wiley doing his best to whip up public sentiment, appearing before women's clubs, doing interviews, and appealing directly to President Teddy Roosevelt.

Yet even while publicly sparring with Wiley, arguing that benzoates were not only safe but "present naturally in...cranberry" and other fruits, Heinz had been quietly trying to come up with a preservative-free ketchup that would last in kitchen cupboards for a full month. Whether this was a matter of survival as he contemplated a ban, an expression of his ethical beliefs, or a chance to have the ketchup market all to himself is hard to say, but it was probably a little of each. It's worth remembering that this is the man who'd entered the condiment business on a guarantee of purity. Now, however, he was failing to deliver on that promise, and public sentiment for additive-free ketchup was building. Henry Heinz was running out of time.

Why, Heinz and his researchers wondered, did ketchup made in the home without preservatives have a substantially longer shelf life than anything they could produce in the test kitchen? Why couldn't H. J. Heinz make ketchup like *Mrs*. Heinz? Mason and his team started digging through recipes for homemade ketchups (by now a rarity) and found that they tended to have more sugar, vinegar, and spices than commercial varieties. They were also made with ripe tomatoes picked fresh from the garden.

Increasing the vinegar, a natural preservative, lengthened shelf life, but made the ketchup too, well, vinegary, so to compensate, Mason added more sugar. But more sugar promoted spoilage, so additional vinegar had to be added. Which required more sugar. By the time an equilibrium had been reached, Heinz ketchup would have fully twice the sugar and vinegar of every other brand on the market. It would also have more seasoning, as Mason had found that leaving the ground spices in the final product, rather than filtering them out before bottling, increased longevity.

Beyond tweaking the recipe, Heinz modified manufacturing, making his ketchup factories sterile and clean enough to eat off the floor. He replaced the traditional wooden barrels used to store tomato pulp with airtight, lacquer-lined metal tubs, eliminating the air infiltration that led to fermentation. For the same reason, he narrowed the neck of the bottle.

These innovations were inching Heinz scientists incrementally closer to an additive-free ketchup, but the goal still eluded them.

They'd tried everything they could think of, yet, maddeningly, their test batches still spoiled within days, the corks blowing out of the bottles like it was New Year's Eve. Well, they'd tried *almost* everything. They had overlooked one critical factor.

The tomato.

⊛

The overripe, unripe, and wormy tomatoes, unsuitable for canning, that provided the raw material for ketchup had less pectin than peak-ripe tomatoes. Pectin, a gelatinous complex carbohydrate found in many fruits and some vegetables, is a potent thickener, commonly used to firm up jellies and jams. But Heinz researchers discovered that pectin had another important property: *It was a natural preservative.* But getting the right amount of pectin from the tomatoes was tricky: Not only did they have to be at the peak of ripeness, they also couldn't be overcooked because under heat pectin breaks down into pectic acid. Yet undercooking invited bacteria. In any event, the key was to start with fresh, ripe tomatoes.

So H. J. Heinz, like today's canners of San Marzano tomatoes, ended up being very choosy about the tomatoes it bought, paying top dollar and rejecting imperfect tomatoes on the assembly line. And in order to get the freshest tomatoes, Heinz decentralized the ketchup business, putting factories where the tomatoes were. One of Heinz' plants sprouted in the fields of Salem, New Jersey (Colonel Johnson's old neighborhood). Another one, to produce ketchup for the Canadian market, was built in Leamington, Ontario, a major tomato-growing region east of Detroit that will loom large in the tomato's story (and this one) before it's all over.

Baskets of tomatoes arriving via the Allegheny River at the Heinz factory in Pittsburgh. Heinz pioneered the use of whole, fresh tomatoes in ketchup. (H. J. Heinz Company Photograph, Detre Library & Archives Division, Senator John Heinz History Center, Pittsburgh, Pennsylvania.)

Heinz would later go one step further, becoming a major tomato breeder itself, developing varieties specifically for use in ketchup, then supplying seeds and seedlings of these high–pectin, low-gel tomatoes to contract growers, the first processed-food manufacturer in the United States to do so. (Home gardeners can purchase some of these Heinz varieties through seed catalogs today.)

For now, though, having cracked the code of the tomato's built-in natural preservative, the scientists in Mason's laboratory continued running test batches, tensely watching and waiting for signs of spoilage, until in late 1904 they hit upon the formula that produced a preservative-free ketchup guaranteed to last a month after opening—the unrefrigerated shelf life of a bottle bought today. Within two years every single bottle of Heinz ketchup sold would be preservative-free. Henry Heinz had won the benzoate war.

His success sent shock waves through the ketchup industry, but it was what he did next that really alarmed his competitors: Heinz abruptly switched sides in the benzoate battle, joining forces with former foe Harvey Wiley to push for a total benzoate ban with the same fervor he had shown in pursuing a preservative-free ketchup.

The company started a nationwide ad blitz against the use of benzoates in food, spending more on advertising than all other ketchup brands combined. A two-page ad in *Collier's* called benzoate acid a "dangerous drug." Other ads rhetorically asked consumers why they would consider using ketchup made with a chemical that their dear grandmothers would never have used in theirs. Every one of his ads, whether for ketchup or pickles, reminded consumers that *all* of Heinz' "57 Varieties" were free of benzoates and other preservatives, as did a label around the narrow neck of every ketchup bottle.

Heinz had introduced the distinctive bottle, its octagonal shape meant to invoke Doric Greek columns, in 1902. Now he replaced the cork with an airtight white screw cap that further reduced spoilage, and the iconic Heinz ketchup bottle, perhaps the most recognizable food container in the world today, was complete. It would remain essentially unchanged until the introduction of the squeezable plastic bottle in 1983.

But it was what lay *inside* the bottle that was revolutionary. In order to make a ketchup free of preservatives, Heinz had needed to dramatically increase the pectin, sugar, salt, and vinegar. In

Good Ketchup Needs No Drugs

Every housewife knows—every food manufacturer knows—that Benzoate of Soda is not necessary in the right kind of ketchup.

Government officials know it, for the U. S. Department of Agriculture has issued a bulletin showing that ketchup can be prepared and kept without artificial preservatives.

Benzoate of Soda is generally used to prevent inferior, unwholesome materials from further spoilage, and to allow the presence of water in the place of solid food. The drug also permits unsanitary handling and loose manufacturing methods. More than this, eminent medical authorities have declared it harmful to health.

HEINZ
Tomato Ketchup
Contains No Benzoate of Soda.

The tomatoes used in it are especially grown from our own seed. They are the best that soil and climate can produce—fine flavored, meaty, solid.

From the field to the bottle is a matter of but a few hours. The tomatoes are invariably vine-ripened. After sufficient cooking, spices of our own grinding, granulated sugar and pure vinegar are added—but not a drop of anything chemical or artificial—and opened or unopened, Heinz Ketchup keeps.

Your safeguard against Benzoate of Soda—often found in well-known brands—is to read carefully all labels, for on them the law requires the presence of drugs to be stated. Read the small type.

No Benzoate of Soda or other artificial preservative is used in any of Heinz 57. They are guaranteed to please or money back. Thousands of visitors pass through Heinz Model Kitchens every year and witness our care and cleanliness and the quality of our materials.

H. J. HEINZ COMPANY

Members of American Association for the Promotion of Purity in Food Products.

An early twentieth-century ad slams the use of benzoates in ketchup. The familiar bottle design would remain virtually unchanged to this day. (N. W. Ayer Advertising Agency Records, Archives Center, National Museum of American History, Smithsonian Institution.)

the process, ketchup had gone from savory to sweet; from thin to thick. *Heinz had in fact changed the very nature of ketchup.* And the thickness came just in time for the growing popularity of French fries and hamburgers, the latter having just been introduced at the 1904 World's Fair.

Not everyone was thrilled. Some consumers complained that you could no longer taste the tomatoes through the sugar and vinegar, and, indeed, Heinz ketchup has more sugar per liquid ounce than Coca-Cola. Many preferred the more savory version, even if it had preservatives. Competing manufacturers, disbelieving that an all-natural ketchup could last a month, publicly accused Heinz of using a secret, undetectable preservative. What they said about him in private was surely unprintable.

Heinz and Wiley ignored the critics and continued to hammer away against preservatives, and the public was won over by this odd-fellow crusade of two former adversaries—won over, that is, to Heinz ketchup. Sales boomed, reaching a phenomenal $79 million annually by 1908. The preservative-free formulation had one problem, however: With all that pectin, the ketchup—said to have twenty-four tomatoes packed into every bottle—was agonizingly slow to come out, a situation aggravated by the bottle's narrow neck. Undeterred, Heinz cleverly turned the liability into an asset, advertising that his ketchup had "more tomato, less water," and calling on consumers to "notice how slowly it comes out of the bottle," anticipating by three-quarters of a century the company's 1978 "Anticipation" television campaign—in which ketchup users wait eagerly (to the soundtrack of Carly Simon's hit song) for the ketchup to start flowing.

Sometimes you can wait quite a while. But ketchup, it turns out, isn't hard to coax from the bottle merely because it's thick or on the wrong side of a bottleneck. In reinventing ketchup, Heinz had inadvertently created a "non-Newtonian fluid," so called because such liquids do not follow Newton's law of viscosity, which in layman's terms says that only temperature—not stirring or shaking—has an effect on a liquid's viscosity (or thickness). And most everyday fluids do obey Newton's law; shaking a bottle of orange juice does not affect how quickly it pours.

At rest, however, a non-Newtonian fluid such as ketchup behaves almost like a solid. You can invert a bottle of ketchup for some time before it starts to drip out of the bottle. But if given a good shake (or squeeze, in the plastic bottle), its viscosity will temporarily decrease to the point where the ketchup will behave as a liquid, which is why it can go from frustratingly thick to perilously thin so fast, with that final shake sometimes drenching your hamburger, and possibly more, in red.

To get the ketchup safely flowing, the Heinz Company suggests you strike the bottle—hard—on the raised "57" just below the neck, not, as people often do, on the bottom of the bottle, which is too far from the ketchup near the opening to do any good.

But hold on a sec—what on earth is a ketchup bottle doing on my restaurant table in the first place? You'd do a double take if your request for some mayo resulted in a jar of Hellmann's being plopped down, yet a bottle of ketchup is not only acceptable, but expected. After all, it's not just ketchup, it's *Heinz* ketchup, in that white-capped, slender octagonal bottle, a symbol of quality that everyone recognizes and loves. Probably nothing else speaks to Henry Heinz' remarkable success as the sight of his ketchup—in its commercial packaging—on restaurant tables.

In the home, however, squeezable plastic bottles have overwhelmingly replaced glass, reducing the frustration factor. Ketchup today is found in 97 percent of American households, quite a feat when you consider the ethnic and cultural diversity of the nation. Which begs the question of why the condiment that can be nearly impossible to dispense is often indispensable to the enjoyment of so many other foods. Why do we love ketchup so much?

For answers, I've turned to Harold McGee, the popular food science writer whose 896-page reference work, *On Food and Cooking*, covers seemingly every imaginable food topic from the chemistry of tempering chocolate to the science of puff pastry. Before getting to ketchup, however, we begin with its main ingredient. To what, I ask McGee, does the tomato owe its terrific flavor?

"I think it comes down to the balance that it manages to create," he says. "Most foods give us pleasure along certain axes. The tomato seems to encompass all of them. Because it manages to be so balanced. You know, it's sweet, but not too sweet; tart, but it's not too tart. It's savory. It's aromatic, but it's not aromatic in a simple way. It's not just fruity; it's not just green, like a green vegetable. It's not just mushroomy like mushrooms, but it somehow combines *all* of those things into something that just tantalizes our senses and keeps us coming in for more."

Tomatoes, McGee notes, are also high in glutamates, a substance that awakens the savory taste we call umami. Only in the last century recognized as one of the five basic tastes that make up the human palate, and more difficult to define (and detect) than the other four—sweet, salty, sour, and bitter—*umami* is a Japanese word meaning "pleasant flavor," which doesn't add much clarity. I think of it is as the flavor of a satisfyingly rich bowl of homemade chicken soup. Meat, Worcestershire sauce, hard cheeses, and mushrooms are all rich in glutamates. For a fruit, tomatoes are uncommonly high in glutamic acid, which may be why they are eaten as a vegetable, because even when sweet, a tomato still retains its savory character.

Glutamate is the "G" in MSG (monosodium glutamate), long used as a "flavor enhancer," although McGee corrects me when I use that term. "It's a relic of the time when we didn't know that MSG did stimulate a very particular set of receptors on our tongue and therefore counted as an actual taste," he says. "So [flavor enhancer] is a way of saying that we find it hard to describe that taste. But it's really not a useful term anymore. I mean, salt is a taste enhancer because it makes things taste better. And glutamate, I would say, is kind of in the same category; it's an actual separate, identifiable taste. And when it's present, it adds to our overall pleasure in the general taste of the food that we're having."

That is especially true of ketchup. When Henry Heinz started using ripe tomatoes with a higher percentage of solids, he greatly increased the glutamates, introducing umami. Doubling the vinegar and sugar made the condiment both sour and sweet. He also increased the salt, and ketchup had always had some mildly bitter notes. Sweet, sour, salt, bitter, umami: Heinz had come up with a condiment that pressed all five primal taste buttons. A focus group couldn't have done a better job. An admiring Malcolm Gladwell writes:

> The taste of Heinz ketchup began at the tip of the tongue, where our receptors for sweet and salty first appear, moved along the side, where sour notes seem the strongest, then hit the back of the tongue, for umami and bitter, in one long

crescendo. How many things in the supermarket run the sensory spectrum like this?

And what that spectrum provides, McGee tells me, is "a very concentrated source of flavors that are generally not in the food that you're applying it to," whether they be meats or potatoes. "These things are delicious in their own ways, but they're lacking all of the components that ketchup can bring. So, ketchup complements them."

Which is pretty much the very definition of a successful condiment.

Yet the reasons *why* we eat *what* we eat go well beyond glutamates and taste receptors. What, for example, makes so-called comfort foods, like a bowl of soup or a French fry dipped in ketchup, so comfortable?

In a 1988 paper in the *Journal of Gastronomy* titled "Ketchup and the Collective Unconscious," the late food historian and theorist Elisabeth Rozin argues that "eating is a significant and emotionally charged act." Our affinity for ketchup results not merely from the condiment's winning flavor, but from something that horror film directors have known since there were moving pictures: the uncanny resemblance between ketchup...and blood.

And this is a *good* thing? Unconsciously, yes, Rozin maintains, because blood has long been viewed with awe and endowed with totemic powers. "In many cultures," she writes, "because blood is the very source of life...it is reserved for the gods" and "denied for ordinary human consumption. But precisely because it is so powerful and elemental to life, it is attractive and desirable. How does the human mind deal with such ambiguity?"

By inventing substitutes. Nearly every culture on earth has

developed plant-based sauces—whether the soy and fish sauces of Asia, the chili sauces of Mexico, or the tomato sauces of Europe and the Americas—that range in color from burnt orange to deep red and, in fact, *resemble blood*. "Surely," she concludes, "such cross-cultural resemblances point to basic human behavior at work."

Of course, Rozin adds, "it is unlikely that…the Neapolitan eating his plate of spaghetti and tomato sauce, or the Mexican with his tortilla and red chili sauce, or—dare I say it?—the American teenager with his bag of French fries and ketchup would be open to analysis of his meal as a symbolic evocation or re-creation of blood." That poor teenager is just trying to enjoy a balanced school lunch (French fries + ketchup = 2 vegetables, by Uncle Sam's elementary school math) before Michelle Obama snatches it away. Nevertheless, Rozin writes, "The primal motivations may be lost forever to our awareness, but the practices remain, firmly entrenched in our culinary traditions."

As challenging as some might find Elisabeth Rozin's hypothesis, it is not mutually exclusive to Harold McGee's or Malcolm Gladwell's more grounded reasoning. Rozin is just taking it one step further, probing the additional, unconscious forces behind our affinity for ketchup. You can take it or leave it. But what a pity she didn't live to see Brett Kavanaugh's confirmation hearing.

Moving on—quickly, thank you—from bodily fluids, it's surprising, given ketchup's popularity, how few brands there are to choose from these days. Every so often a "gourmet" ketchup will pop up but fail to catch on. People just seem to like Heinz, which, following the benzoate wars, never relinquished its lead in the ketchup race, today holding 60 percent of the American market and selling 8 out of every 10 bottles of ketchup consumed in Europe. This, despite the fact that Heinz and Wiley *lost* their battle to ban benzoates.

As late as January 1906, the passage of a food safety bill was looking doubtful. The Pure Food and Drug Act did pass in the Senate, but the bill had been tied up in Congress for twenty-seven years, and it looked like it was going to die again in the current session. This was despite the support of President Theodore Roosevelt, who, as commander of the Rough Riders during the Spanish-American War, had seen more of his soldiers die from American canned meat than from bullets.

Then, just after debate had begun in the House, a twenty-seven-year-old muckraking journalist named Upton Sinclair published *The Jungle*, a shocking account of the hideously unsanitary conditions in the meatpacking industry. The book was a national sensation, raising public and political awareness of the dangers lurking in the nation's foods. This surprised no one more than Sinclair, a committed socialist who had written the novel to draw attention to the plight of the immigrants working in those plants. But it was the few pages on the plight of the slaughtered pigs and cows—rotten meat mixed with chemicals, rat droppings, and sawdust—that captured the public's imagination (and near hysteria), tipping the scales in favor of food safety reform. On June 30, 1906, the nation's first bill regulating food safety, the Pure Food and Drug Act, was passed.

With no mention of benzoates.

The law focused on food ingredient *labeling*, rather than *control*. Even the narcotics used in patent medicines were still allowed, as long as the label indicated their presence. Meanwhile, the debate on the use of benzoates continued into 1909, when a Federal

Referee Board, relying on a recent study that took a less ham-handed approach to ascertaining benzoate safety than Wiley's poison squad, ruled that benzoates were safe in small quantities.

The federal government would eventually get around to regulating ketchup (during, surprisingly, the Reagan administration), but in a vastly different way: The Code of Federal Regulations, Title 21, Section 155.194: Catsup (notice the oddly archaic spelling choice) has since 1983 specified what can and can't be labeled "catsup," with by far the longest section of the code dealing, appropriately enough, with its flow rate:

> The consistency of the finished food is such that its flow is not more than 14 centimeters [5½ inches] in 30 seconds at 20 deg. C when tested in a Bostwick Consistometer in the following manner...

After which follows a full page of instructions on how to properly use a Bostwick Consistometer, although it leaves out the most important, non-Newtonian part of the test: *Don't shake the catsup!* And yet the highly viscous nature of ketchup was never designed—it was an unintended and not entirely welcome consequence. Almost certainly, Heinz' original, artificially preserved ketchup, in 1905 America's best-selling ketchup, would've flunked the Bostwick test, and thus could not today be called "catsup." Or even "ketchup."

Guess how some ketchup manufacturers today make their ketchup thick enough to satisfy the government. Yep, by using a *food additive*, usually xanthan gum. A Heinz representative nearly bristled when I asked if their ketchup is still all-natural (it is). However, this common thickener, found in ice cream and salad dressing, might be required in cheaper ketchups because the regulations do still allow "liquid obtained from the residue from preparing such tomatoes for canning, consisting of peelings and cores with or without such tomatoes or pieces thereof." In other words, floor slop.

But what does 21 CFR 155.194: Catsup have to say about preservatives, specifically benzoates?

Nada. In fact, sodium benzoate is a more common food preservative today than Harvey Wiley could ever have dreamed, added to soft drinks, fruit juices, salad dressings, soy sauce, and other condiments, as well as toothpaste and baby wipes. Although, in what must be some kind of endurance record, the additive is *still* controversial, mainly because it can combine with vitamin C (which happens to be found in many of the drinks preserved with sodium benzoate) to form benzene, a carcinogen. Coca-Cola removed sodium benzoate from its flagship colas in 2008 to avoid controversy, while leaving it in its other, less hallowed soft drinks.

Henry Heinz may have lost the regulatory battle on benzoates, but he decisively won the war for the public's hearts and minds. Thanks in large part to his vision, tomato ketchup (more often than not with his name on the bottle) has spread around the world, remaining the world's most popular condiment. And let's not forget that into every bottle of Heinz ketchup go two dozen tomatoes. Or rather, their equivalent in paste, which the company now uses exclusively, making H. J. Heinz the largest buyer of processed tomatoes in the world, over two million tons annually. The adoption of paste freed the company from having to locate its ketchup factories near tomato fields, and as a consequence its ketchup plants have closed one by one. Today every bottle of

Heinz ketchup sold in the US comes from a single factory in Fremont, Ohio. (Talk about a potential bottleneck.)

Henry Heinz died in 1919 at the age of seventy-four, and the company continued to be run by family members into the 1950s. H. J. Heinz was purchased by Berkshire Hathaway and a Brazilian investment firm for $23 billion in 2013, merging two years later with food giant Kraft to become the world's fifth-largest food company.

Yet Henry Heinz might be resting uneasily in his grave: A number of Kraft Heinz products contain sodium benzoate.

Six

ON TOP OF SPAGHETTI

At Long Last, Tomatoes Find Pasta, and a New Cuisine Is Born

"The angels in Paradise eat nothing but vermicelli in tomato sauce!" the mayor of Naples defiantly proclaimed as Italians poured into the streets, pledging to fight to the last strand the latest fascist proposal: a ban on pasta.

Italians had tolerated Mussolini's thuggish Blackshirts, the violent suppression of labor unions, and the murder of dissidents. But this time the fascists had gone too far. Filippo Tommaso Marinetti, a founding member of the Fascist Party who'd helped boost Mussolini into power eight years earlier, had published a manifesto in late 1930 that called for "the abolition of pasta, the absurd Italian gastronomic religion," claiming that it left Italians heavy, shapeless, and (lest anyone miss the point) unprepared for war.

As Neapolitans vented their outrage, choosing pasta over patriotism, Mussolini might have wondered if this was the kind of policy that could get your head planted on a pike. Yet, as passionate as Italians—especially southern Italians—were about their beloved vermicelli and tomato sauce, *pasta al pomodoro* was an almost shockingly recent newcomer, having become popular only during the past half century. Although the Italian love affair with pasta goes back much further than that, to the High Middle Ages, when city-states like Venice and Pisa were major economic and military powers, and the most celebrated explorer was a Venetian merchant and envoy to Kublai Khan who introduced to Europe such Asian wonders as porcelain, coal, gunpowder, and paper money. And, it was once widely believed, something else.

Marco!

   Polo!

Marco!

   Polo!

The explorer's name is mostly heard today when kids gather in swimming pools, but when I was a lad, he was famous for introducing pasta to Italy. The legend has its origins in Polo's memoirs, in which he reported finding pasta in China, adding that it was sourced from trees—meaning he either mistook some flora (possibly the starchy fruit of the sago palm) as the origin of the flour, or while in China he'd also discovered opium. Either way, while the faithful may find enough of a credible shred of evidence to justify clinging to the cherished Queen Margherita and Colonel Johnson legends, the story that Italians owe their pasta legacy to the Chinese by way of Marco Polo is demonstrably false, because on his return to Italy in 1295, Polo compared the noodles he'd eaten in China to . . . *lasagne*.

Still, somehow an entire generation of Americans, including this one, grew up thinking that the Chinese not only introduced pasta to Italy, but provided the *name* for the most common variety.

This is thanks to the 1938 Hollywood biopic in which Gary Cooper, playing Marco Polo (not to be confused with playing "Marco! Polo!"), is introduced to "spa-GET," pronounced by Polo's Chinese host as if he'd just stepped out of Tony Soprano's Bada Bing! club. You almost expect the next thing out of his mouth to be, "You goombah!"

The Italian version of pasta, like both pizza and tomatoes, originated around Naples, in part because the same warm winds and sunny skies that dried tomatoes on terra-cotta rooftops were also ideal for drying pasta, a surprisingly complex operation that requires the pasta to be dried neither too quickly nor too slowly, lest you wind up with a brittle or moldy product. There was a saying, "I maccheroni si fanno col sirocco e si asciugano con la tramontana," meaning, "The pasta should be made with the sirocco and dried with the tramontana"—the prevailing southerly and northerly Mediterranean winds, respectively—and Campania, the region of southern Italy encompassing Naples, Salerno, and the Amalfi Coast, had plenty of both, the mild ocean winds alternating with the dry breezes from Vesuvius. By 1400, pasta made with durum, a high-protein variety of wheat grown locally since Roman times, was being produced commercially, and within two hundred years entire towns on the Bay of Naples and the Amalfi Coast were dedicated to the pasta industry, exporting thirty thousand pounds a year by 1633.

But, in an odd twist, it was Italy's perpetual rival, the French, who indirectly helped turn Naples into a pasta machine. The Crusades brought silk production to Italy in the twelfth and thirteenth centuries, and Naples, a growing city with an international market, available labor (including Jews employed as fabric dyers), and a port, became one of the major silk producers in Europe. Italy had a virtual monopoly on European silk until the late

1400s, when King Louis XI recruited a Calabrian silk weaver to Lyon, kick-starting the French silk industry. This competition proved fatal to many Neapolitan silk weavers, already reeling from an outbreak of disease that had decimated their silkworm stock. Consequently, Naples, nearby Gragnano, and the other silk powerhouses pivoted to the production of pasta.

Neopolitans embraced pasta with the kind of enthusiasm they would later show for pizza, although the poorest peasants could afford it only occasionally, or settled for the broken scraps from the bottom of the barrel. Never ones to get much respect from their northern neighbors (after unification, their northern countrymen), Neapolitans were derided as *mangiamaccheroni*, "macaroni eaters" (an insult that northerners would, to their bafflement,

Pasta drying in a Naples street, ca. 1897. (J. F. Jarvis, publisher. Library of Congress, LC-DIG-stereo-1s28228.)

find flung back at themselves in other languages after they'd emigrated). But the sobriquet, if demeaning, was not inaccurate, as visitors to the city reported with amazement the proliferation of pasta: drying on wooden poles, strung across doorways, and hanging from open windows. By 1845, Naples, a city of less than half a million, had 280 *maccheroni* shops, about four times the number of pizzerias.

Initially, *maccheroni* was cooked much differently than today, boiled in broth or water, often for an hour or two, until thoroughly soft, and topped with a little oil, pork fat, vinegar, grape must, or (if you had an extra coin in your pocket) grated cheese. Like pizza, Neapolitan *maccheroni* was street food—served and eaten with bare hands, a custom that wasn't restricted to the street. A late-1700s Irish dinner guest of King Ferdinand IV reported losing his appetite at the sight of the Neapolitan king dipping his meaty hands into a bowl of pasta, "twisting and pulling it about, and cramming it voraciously into his mouth, most magnanimously disdaining the use of either knife, fork, or spoon," a habit he was also wont to display, in full view of his subjects, in his box at the San Carlo Theatre.

It wasn't until the nineteenth century that the custom of eating pasta slightly hard—*al dente*—became common, although the term itself didn't become widespread until after World War I. Historian David Gentilcore, noting that the preference for firmer pasta coincided with the rising popularity of street *maccheroni*, speculates that the two are connected. Certainly, eating vermicelli or spaghetti with your fingers is easier to do if the long strands are not falling apart while being lifted to your mouth.

Making *maccheroni*—the word originally referred to any dried pasta made with durum wheat—was an arduous task. The dry, stiff dough must be thoroughly kneaded, a job that was

Neapolitan pasta eaters, ca. 1865. (Library of Congress, LC-DIG-ppmsc-06572.)

accomplished by having men stomp around on it in their bare feet for an entire day before the advent of machinery (albeit human-powered, but at least not toe-powered) relieved them of the task. The thick dough was then extruded through bronze dies (sturdy plates containing holes or slots), either by a couple of men or one horse turning a large screw by means of long levers, producing strands of vermicelli or hollow tubes of various sizes.

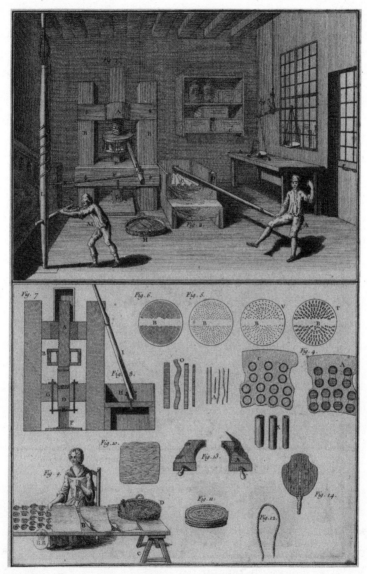

An eighteenth-century macaroni press, from Paul-Jacques Malouin,
Descriptions et details des arts du meunier, du vermicellier et du
Boulanger, *1767. (Bibliothèque nationale de France.)*

The names bestowed on the seemingly endless variety of pasta shapes and sizes (some three hundred to date) are often delightfully descriptive, even literal: *Spaghetti* means "little strings," and the bow tie–shaped *farfalle* is simply the Italian word for "butterflies." And when a Roman shopper examines boxes of pasta in a supermarket, what we see as *vermicelli* is to her, quite literally, "little worms." No wonder the Italian is rarely translated into English upon export.

By the early 1800s, both tomatoes and pasta were eaten widely throughout the Italian Peninsula. But it still seemed not to have occurred to anyone to combine the two into *pasta al pomodoro*. Sauces made from tomatoes simmered with onions, garlic, and seasonings had been popular since the late 1700s, but were served exclusively with meat or fish. ("Pasta and tomatoes? Are you mad, signore? It just isn't done!") It wasn't until the 1880s—not even 150 years ago—that tomato sauce became the standard topping for pasta. This leaves the tantalizing question of why this happened *when* it did, and how did tomatoes on pasta go from "Are you mad, signore?" to *pasta al pomodoro*. What changed?

Pigs.

At least that's what Giulia Marinelli had told me at the Museo della Pasta, which sits directly atop the Museo del Pomodoro near Parma, in a convenient (if logically reversed) arrangement.

Wondering if perhaps I'd misunderstood, I asked, "What do pigs have to do with tomatoes?"

"Up until the nineteenth century ordinary people dressed their pasta with lard—pork fat—because it was very good. But in the middle of the nineteenth century the breed of pigs changed.

Black pigs were replaced by Large White, Landrace, or Duroc breeds, because with those pigs the prosciutto is lighter in taste and the pig grows much faster than the Black one. But the lard is not as good."

The porcine swap began in Parma, which is famous for *prosciutto di Parma* (Parma ham), but soon spread throughout Italy, and the lousy lard, eliciting squeals of protest from unhappy *mangiamaccheroni*, may well have prompted Italians to explore other ways to sauce their pasta. At the same time, Giulia said, tomato breeding programs both in the north and the south of Italy were producing more flavorful varieties of tomatoes, and the stage for a culinary revolution was being set. But who would fire the first shot? Which Italian chef would go down in history as being credited with the momentous invention of what would become the signature dish of Italy, *pasta al pomodoro*?

Alexandre Balthazar Laurent Grimod de La Reynière doesn't sound Italian—it doesn't even sound like a single individual— but the Frenchman's 1807 *L'Almanach des gourmands* contains the first known published mention of saucing pasta with tomatoes. The fact that the honor belongs to a Frenchman must, I imagine, bring great satisfaction to French patriots who bristle at the legend that, after being married off to the French king Henry II in the sixteenth century, the fourteen-year-old Catherine de' Medici (another cousin of sorts to Cosimo, two months her junior) employed her Italian palate and Mediterranean wiles to essentially invent French cuisine.

Grimrod was well-known in France, where he was that country's first restaurant critic and a major (if the term had been around then) "influencer," often credited with being the father of modern French cuisine—a paternity that others, notably Georges Auguste Escoffier, might have a stronger claim to. Whether Grimrod's suggestion to add diced fresh tomatoes to vermicelli in place of the usual cheese was his own notion or something he'd imported from the Italian Peninsula, the convergence of pasta and *pomodoro* almost certainly took place not in France, but in Italy—specifically, somewhere in Italy that had both ingredients in abundance.

That sounds a lot like—you guessed it—Naples, making you wonder if all they did in that city was eat. In fact, the Neapolitan diet caught the attention of the American physiologist Ancel Keys (for whom the US Army K ration is thought to be named), who, during a visit to Naples in the early 1950s, was struck by the surprisingly robust health and life expectancy of the carbloading, olive oil–loving Neapolitans, even among the poor. This led to his landmark discoveries about the effects of diet on cardiac health. Keys' recommendations for dietary reform would be published as the "Mediterranean diet."

A guide to Neapolitan home cooking published in 1837 by Ippolito Cavalcanti, a duke from Calabria, includes a strikingly modern recipe for baked *vermicelli al pomodoro*, instructing the reader to boil the pasta until just firm, and to thoroughly cook down the tomatoes into a thick sauce. By the time that an 1891 Italian cookbook, *Science in the Kitchen and the Art of Eating Well: A Practical Manual for Families*, was published, the practice of dressing pasta with tomato sauce was so common that the author included not one but two recipes for *maccheroni alla napolitana*. The first is a tomato and meat sauce (although the meat is removed from the finished sauce and eaten separately); the second recipe is a classic *pasta al pomodoro*, made with tomatoes, a sautéed onion that is discarded before serving, butter, olive oil, and grated cheese. The recipe suggests serving it over a short pasta, such as penne.

This cookbook was the work of Pellegrino Artusi, a seventy-year-old former silk merchant (the French hadn't grabbed the *entire* silk market), who'd decided to keep himself busy in retirement by bringing all of Italy's regional cuisines together into a single collection, thereby creating (or at least identifying) a *cucina italiana* for the young nation, which in the late 1800s was still more unified in name than in fact. After being turned down by numerous publishers, who (ha!) knew a stinker of a book when they saw one, Artusi, who had traveled widely throughout Italy (and kept notes) assembled his 790 recipes and self-published Italy's first national cookbook.

One hundred thirty years later, *l'Artusi*, as it is commonly known, is still selling briskly, having long ago become the most popular Italian cookbook of all time.

Despite Artusi's preferences for northern cooking over southern, and his disregard for dishes "limited to particular environments or social levels" (what we might call "peasant food"), the book is valuable today as a rough culinary snapshot of the entire nation, from Milan to Sicily, in 1891. And it looks an awful lot like the cuisine of Italy today, with recipes for *tortellini alla bolognese*, *risotto alla milanese*, and *ravioli alla genovese*.

The popularity of tomatoes—and tomatoes with pasta—continued to accelerate in the twentieth century, with Cirio, the canned food company that introduced the San Marzano tomato to Campania, playing a major role. Cirio promoted the use of canned tomatoes and tomato products through colorful advertising, free recipe pamphlets, and contests. A 1936 competition for the best canned tomato recipes drew three thousand contestants. Cirio's iconic and creative advertising posters are reminiscent of the art deco aperitif posters sought by collectors today—and some were in fact painted by the same hand, that of the great illustrator Leonetto Cappiello.

Leonetto Cappiello (1875–1942), considered the father of the modern advertising poster, created this 1921 lithograph for Cirio. (Museo nazionale collezione Salce di Treviso, by permission of the Ministero della Cultura.)

It would seem that pasta and tomatoes were by this point inextricably intertwined and destined to be part of the Italian diet for the foreseeable future. Yet Cappiello's exuberant posters of the early 1920s belied the fact that pasta, tomatoes, and the entire canning industry were all in trouble, and headed for more.

⌖

The Po Valley, an east-west swath across northern Italy running from the western Alps to the Adriatic Sea, is the country's most important agricultural region and a major tomato-growing and -canning center. It was also where the budding postwar socialist movement was the strongest and most strident, and where labor strikes in 1919 and 1920 had left tomatoes rotting in the fields and anxious landowners looking for a solution.

They didn't have to look far. Benito Mussolini, a thirty-seven-year-old disillusioned former socialist and Po Valley native, had been making a name for himself and his recently formed Partito Nazionale Fascista by promising to restore Italy, staggering out of the trenches of World War I, to the glory of ancient Rome. Mussolini vowed to usher in a re-Renaissance of sorts, although this one would leave Italy with fascist architecture instead of the Sistine Chapel. He also promised to stamp out socialism, a pledge that resonated among the land- and factory owners of the Po Valley. With their support, Mussolini seized power in October 1922.

Mussolini viewed food as a tool to control the immediate needs of the population and to promote a fascist agenda of self-dependency, austerity, and increased productivity and *re*productivity (to replace all the Italians who'd emigrated in the previous decades). Of particular concern to the fascists was the country's dependence on foreign wheat. When farmers were compelled to grow wheat or rice in place of valuable cash crops—like tomatoes—even in areas where the climate or soil was not suitable, tomato harvests fell by more than half during Mussolini's reign, while grain production increased only slightly. Canned tomato production additionally suffered from his policy of limiting women in the workplace, resulting in labor shortages. Tomato exports, once an important source of income, plunged by a third.

Italy, in the face of postwar hunger and malnutrition, was producing less food, not more. Mussolini's response to the crisis was to launch a campaign encouraging his countrymen to eliminate waste and reduce their food intake, enlisting scientists to speak to the health benefits of a diet containing fewer calories and nutrients. Unleashing his inner Dante, Mussolini even published a poem—yes, Il Duce wrote poetry—beseeching Italians not to waste bread. To reduce wheat imports, he promoted the consumption of domestically grown rice, almost exclusively a northern Italian staple, over pasta. Declaring November 1 as National Rice Day, he sent rice trucks throughout the country to distribute free samples and recipe booklets. Then, in late 1930, an old pal of his from the early, heady days of fascism, Filippo Tommaso Marinetti, did him one better, choosing the Christmas holidays as the ideal time to call for the complete banishment of pasta.

Marinetti's *Manifesto of Futurist Cuisine* appeared on December 28, 1930, in Turin's daily *Gazzetta del popolo*. Subsequent reprinting gave it nationwide exposure. Marinetti, in addition to being an early fascist and Mussolini enabler, was best known as one of the founders of futurist art, an early twentieth-century movement that aimed to break with the stodgy past and bring the speed, energy, mechanization, and efficiency of the twentieth century into the arts. And to Marinetti, food *was* art. His "Futurist cuisine," which sounds more like "Dadaist cuisine," included a "tactile dinner" at which the guests changed into pajamas on arrival, each pair covered with a different tactile material such as sponge, cork, sandpaper, or felt, and then, suitably attired, proceeded to eat with their fingers in complete darkness, the better to experience the textures of the food and the jammies.

Other dinners featured settings in mock aircraft whose engine vibrations were said to stimulate the appetite; a table set with foods that were only to be salivated over, not eaten; food in concentrated pills (hello, Dr. Miles' Compound Extract of Tomatoes!); and such mouthwatering concoctions as a cylinder of ice cream topped with plum-filled hard-boiled eggs.

To some Italians, Marinetti was a visionary. Indeed, many of his recipes anticipated nouvelle and molecular cuisine, and dining in the dark or while blindfolded has seen a small revival in recent years. To most, however, he was a harmless avant-garde crackpot barely, if at all, on their radar—until he trained his sights on their beloved *pasta al pomodoro.*

His *Manifesto*, in calling for the abolition of pasta, claimed that his countrymen's devotion to the "biquotidian pyramid" of pasta would produce generations of Italian "weakness, pessimism, nostalgic inactivity and neutralism." (To be fair, nothing says "after-dinner nap" like polishing off a plate of spaghetti.) And just look at what pasta has done to the Neapolitans, Marinetti warned. Daily consumption of pasta had led formerly "heroic fighters and moving orators" to "develop the typical ironic and sentimental skepticism that so often stifles their enthusiasm." Italians, growing fat on pasta, should be preparing for—that is, slimming down for—the "very light aluminum trains that will replace the present heavy iron-wood-steel trains." Italy needed a new cuisine, one whose "goal is to create harmony between men's taste and their lives, today and tomorrow."

"*L'Artusi*'s day is over," Marinetti declared.

It is tempting to make light of Marinetti's assault on pasta (and the *Chicago Tribune* did, with the headline "Fascist Writer, All Wound Up in Health Subject, Begs Countrymen to Swallow New Theory"), but there was a darker side to Marinetti's campaign, which, in calling for Italians to eliminate pasta and shed pounds, was perfectly aligned with Mussolini's policies of dietary austerity and self-sufficiency. And the futurist's complaint about Neapolitans growing lazy on pasta echoed Mussolini's contempt for Italians who were rotten with "cowardice, laziness, and love of the quiet life." Most tellingly, when Marinetti spoke of rice as a "patriotic" choice and declared, "Pasta is no food for fighters," it was clear that futurism and fascism had met.

Marinetti, undeterred by international ridicule and the Neapolitan protesters who roused themselves from their post-pasta naps to rally in the streets, kept pressing his case. Ultimately, the present caught up with the futurist when Hitler declared modern art to be degenerate, spurring Mussolini to dutifully stamp out futurism, the most modern art of all. As for pasta, Il Duce, himself quite fond of *pasta en brodo*—noodles in broth—dealt with the self-sufficiency issue by increasing durum wheat production in the rice-growing areas of central and northern Italy (although not by nearly enough; Italy today imports about 40 percent of its durum, meaning that when you buy imported Italian pasta in your supermarket, you are often eating North American wheat). Thus, Neapolitans and the angels in paradise all continued happily eating their vermicelli with tomato sauce. But almost before you could boil water for spaghetti, there was yet another threat to *pasta al pomodoro*: a shortage of tomatoes.

Probably the only thing as unimaginable as Italy without pasta is Italy without tomatoes, yet it almost became a reality during

World War II. The trouble stemmed from the May 1939 Pact of Steel that Italy had signed with Germany, formalizing their alliance. Originally proposed as the Pact of Blood, it might as well have been the Pact of Tomatoes, because the fine print (so fine that few even knew of it) included a secret economic alliance that sent a full 90 percent of Italy's tomato crop to Germany during the war. The Germans, unsurprisingly, were said to prefer unblemished, perfectly uniform specimens.

Such basic staples as canned tomato paste became scarce, because even if manufacturers managed to get their hands on tomatoes, they certainly weren't getting any more tin from England with which to can them. Yet Italian ingenuity prevailed, as companies with longer memories turned the clock back and started making *conserva nera*, sold in rolls or sheets, just as in the 1800s. So much for futurism.

⊛

Mussolini, meanwhile, was attempting to make good on his promise to restore the territory and glory of the Roman Empire—not by reconquering Gaul and England, but by consolidating and expanding Italy's colonial holdings in Africa. This included the creation of the colonies of Libya (reviving the ancient Greek name for the region) and Italian East Africa (through the merger of Somalia and Eritrea with Ethiopia, which Mussolini invaded in 1935).

Pasta al pomodoro, naturally, traveled to Africa with the Italian aggressors and was incorporated into the traditional cuisine by the native populations. This explains the otherwise inexplicable Somali dish of spaghetti on *injera*, the national crepe-like flatbread made from the ancient grain called *teff*. The flat injera is topped with, as Marinetti might say, a "pyramid" of swirled spaghetti in a spicy, meaty tomato sauce, sometimes garnished with a chopped banana, folded, and eaten with the hands—the ultimate Afro-Italian fusion dish.

Italy's brief colonization of Libya, cut short by Allied tanks in 1943, left a lasting cultural impact in that country as well. Thirty years after the Italians had left, Muammar Qaddafi's promise to "de-Italianize" Libya apparently didn't extend to its cuisine. "Like all people in Libya, he loves Italian food, especially pasta," Qaddafi's Ukrainian nurse said of the leader before he was deposed in 2011. Mussolini had encouraged Italians to settle in the Libyan colony ("the real America," according to a fascist slogan) as a way of both stemming the tide of immigration to the Americas and solving Italy's food shortages, which had become exacerbated by an international trade embargo following the invasion of Ethiopia. One of his goals was to build an export tomato industry, partly on land seized by Italian settlers, who in the province of Cyrenaica displaced fully half the local population. Far from feeding Italy, the twentieth-century colonization of Africa had the opposite effect, as the colonies wound up swallowing one-quarter of Italy's exports.

Italy didn't introduce tomatoes to Africa; they had preceded Italians to the continent by a hundred years, although exactly how they arrived remains a mystery, leaving historians to speculate about a vague brew of "invaders, explorers, missionaries, and traders." Some credit eighteenth-century Portuguese explorers, but the earliest record of African tomatoes isn't until 1839, in Liberia, which had just been founded as a settlement for freed American slaves and freeborn Black people. This suggests the intriguing possibility that tomatoes were introduced to Africa by former American slaves, possibly some of the same slaves who introduced tomatoes to the Southern United States.

Tomatoes are a staple of many African diets today; in Ghana they account for 38 percent of all vegetable expenditures. Beltway breeders in Maryland might be gratified to know that one of the most commonly grown Ghanaian tomato varieties is none other than their venerable Roma. Tomatoes show up frequently in African soups and stews, and in the iconic West African dish jollof rice. Made with onions, peppers, spices, tomatoes, vegetables, and meat, "jollof rice is to West Africa what paella is to Spain, risotto to Italy, biriyani to India, and fried rice to China," according to Ghanaian-born journalist Patti Sloley. So popular are tomatoes in some African nations that the continent must import processed tomato products to satisfy demand. Most of these come from China. Tomatoes originally came to China from the Philippines, which the Spanish colonized in 1564. As in Italy, the tomato was initially considered a type of eggplant; the Chinese, not mincing words, called it *fānqié* or *fan chieh*: "barbarian eggplant."

Tomatoes were first grown in China for the restaurants that catered to Westerners. It wasn't until the twentieth century that the Chinese ventured to incorporate the barbarian eggplant into their native cuisine, to a point. Even though China has had both pasta and tomatoes for centuries, the two once again seem reluctant to meet. The adoption of tomatoes into Chinese cuisine in general has never risen to the level you might expect of the country that leads the world in tomato production (nearly all of it for export of processed products). One notable exception is a popular Chinese comfort food: scrambled eggs and tomatoes. Even though it sounds like something your neighborhood café might whip up on a Sunday morning, it's an Asian original.

Conversely, one of the world's most popular southern Asian dishes is nearly as Western as mayonnaise. That would be what former UK foreign secretary Robin Cook has called "a true British national dish"—not fish and chips, but chicken tikka masala, an Indian take-out favorite consisting of boneless chicken in a tomato-based curry sauce. How an Indian dish using a Meso-american vegetable came to be beloved in Britain doesn't have a one-sentence or even a one-*century* explanation, but the truth about it is hidden in the rarely quoted remainder of Cook's sentence. Chicken tikka masala is truly British, Cook said in a 2001 speech in praise of British multiculturalism, "not only because it is the most popular, but because it is a perfect illustration of the way Britain absorbs and adapts external influences."

That might've raised a few eyebrows in India, because it wasn't exactly the British who were absorbing and adapting on the way to tikka masala; they were delivering the blows. The full recipe, as it were, is worth taking a brief look into, because its main ingredients are colonial occupation, immigration, and invention. In other words, it's the history of the tomato.

Occupation: In the 1500s, tomatoes were introduced to Portugal from Spain, with whom it shared the Iberian Peninsula and an aptitude for seafaring conquest. Tomatoes then traveled with Portuguese colonists to the Indian subcontinent in the late sixteenth century, where—not for the first time in our story—the tart red fruits were initially received by the locals with a mixture of bafflement and disdain. And that was pretty much their status for the next two hundred years, until the British arrived. Of course, the Brits wanted to eat their favorite British foods, and by the nineteenth century that included tomatoes, which they started to cultivate (or, more likely, had their subjects cultivate while they played cricket).

This is, in many respects, the typical colonial culinary story, one that has been repeated countless times with countless foods and various colonies, but in Bengal, as in other territories, the British colonial government wasn't content to merely look after the diets of the English. "Transforming the palate of the colonised was also an agenda of the colonial state," writes historian Utsa Ray. This included "correcting" the diet of the "emaciated rice-eating" Bengalis to include such Western foods as potatoes, tomatoes, cauliflower, carrots, peas, and even manioc, the South American root also known as *cassava*. Thanks to the rather persuasive powers of the British Empire, all these vegetables caught on to some degree. Potatoes in particular are common in Indian home cooking, although Bengalis had a more difficult time finding a use for the tomato.

Immigration: During the second half of the twentieth century, the flow of colonization was reversed, and instead of British subjects settling in India, Indians started emigrating to Great Britain. Many were brought in to help rebuild England after the Second World War, while others came to cook for the immigrants—and before long, for the English as well. Prior to the war, there were six curry houses in Britain. Today there are twelve thousand because Brits, known for their bland diet (think mushy peas—that's not a description, it's the *name* of a popular side dish), found the vibrant spices in Indian food a revelation, becoming fans of curries and other South Asian foods.

Few of these contained tomatoes in any fashion.

Invention: I shouldn't have to warn you by now that food origin stories can be dicey, but one much-recited version of the birth of chicken tikka masala goes like this: One rainy night in Glasgow, Scotland, ca. 1971, a tired bus driver who was eating dinner in an Indian restaurant sent his chicken curry back to the kitchen, complaining that it was dry. The chef, a Bengali—a descendant of the Bengalis induced to eat tomatoes and other Western vegetables by their British occupiers—had been sipping on canned tomato soup while nursing a stomach ulcer when the unhappy bus driver's curry reappeared in his kitchen. Annoyed and ill, the chef dumped some of his tomato soup into the curry and sent it back out. The bus driver, delighted with the result, started coming back for more, and soon his mates were asking for it, and next thing you knew, chicken tikka masala, a fusion not only of Indian and European cuisine, but of colonialism, immigration, and indigestion, was added to the menu. It has since become the most popular Indian dish in the world—outside India, that is.

Colorful details of stormy nights and dyspeptic chefs aside, chicken tikka masala almost certainly did originate *somewhere* in a Bengali restaurant *somewhere* in Britain. In another variation of the story, "the most likely," according to Indian chef and writer Anita Jaisinghani, the city is London, and the soup, undiluted and straight from the can, is—thank you, gods of writing—Campbell's.

If the Campbell's twist is true (and I'm going to say it is; try to prove me wrong), then our favorite soup company was responsible for *two* major tomato-based innovations within the span of just a few years, the other being SpaghettiOs, introduced in 1965 after a yearlong internal study to develop a pasta shape that children could eat without making a mess. (They might've saved themselves a lot of time and money had they first sat down to a breakfast of Cheerios with their kids.)

Campbell's, although known for its soup, has been putting spaghetti into cans since 1915, when it purchased Franco-American, a soup and convenience-food company founded by French immigrant Alphonse Biardot in 1886. Just after the turn of the century, Franco-American introduced a product labeled Spaghetti à la Milanaise, giving the name a Gallic twist, as restaurants and cookbooks often did, to appeal to an American public that was still more open to French food than Italian (and because his company was, after all, called *Franco*-American).

Biardot may have been the first entrepreneur to put spaghetti and tomato sauce into cans, but the most successful was his fellow immigrant and near anagram Hector Boiardi. At the age of seventeen, Boiardi left his home of Piacenza, Italy (just outside Parma), arriving at Ellis Island in 1914. He quickly got an entry-level job in the kitchen of New York's famed Plaza Hotel, where, within a year (possibly because the First World War emptied the kitchen of more senior talent), he was promoted to head chef.

After the war, Boiardi made his way to Cleveland and opened an Italian restaurant, where his sauce was so popular that patrons often asked if they could take some home. When demand outstripped Boiardi's supply of the old milk bottles he used for takeout sauce, he opened a factory in 1928 to can the sauce (now with cooked pasta included) properly, using an easier, phonetic spelling for his name: Chef Boyardee.

His cans of spaghetti, ravioli, and lasagna all bore the smiling face of Chef B., the spitting image of what Americans expected an Italian chef to look like: his twinkly eyes, mustache, towering white toque, and neckerchief assuring consumers of the goodness inside the can. As the US declared war on his homeland, Boiardi contracted with the army of his adopted country to produce wartime rations, at the height of the war turning out some 250,000 cans of spaghetti and tomato sauce *a day*. Tomatoes in cans hadn't been so popular since the Civil War.

"The war experience was largely responsible for bringing the Chef Boyardee name to national prominence," Dan Skinner, a representative of Conagra Brands, which today owns the label, told me. "When soldiers returned home, the brand already had positive association, and Hector Boiardi himself was hailed as a national hero for his wartime efforts." In fact, Boiardi was awarded the prestigious Gold Star by President Truman.

Returning GIs continued eating canned Chef Boyardee products, as did their children, and their children's children. Today, four of the Chef's spaghetti and ravioli products rank among the leading twenty canned foods in America, their combined sales making Chef Boyardee pasta in tomato sauce the top-selling canned food in America.

How could you not buy canned spaghetti from this man? This image of Hector Boiardi has sold billions of cans of Chef Boyardee. (Chef Boyardee is a registered trademark of Conagra Brands, Ltd. Logo reprinted with permission.)

This achievement is all the more remarkable considering that when Boiardi arrived in America on the eve of World War I, pasta was rarely found outside Italian American neighborhoods. It was not unknown, however. As far back as 1787, Thomas Jefferson, upon his return from Italy, had sketched out a design for a "macaroni machine," before having an actual one shipped to him from Naples.

A little over a century later, a 1903 article in the *Kansas City Star* offered housewives detailed advice for preparing "macaroni, spaghetti, and vermicelli," noting that "the best macaroni in the world is made from hard Italian flour," while predicting that improvements in the American product would "soon render importation as unnecessary as 'carrying coals to Newcastle.'" That newspapers needed to introduce Americans to pasta as late as the twentieth century indicated it was still an exotic, unfamiliar food. That situation would change dramatically with the advent of something nearly as unthinkable as Italy without pasta: America without alcohol.

On January 17, 1920, the Eighteenth Amendment to the US Constitution—Prohibition—went into effect. If this seems about as relevant to pasta as our Italian pigs, well, it is. The national ban on the production and sale of alcohol resulted in the astronomical growth of illegal speakeasies—thirty-two thousand of them in New York alone—many of which were operated by Italian Americans. Unlike saloons, speakeasies welcomed women. Now, give a man in a bar a few cold beers and a bowl of peanuts, and he'll be content for hours, but women of the Roaring Twenties were more likely to want a meal. Speakeasy owners served what came naturally: spaghetti with tomato sauce, often with the house wine—in this case meaning *made* in the house. Consequently, more than a few Americans had their first taste of Italian food not in a corner Italian restaurant, but in an illegal speakeasy. National pasta consumption, near zero when the taps were turned off in 1920, rose to 3.75 pounds per person annually by the end of the decade.

Pasta became mainstream enough to start appearing in the movies. Those who didn't catch the reference in 1925, when a starving Charlie Chaplin cheerfully twirled the shoelaces of his shoe like a forkful of spaghetti in the silent classic *The Gold Rush*, were certainly in on the joke six years later when Chaplin, eating a bowl of pasta at a swanky dinner party in *City Lights*, winds up

Spaghetti was popular enough by 1931 that Charlie Chaplin could give it a cameo in City Lights. *(City Lights Copyright © Roy Export S.A.S. All rights reserved.)*

unwittingly gobbling down a long paper streamer that has inter-twined with his spaghetti. By this time, 1931, America was in the grips of the Depression, and for many American families, spa-ghetti dinner, inexpensive and nourishing, had gone from nov-elty to necessity. Pasta—which nearly always meant spaghetti and tomato sauce—had arrived.

Like the Bengalis who invented tikka masala, or Chinese chefs who gave us chop suey and beef with broccoli, Italian immigrants to the Americas used local ingredients in adapting their tradi-tional recipes to their new country. This included something that Italians had rarely enjoyed in Italy: meat. Said one Argentinean immigrant from Piedmont, "Meat was like polenta to us," more available and cheaper than vegetables. A New York shoeshine boy marveled that "we had enough to eat, and we had meat quite often, which we never had in Italy."

This abundance would lead to the creation of a dish that, for many foreigners, represents *the* quintessential Italian dish, although, paradoxically, it is virtually unknown in Italy: spaghetti with meatballs.

Created in New York by Italian immigrants, spaghetti and meatballs is just one example of global Italian "classics" that origi-nated outside of Italy. Any tomato-based dish that contains sub-stantial amounts of meat, including chicken parmesan or a sausage hoagie—is almost certainly an Italian American invention. That most definitely includes Sunday gravy.

Despite its name, Sunday gravy is not gravy at all, but a rich pasta sauce (usually made on Sundays for the extended family) in which various cuts of meat are simmered for hours in Italian canned tomatoes. A typical gravy might include meatballs, sau-sage, and cuts of pork, veal, and beef, even—as in the childhood

home of my sister-in-law, an Italian American from New Jersey—
braciola, a rolled, stuffed flank steak, which is a stand-alone entrée
on its own.

Sunday gravy could never have existed in the old country,
where a single dinner would have used up an entire year's worth
of meat, but even less extravagant Italian American dishes, while
hugely popular in America, are still rarely found in modern
Italy. A Sicilian restaurateur named Niccoló de Quattrociocchi
reported in his 1950 memoir that during a visit to America, he
"was introduced to two very fine, traditional American special-
ties called 'spaghetti with meatballs,' and 'cotoletta [veal cutlet]
parmigiana,'" adding, "I found them both extremely satisfying
and I think someone in Italy should invent them for Italians over
there."

Last time I checked, no one had, so if you should have a han-
kering for "spag and balls" after touring the Roman Forum, your
best bet is to order a bowl of *spaghetti al pomodoro* and a side of *pol-
pette*. Then, when no one is looking, dump the meatballs into the
spaghetti. The angels in paradise won't mind.

Seven

BIG BOY

The Hybrid Tomato Propels Home Gardening into the Space Age

The year was 1866. Two men, separated by an ocean, each working tirelessly in his garden, were ignorant of each other's existence. One had a very big problem that he couldn't explain; the other had the explanation but didn't know what to do with it.

The problem vexing an Ohio seedsman named Alexander W. Livingston was that although crossbreeding tomatoes—that is, creating a hybrid from two different varieties—often produced superior fruits, Livingston could not develop seeds to sell from the resulting hybrids. The fruits produced in the next generation did not "breed true" to their parent, displaying significant differences from the very tomato they had come from. Livingston couldn't even guarantee that the color would be the same! More baffling, he found that "even where for several generations these bad qualities are not seen, for some unaccountable reasons they will begin to appear again." This maddening situation would send most men packing, and indeed Livingston did give up on hybridization—after *fifteen* years. Such determination takes a man of preternatural patience, intelligence, and powers of observation, all traits attributed to Livingston by the admiring author of *Livingston and the Tomato*—none other than Alexander Livingston himself.

Across the Atlantic, an Austrian monk as modest as Livingston was boastful, but otherwise similar in temperament—remarkably patient, thoughtful, and observant—had, after years of painstaking experimentation with peas, figured out exactly how plants inherit traits from their parents, as well as the reason for the unruly behavior that Livingston had observed in his tomatoes. In fact, not only could Gregor Mendel have told Livingston *why* his tomatoes didn't always inherit characteristics from their parents, but he also could've accurately predicted the percentage of offspring that *would*, having discovered the laws of inheritance.

Unfortunately, the odds of Livingston or any other breeder in 1866 learning of Mendel's work were slim, because the vehicle through which the Augustinian friar chose to announce his groundbreaking findings was an obscure journal, *Verhandlungen des naturforschenden Vereines in Brünn* (*Proceedings of the Natural History Society of Brünn*), the equivalent of announcing the cure for cancer in your workplace newsletter.

I like to imagine an alternate universe in which Livingston has sailed to Europe for an international horticultural conference at which Mendel, overhearing the American complain about his "untrue" tomatoes, comes over and says, "Let's talk."

The monk explains, "All traits are expressed not by one, but by *two genes*, one from each parent," as Livingston strokes his long, bird's-nest beard, taking in this revolutionary notion. "And some genes—for example, red tomato color—are dominant, while others—yellow—are recessive. If there is one of each, the dominant gene will rule over the recessive gene. So, a tomato with one red and one yellow gene will always be red. Only a tomato with a pair of yellow genes will be yellow. Even a red tomato can have a yellow gene lurking about, however, and if through later fertilization it joins up with another yellow gene, the pair will yield a yellow tomato."

"My word!" the Ohioan exclaims, his buckeyes widening. "So that's why lumpiness and tough skin keep coming back, generations after I think I've eliminated them. *Pater*, you need to publish this."

Mendel's face falls. "I have," he says. "And I sent copies to both the Royal Society and the Smithsonian. You never saw it?"

Almost no one saw it, even in Europe. Cited only three times in the three decades following its publication, Mendel's monumental discovery is what geneticist Siddhartha Mukherjee calls "one of the strangest disappearing acts in the history of biology," reminiscent of the tomato's own vanishing act three centuries earlier. Yet what Mendel had discovered would become, decades after his death, the very foundation of modern genetics.

Gregor Mendel was born in July 1822 in the Austrian town of Heinzendorf bei Odrau, today part of the Czech Republic; less than three months later, John and Mary Livingston, of Reynoldsburg, Ohio, had a son they named Alexander. Both families were struggling farmers, the Mendels on land their ancestors had worked for generations; the Livingstons on land they had cleared on the American frontier.

As a child, Gregor Mendel worked as a gardener and learned beekeeping. When his attempts to gain an education were thwarted by his family's poor finances, he became an Augustinian monk, which afforded him free university schooling and, he wrote, spared him "the perpetual anxiety about a means of liveli-hood." The future father of genetics was a poor student, twice failing his final exams. He had better luck with his religious studies than with physics, eventually becoming the abbot at St. Thomas' Abbey in Brünn. The abbey had a five-acre garden, and in 1856 Mendel begin to tinker with hybridizing peas, eventually growing some twenty-eight thousand plants in order to under-stand how peas inherited such characteristics as color, height, seed shape, and flower position.

In that same year, Alexander Livingston, who'd been working for a seed grower, went into business for himself, purchasing the entire stock, four hundred boxes of seeds, of the Buckeye Gar-den Seed Company. Livingston's frontier education was limited but practical, he writes, consisting of being taught to "spell, read, and write well and to cipher in arithmetic as far as the Rule of Three," a mathematical tool that allows one to solve such real-world problems as: If I need 20 pounds of seeds for 4 acres, how many pounds do I need for 7 acres?

The success of his consignment seed sales allowed Livingston to buy a farm and start growing his own crops for seed. But Liv-ingston, it turns out, was cultivating more than plants. His farm was also a stop on the Underground Railroad. The seedsman hid and fed escaped slaves, using his vegetable wagon to transport the fugitives to the next station.

Since 1848—eight years before Mendel started his experiments—Livingston had been experimenting with hybrid-izing tomatoes, not in a scientific vein, but simply to develop a better product. Why, of all vegetables, the tomato? Because, he suggests, it was a forbidden fruit. As a child, Livingston recalls, when he'd once brought home some "love apples" he'd found growing wild in a field, his mother recoiled, crying, "You must not eat them, my child! They must be poison, for even the hogs will not eat them!"

"From that early date on," Livingston writes, "the tomato became an object of special interest to me." (Mothers, take note.)

Tomatoes, you might recall, were also an object of special interest to the tomato hornworm, and Livingston's original thinking is demonstrated in the method he devised of controlling the destructive critters: Attract and eliminate them in the moth stage, before they can lay the eggs that develop into the destructive caterpillars:

> The first thing to do is to raise a good-sized bed of petunias near the tomato field, so as to have them in full bloom by the time the tomato plants are growing nicely in the field...In the evening you will soon discover a large miller [moth]— almost as large as a hummingbird—attracted to the sweet-scented flowers...Now while he hovers over a flower [and] eats thus is your opportunity, having a short, broad paddle in hand, slap one on the other with said miller between them.

Livingstone sensibly recommends the employment of some "spry" boys and girls to handle this task.

The hornworms were a minor annoyance compared to the vagaries of hybridization. Livingston gave up the maddening business after "years of the most scrupulous care and labor," concluding, "I have no confidence in hybridizing or crossing as a method of securing new varieties. I am not likely to forget my failures of fifteen years, nor the lesson which they taught me."

The lesson was that the time-honored breeding technique of

selection was more reliable than *hybridization*. Since the dawn of agriculture, humankind has been trying to improve on agricultural food sources by selecting for propagation those grains, fruits, and vegetables that demonstrate superior traits, whether they be flavor, appearance, drought resistance, earlier ripening, or greater yield.

This process of selection, sometimes called artificial selection (to distinguish it from Charles Darwin's *natural* selection, where forces of nature, not humans, do the selecting), is how most new tomato varieties were developed in the nineteenth century. Some were discovered by chance mutation—and tomatoes have a proclivity to mutate—or by travel, but most were literally the fruits of the painstaking labors of breeders. Relying on trial and error, tomato breeders like Livingston would plant thousands of seeds of their favorite tomato varieties, then take the best tomatoes of those plants—say, the first to ripen if you were trying to breed an early tomato—grow out their seeds, take the earliest of those, and so on, for several generations.

Without a full understanding of botany and genetics, breeders looked for the best individual fruits. If one particular tomato ripened several days before the others on that plant, that tomato would be selected for further propagation. What these early breeders didn't know, however, is that all the tomatoes on a given plant are genetically identical; the differences found between fruits on the same plant are due to environmental influences or the complex ways in which genes express. Thus, choosing the earliest-ripening tomato from a given plant in the hope that its progeny will also be early bloomers is, as one breeder told me, akin to selecting one of your identical-twin daughters to give you grandchildren because she started walking before her sister.

Alexander Livingston, the most successful tomato breeder of the late nineteenth century, from his 1893 autobiography, Livingston and the Tomato. *(Library of Congress, courtesy of HathiTrust.)*

One day, while working in his tomato field, Livingston noticed one plant among the thousands of others that, because of a mutation, had smoother, more evenly shaped fruits, unlike the ridged or lumpy tomatoes that predominated. "Like an inspiration," he writes, the notion came to him, apparently in all caps: "WHY NOT SELECT SPECIAL TOMATO PLANTS INSTEAD OF SPECIMEN TOMATOES?"

> I acted at once on this idea. The seeds from this plant were saved with pains-taking care, and made the basis of future experiments. The next spring, from these seeds, I set two rows across my garden...and to my glad surprise they all bore perfect tomatoes like the parent vine.

> The tomatoes from the original plant were too small for market, but these second-generation tomatoes

> were a little larger, for which I also rejoiced...The seeds from this crop were again carefully harvested, but from the

first ripe and best specimens I selected stock for my own planting. By good cultivation and wise selection from season to season, not to exceed five years, it took on flesh, size, and improved qualities.

In 1870, Livingston released the result, which he named the Livingston Paragon tomato, calling it, in his characteristically modest prose, "the first perfectly and uniformly smooth tomato ever introduced to the American public, or, so far as I know, to the world." In addition to being smooth and uniform, it was also, as they say, "a good cropper" and continued producing late into the season, when market prices were higher. But its main asset—and influence to this day—was its appearance. It was gorgeous. No longer the deeply furrowed fruit of Raphaelle Peale's canvas, it was essentially what we think of today when we picture a tomato. Notably, Livingston, in his description of the Paragon, does not even mention its flavor, setting us on a perilous path that would, a century later, lead to the perfectly smooth, red, uniform—and tasteless—supermarket tomato.

Remember that.

Livingston, the most renowned tomato breeder and seedsman of his day, would go on to release fifteen new varieties through this same method, all named after himself. Thus, we have Livingston's Favorite and Livingston's Perfection, which (belying the adage that you can't improve upon perfection) was followed by Livingston's Beauty, Livingston's Golden Queen, Livingston's Potato Leaf, and Livingston's New Stone—to name just a few. As Livingston was growing tomatoes for seed, not for sale, he found himself with tons of mashed pulp left over after the seeds were extracted. Fortunately, there was a ready buyer for tomato pulp in the adjoining state of Pennsylvania; many of Livingston's tomatoes wound up in Heinz ketchup bottles—until, that is, Heinz swore off preservatives in 1906, which also meant swearing off the use of tomato slop.

Several Livingston tomatoes would wind up being commercially grown and canned in northern Italy; another, the Globe, would, twenty years after his death, be bred with a cultivar called Marvel to yield a hybrid named the Marglobe. Released in 1917, the Marglobe was valued by commercial growers for decades because it was resistant to fusarium wilt. Many hybrids today owe their heritage to this tomato, which secured its place in history in 1951 when tomato researchers, needing a reference point from which to describe newly discovered varieties, selected the Marglobe, with its Livingston bloodline, as the "standard" tomato—that is, the definitive concept of what a tomato should look and act like.

Despite his success—and his relentless self-promotion—A. W. Livingston has been forgotten except by the most fervent gardeners who still buy Livingston seeds from the mail-order catalog that bears his name (although the company is no longer associated with his family). Livingston's track record is all the more remarkable given that he was working with an extremely small genetic pool and relying totally on selection—on luck and a sharp eye—to identify tomatoes with different gene expression or mutations, a chance that he put at "one in a thousand plants." Livingston may have abandoned hybridization for good reason, but to use a modern analogy, the practice of artificial selection was like going on a thousand blind dates, hoping one of them would just happen to work out; hybridization was OkCupid, a targeted match based on specific criteria. But during Livingston's lifetime, Cupid's quiver remained empty. The arrows needed to unlock the tomato's heart were hidden in plain sight in Mendel's paper, collecting dust in several libraries around the world.

Livingston died in 1898, four years after Mendel. Two years later, Mendel's writings and his laws of inheritance would be rediscovered, and Cupid would start making matches such as the world had never seen, ushering in the age of hybridization.

The first plant to be commercially hybridized in America was corn, which, like the tomato, possesses both male and female parts and is self-fertilizing, although it can also be fertilized from another plant. Among the first who recognized that corn could be hybridized was a man whose name is not generally associated with science: Cotton Mather, the Puritan minister better known for lighting the fires of the Salem (Massachusetts) witch trials. In 1716, Mather conducted one of the first known experiments with crop hybridization, planting rows of red and blue corn upwind of standard yellow corn. The resulting multicolored cobs on the downwind yellow corn provided unassailable proof, he wrote, of wind-driven cross-fertilization occurring in nature. History might have taken a different path had Mather's search for unassailable proof extended beyond the cornfield; regardless, the minister was on to something.

Corn also attracted the interest of Charles Darwin, who observed in 1876 that corn cross-fertilized with another variety was superior to self-fertilized, or inbred, corn. This phenomenon was later given the name "hybrid vigor" because the crossbred plants were often far healthier and more productive than either parent. Darwin's favorite example of hybrid vigor was the mule (a cross between a female horse and a male donkey). "That a hybrid should possess more reason, memory, obstinacy, social affection, powers of muscular endurance, and length of life, than either of its parents," he wrote, "seems to indicate that art has here outdone nature."

In the case of corn, hybrid vigor meant healthier plants, greater drought resistance, and, most notably, larger yields. This discovery was nothing short of revolutionary. In 1935, only 10 percent of the corn grown in Iowa was from hybrid seed. A mere four years later the figure had soared to 90 percent. By the end of the twentieth century, the yield per acre of corn in the US had risen from 20 bushels to 120, a sixfold increase.

Breeders of other crops took notice, and the decade after the Second World War represented, you might say, the salad days of hybridization. And the salad was about to get a fresh tomato.

Born in 1915 in what was then Ottoman-ruled Palestine, Oved Shifriss was raised in a moshav (a partially collectivist agricultural community) in Ein Gadim, one of the first Jewish farming settlements. At the age of twenty-one, Shifriss left his studies in agriculture at Hebrew University and boarded a ship bound for America, where he earned his doctorate in plant breeding at Cornell before taking a position in 1942 as director of vegetable breeding at W. Atlee Burpee & Company, the world's largest seed company.

"He was only twenty-nine," I say to Burpee CEO George Ball over the phone. "Isn't that young for someone in that role?"

"Oh, no, no, no," Ball says emphatically. "That's actually when you want someone. Plant breeding is as much art as it is science. In fact, I would argue, it's even more art because of the lyricism involved. I'm speaking of the impression that the plant makes on you. Flower breeding is complicated enough. But vegetable breeding, because there are so many other characteristics besides appearance, just poses a particular challenge. It's an enormously complicated thing. And so, therefore, there tend to be prodigies in it. And Oved was a prodigy. He was brilliant."

What Oved Shifriss did while in his thirties, not long out of graduate school, was to create for home gardeners the most important, game-changing tomato hybrid the world has ever seen: the Big Boy tomato.

It's hard to imagine what could be revolutionary about a back-yard tomato, but Ball's voice becomes animated when I pose that question. I'm expecting him to talk about yield or size or disease resistance, but that's because I wasn't around in 1949, when the Big Boy made its debut, and when growing tomatoes was quite a different proposition than it is today. The tomato plants available to gardeners then grew tall, so tall and sprawling, Ball says (up to fifteen feet—five feet higher than a basketball hoop), that gardeners had to employ stepladders to tend the plants, whose jungly vines were often supported by large beanpole tepee-like constructions.

"Stepladders?" I say, trying to picture myself pruning and tying vines fifteen feet in the air, grabbing the flimsy tepee for support while Anne pleads with me to come down before I kill myself.

"Stepladders. And the overwhelming percentage of home gardeners in those days consisted of older people. *There is no question of that.* I've looked at the data. And Oved, he was a very curious person. He would go down from the farm to Burpee headquarters in Germantown [Pennsylvania] and read the mail, and there was the not infrequent letter that read, like, 'My husband can't grow tomatoes anymore. Do you have something that he could grow? He cannot go up a ladder because he fell.' There were lots of these

Prior to the Big Boy, harvesting tomatoes often required a stepladder, as in this 1936 photo of a Madison, Wisconsin, gardener. (Wisconsin Historical Society, WHI-15357.)

letters: 'Dear Mr. Burpee, do you have anything that doesn't need a ladder?'

"So, the big thing about Big Boy was that he brought it down in height, like *way* down." Shifriss also tamed it. Less rambling than typical tomato plants (although the Big Boy is indeterminate), the vines could all be tied to a single stake, instead of needing the support of a tepee or something similar. (The commercialization of the tomato cage, another game changer for gardeners, was still some years away.) Ball pauses as he considers the impact: "It was just a revolution, an absolute revolution."

As for the tomato itself, Ball says, "It was this wonderful, luscious, round slicer," with a great aroma and fruits of up to a pound, "that you could use for anything. You could use it for your sandwiches, you could use it in your salad—just a perfect tomato for general gardening and culinary purposes." It also boasted superior disease resistance for its day.

It quickly became *the* tomato of the gardening masses, whose numbers not coincidentally increased. "Up until Oved bred the Big Boy, the tomato was very much the preoccupation of an aficionado hobbyist," Ball told the *New York Times* following Shifriss' death in 2004. "Suddenly anybody—Mom, Dad, the Boy Scout next door—could garden with the tomato. For gardening, it was as innovative as the V-8 engine or the microchip."

It's not clear that Shifriss immediately realized what he had on his hands, writing in his laboratory notes, "Hybrid tomatoes are relatively recent in origin and only time will tell how well they will take hold in the trade."

"How long did it take Oved to develop the Big Boy?" I ask Ball.

"Easily eight to ten years." It's not so hard to make a shorter tomato plant, Ball explains, but it *is* hard to make a shorter tomato plant that doesn't lose all its other desirable qualities: flavor, successful blossom set and fruiting, disease resistance, fruit appearance, and size. "There are literally dozens of things you have to evolve, and get all these things right, in one variety. And that's why it's so complicated and so difficult. And why so few people do plant breeding."

New Giant Hybrid Tomato
1131 BURPEE'S BIG BOY
Largest fruits of all our hybrids; some weigh 1 lb. and more,—average is about 10 ozs. Perfectly smooth, firm, scarlet-red, thick-walled fruits with meaty flesh of fine flavor and excellent quality. Plants are large, extremely vigorous, with moderately dense foliage that protects the fruits from sun-scald. Valuable for home and market. **Pkt.** (30 seeds) 50¢; **2 pkts. 95¢; 3 pkts. $1.35; 5 pkts. $2.20**

744 BURPEEANA EARLY DWARF PEA
A really high quality, early dwarf, wrinkled pea for the home garden, market grower, canner and freezer. Pods are dark green, 3 in. and more long and tightly filled with 8 to 10 sweet, tender peas. Vines grow 1½ to 2 ft. tall depending on location, and are exceptionally prolific. In comparison with other varieties of the same class, Burpeeana Early Dwarf is most outstanding for its high production of pods which are ready to pick in about 63 days. Experiment stations, to whom we sent seeds for testing purposes, reported most favorably on it. **Pkt. 25¢; ½ lb. 55¢; lb. $1.00; 2 lbs. $1.90**

The Big Boy tomato, which revolutionized home gardening, made its debut on the back cover of the 1949 Burpee seed catalog. (Courtesy of W. Atlee Burpee & Company.)

In addition to tomatoes, Oved also found time to develop some of the world's first successful hybrids of cucumber, eggplant, muskmelon, and watermelon. In all, he is credited with the creation of twelve hybrids in his short time at Burpee, but nothing comes close to the success of the Big Boy.

Yet Oved Shifriss had even bigger things in mind. The creation of the Big Boy in the late 1940s coincided with the birth of a nation, and when the smoke had cleared in the Middle East, Oved's Palestinian birthplace was now in the state of Israel. Shifriss returned to his homeland to do his part to make the desert bloom, founding and directing the plant genetics program at the Weizmann Institute of Science in Rehovot. He lived there for the next six years, his pet project being the development of a castor bean as a petroleum substitute.

In 1958, Shifriss returned to the United States, taking a professorship at Rutgers, where he taught and continued with research and breeding until his retirement in 1984. Shifriss had by then turned his attention from tomatoes to squash, leading to another important, if less celebrated breakthrough: a line of yellow squash resistant to the cucumber mosaic virus, a disfiguring disease that had previously made yellow squashes too risky to grow commercially. Up until a year before his death at eighty-nine, Oved Shifriss could still be found in research fields and greenhouses, pursuing his dream of creating a new squash variety that he hoped would become a nourishing staple crop around the world, on a par with corn, rice, and potatoes—that is, a Big Boy for squash.

Speaking of big boys, I ask George Ball, "Do we know where the name came from, or did Oved take a secret to his grave?"

I realize I've touched a nerve, as Ball launches somewhat haltingly into the story. "Well, yes. And that's no. I'm going to tread lightly here because there are a lot of people who, including *USA*

Today—I was shocked when they—when we had to let one of the family members go after I bought the company in '91." That was Jonathan Burpee, the grandson of founder W. Atlee Burpee. "It's kind of a misbegotten—it's not a bad story; it's just a little thing they put on the front page."

A "little thing" on the front page? Now with my full attention, Ball continues. "I don't know exactly how old he was." (He was fifty-one.) "But we had to let him go. Just because, you know, it was time. And the company had been sold [to General Foods] twenty years earlier. And so, we gave him a wonderful package" and said goodbye.

Except Jonathan said goodbye in newspaper headlines like: "BURPEE BOUNCES BIG BOY" and "BURPEE'S BIG BOY GETS THE BOOT," claiming aggrievedly that he was the eponymous "Big Boy," the boy for whom the most famous tomato of all time was named. Not true, says Ball emphatically. "Oved bred it and Oved named it," and he named it after his *own* son, Jordan. "And Jordan *was* a big boy!" And a playmate of Jonathan, whom he towered over.

In any event, "Big Boy" turns out to have been an absolutely brilliant name, alliterative, easy for English speakers to remember and for foreigners to pronounce. Ball says that when he travels the world to sales conferences and the like, people with hardly any English will approach him and say, "Big Boy!" Turns out, the word that's tricky to pronounce, even for native speakers, is "tomato."

"I've been breeding to-*mah*-toes, really, since 1978," Simon Crawford tells me over a video link from his office in Yorkshire,

England. (America is among the minority of English-speaking nations to pronounce the word like "potato.") Crawford, who served as Burpee's director of breeding until becoming managing director of Burpee Europe, where most of their breeding is now done, is the new (clean-shaven) face of the modern seedsman and breeder, as well as the living embodiment of the global nature of the seed business today. He has traveled the world, living in Illinois and the Pacific Rim before returning to his native England. The list of countries he has lived in or visited reads like a world atlas.*

Burpee, founded in Philadelphia in 1876 (while Livingston was at the peak of his career), has its European headquarters in England; its breeding research and development labs in the Netherlands; does heat tolerance testing in India; and conducts field tests of all new hybrids for the North American market in the United States. Like Livingston, Crawford has been involved in virtually every aspect of the seed business, but his passion is tomato breeding.

Despite my hours of reading, poring over websites, and trying to grasp technical papers, I understand hybridization about as well as Adam and Eve understood family planning, so Crawford has his work cut out in explaining to me how it is done. He seems up to the task, possessing the calm and knowledgeable demeanor of a BBC gardening show host—until, that is, he starts talking about emasculation and vibrators, two words not often heard on the BBC.

---

* Sydney, Melbourne, Perth, and Brisbane, Australia; Auckland and Palmerstone North, New Zealand; Chiba and Aomori, Japan; Hong Kong, Kunming, Beijing, and Shanghai, China; Bangalore and Delhi, India; Jakarta and Malang, Indonesia; plus Singapore, Thailand, South Korea, Mexico, Ecuador, Colombia, Chile, Brazil, Argentina, the United States, and virtually all of Europe.

"Tomatoes self-pollinate as a matter of course," Crawford begins, because every tomato blossom has both male and female organs. Over the centuries of tomato domestication, the stigma, the part of the female pistil that receives the pollen, has grown shorter, receding inside a nearly closed staminal cone, creating a kind of chastity belt that keeps out—or at least deters—insects from bringing in pollen from other blossoms. Bees, specifically bumblebees, with their rapidly beating wings, still have a role to play, however. When they land on a flower, the vibrations from their wings shake loose the pollen, which falls onto the stigma. The fertilized ovary at the base of the blossom then develops into a tomato. This self-fertilization results in every tomato and every generation (barring mutation) being a clone of the preceding one.

But let's suppose you don't want a clone. What if you want to combine, or "cross," two different tomato varieties to get some of the qualities of each—to create a hybrid?

"You start by looking at what characteristics you want," Crawford begins. "So, let's say you want a plum tomato with higher sugar levels than the average plum tomato. You might start with something like a San Marzano type, and cross that with something that has more sweetness, like a cherry tomato."

The parents-to-be are grown in separate insect-proof greenhouses to prevent any chance of premature cross-pollination, as segregated as the boys and the girls at a fundamentalist summer camp. Although it's about to get even worse for one of the groups. "To prevent self-pollination you have to emasculate the flower of what you choose to be the female plant before it can release any pollen. That has to be done using a pair of forceps or tweezers."

Meanwhile, in the boys' cabin they might be having a little more fun. "You collect pollen from the male parent using a small vibrating device similar to an electric toothbrush, with a little tube on the end. And then you pollinate the females with that pollen," using a small artist's paintbrush or similar tool.

It sounds simple enough. But creating a successful tomato hybrid is not as straightforward as sending a mare and a donkey out into the clover and hoping the mood strikes, because, for one thing, you're looking for very specific traits in the offspring; not just any old mule will do. Besides, crossing your tomatoes won't combine only *desirable* traits; some resulting tomato hybrids will have acquired *undesirable* traits while losing their best qualities. Your first cross may indeed produce some sweeter plum tomatoes, but it's not until growing them out and testing that you'll find out they wilt like a Victorian maiden on a hot day. Or they have no disease resistance. Or the texture is mealy. Even worse, Crawford points out, in this hypothetical example the crosses will produce more cherry tomato offspring than plum because the gene for the plum form tends to be recessive.

So, the breeding process begins with not one but several different plum tomato–cherry tomato crosses. To say there's a lot of (educated) trial and error involved is a gross understatement. And once you have promising parent lines—having now *increased* genetic diversity—you need to start working to *reduce* genetic variability in each of your parents to almost zero so that their "mating" will always produce identical offspring—your marketable hybrid.

This is the repeatability problem that bedeviled Livingston, who couldn't understand why "even where for several generations these bad qualities are not seen, for some unaccountable reasons they will begin to appear again." But we know something that Livingston didn't, namely that those troublemakers, those "lurking" recessive genes, need to be eliminated. You need, for example, to ensure that your red tomatoes all have a *pair* of dominant red genes and are not red simply because they have one red and one yellow gene. How do you know? Let them self-pollinate, and only if *all* the resulting plants bear red tomatoes will you know you've eliminated the yellow gene.

And so on. This is what took Oved Shifriss nearly a decade, the initial crosses followed by the successive inbreeding of each parent line—that is, self-pollination, growing to maturity, and selection of the best plants, followed by another cycle of inbreeding, until all of the offspring are identical and possess the traits you want. This generally requires about eight generations. "It's this inbreeding process that gives you lines that are completely uniform, what we describe in genetic terms as 'homozygous,'" Crawford explains. And, of course, you need homozygosity for not just a single trait, like color, but for each and every one of the characteristics important to your new hybrid.

It is a complex ballet, a dance in which one partner demands genetic purity while the other craves diversity, a pas de deux featuring a waltzer and a break-dancer. Even with modern tools, such as genetic markers that can allow breeders to infer the presence of genes without waiting for ripe tomatoes, development of a new hybrid today takes from five to seven years and involves up to a hundred thousand plants. In an age of instant gratification, where apps are developed in days and messages delivered in milliseconds, plant breeding seems to belong to another century. But getting the right traits into a tomato is one thing; what traits, I ask Ball and Crawford, make for a good breeder?

"Curiosity," George Ball says without hesitation. "Curiosity is absolutely the first button pressed when you find a great plant breeder. And a close second is a great eye. So if you've got those two things, you're probably going to be a good plant breeder, if you can keep a lot of information in your head, too, because it's very much like an engineering science. Genetics automatically throws you into an engineering situation, where you have to create something new out of something very complex."

Simon Crawford adds, "It's discipline, organization—and good record keeping is essential. And a good eye for a plant, and commitment to just get out there. Plant breeders need to get out into the field; you can't just sit in the lab. You've got to get out there and look at the crops—actually handle the crops—and get involved with them. So, you've got to have a good appreciation of growing horticulture generally. Nutrition, disease control—all of these aspects are essential to a plant breeder."

Crawford was studying botany and genetics at the University of London when he became interested in plant breeding. "So, I read books on it and then after graduation I started to work for a small UK seed breeding company. I was then let loose in the greenhouse and haven't looked back since." His greenhouse years were fruitful; among his successful tomato hybrids are Cloudy Days (designed for the drizzly English climate, it has one of the few hybrid names to actually make any sense); Honeycomb; Cherry Baby; Gladiator; Medium Rare (a pinkish beefsteak tomato that bears eighteen-ounce fruits); and Tumbler, a compact hybrid, intended for hanging baskets, that produces heavy clusters of cherry tomatoes in just forty-five days (nearly a month earlier than most).

"It's a great adventure," Crawford says of breeding. "You try to plan but there are always surprises around the corner, good and bad. I remember the first time I tasted Sungold," a golden cherry tomato hybrid that has become a favorite in backyard gardens around the world. "I was shocked. The taste was so sweet and tangy I almost couldn't believe my own senses. Sungold was bred by Tokita in Japan, and since that day about twenty years ago I have been in awe of their breeding. They are true innovators, not copiers. They are able to think independently, and that is another key lesson for plant breeders."

Yet for every Big Boy there are a hundred Little Disappointments. To be a breeder is to deal with the unpredictable and the unexplained, anticipation and apprehension, success and failure. For people like Simon Crawford, it's worth it: "Making the cross is great and exciting but seeing that first fruit ripen in the summer following the cross—that is the most satisfying part of the job."

Oved Shifriss was far from the only person in America successfully hybridizing tomatoes in the twentieth century. Yet the figure who made some of the greatest contributions to tomato hybridization wasn't a breeder at all.

Charles M. Rick—Charley Rick to everyone—was a botanist and plant geneticist who accepted a faculty appointment in 1941 at the delightfully named Division of Truck Crops at the University of California, Davis. Seven years later, Rick, often described as a hybrid of Charles Darwin and Indiana Jones, made the first of thirteen trips to South America—mostly Peru and Ecuador—to collect and catalog hundreds of wild relatives of the cultivated tomato. His early trips were not easy, beginning and ending with several weeks on a freighter, but that didn't deter Rick from bringing his family along and driving into the coastal Andes in a rickety Volkswagen minivan in search of tomatoes. (Afforded an early taste of adventure and discomfort, his son, John, would become an archaeologist.)

When Rick began his South American explorations, the tomatoes being bred and grown in the United States were all descendants of just the handful of cultivars collected by the Spanish during the conquest of Mexico four hundred years earlier. And *those* had been bred from a smaller number of the wild tomatoes growing in the Andes. The diversity of this already small sample was squeezed down further in Europe through centuries of artificial selection before even reaching America, leaving the domesticated tomato with just an estimated 5 percent of the total genetic material of the wild population.

Rick went out in search of the other 95 percent, collecting hundreds of previously undiscovered wild tomato varieties, some of which were not "tomatoes" at all—that is, not belonging to the species *Solanum lycopersicum*—but related closely enough that they could be interbred with the domesticated tomato. This included the species thought to be its ancestor: the diminutive currant or pimp tomato, *Solanum pimpinellifolium*, with fruits not much larger than a pea. Beginning with the seeds of the tomato varieties he harvested in South America, Rick created the Tomato Genetics Resource Center at UC Davis. Its seed bank, which mails out as many as a thousand seed packets a year, is freely available to any breeder or researcher. The center, now directed by one of Rick's former graduate students, Roger Chetelat, claims to have the largest collection of tomato seeds in the world.

Part of Charley Rick's success stemmed from his approach of looking at tomatoes in the context of their surroundings. When he found a tomato plant growing in a desert, he figured it must have a valuable drought-resistant gene; when he discovered tomatoes in one Peruvian village irrigated by recycled wastewater, an environment ripe for nematodes, he figured they had to have some natural resistance to that destructive worm. Once these genes were identified, they could be bred into other tomatoes, although it isn't as simple as swapping out a part in a '57 Chevy. More often than not, genes are difficult to isolate, and they carry deleterious effects as well as benefits. So that drought-resistant gene sequence may also carry a bitter flavor or be susceptible to disease.

Rick twice visited the Galápagos Islands, where Darwin, while studying different species of finches, had his epiphany about natural selection and evolution. Rick brought home the seeds of the Galápagos tomato, similar to a cherry tomato, only to find that they wouldn't germinate, resisting all the tricks of the trade. He soaked the seeds in solvents and scraped them with sandpaper, but still, they wouldn't sprout. Knowing that some seeds need to pass through an animal's digestive tract to become viable, he next tried feeding them to (and subsequently retrieving them from) mockingbirds and iguanas common to the Galápagos, to no avail.

Finally, he thought of the Galápagos giant tortoise. There weren't any on the Davis campus, but Rick knew an expert in finch evolution from San Francisco named Robert Bowman who kept a pair in his backyard. Rick mailed Bowman some seeds to feed to the tortoises, and in return, every few days Bowman mailed Rick a fresh mound of tortoise dung, tightly sealed to escape detection. (Sending feces in the US Mail was as illegal then as it is now.) Rick would then painstakingly pick through each pile of feces with a pair of tweezers, yet he couldn't find any of the tiny seeds in the many samples he'd received, and his supply was starting to run low.

An animal scientist Rick knew suggested employing a marker dye to make detection easier, so the tortoises were fed lettuce spiked with red dye and Galápagos tomato seeds, and after a month (tortoises, true to their reputation, are slow in *every* way), the red seeds showed up. And germinated. More than providing an entertaining anecdote about Charley Rick's legendary determination, the Galápagos tomato turned out to have a trait critical to one of the major innovations of the twentieth century: the mechanically harvested tomato.

When you pluck a tomato off a vine (especially with one hand), you often get a small piece of the green stem (the pedicel) with it. This is because of a weak spot, or "joint," that forms in the pedicel as the fruit matures, a feature that evolved to help a vegetable plant or fruit tree shed and disperse its ripe fruit. A nuisance to tomato harvesters and processors because it must be removed in the field so that it doesn't damage other tomatoes on their way to the packing house or cannery, its presence had long inhibited the use of a mechanical tomato harvester.

The Galápagos tomato, *Solanum cheesmaniae*, however, is "jointless." When this trait was successfully crossed with the domesticated tomato, the fruits of the resulting hybrids would separate from the vine at the next-weakest point: where the stem meets the tomato. When bred into a tomato with a tougher skin, the jointless characteristic allowed the use of a mechanical harvester, a tractor-like device that crawls down the rows, slicing the roots with sharp blades, then ripping the entire tomato plant out of the ground and shaking it vigorously over a bin until the tomatoes separate cleanly.

To California growers, with whom UC Davis and Rick worked closely, the mechanical harvester was a godsend, relieving their chronic migrant labor shortages, which were partly a result of federal policies of the 1960s that restricted Mexican farm labor. The harvester took over the American tomato processing industry almost overnight. (The machinery is too rough on tomatoes grown for the fresh market, which demand more selective harvesting and unblemished fruit.) Not everyone was happy at this development, of course; mechanized harvesting accelerated the decline of the family farm in California, as small farms couldn't afford the $50,000 to $200,000 cost of the machinery (and couldn't compete without it). Within five years of the machine's release, 4,428 of California's 5,000 tomato growers had gone out of business, taking 32,000 jobs with them.

Charley Rick's work touched almost every aspect of tomato breeding and genetics, not the least of which was making the tomato one of the most understood genomes in the plant world. Had he been born just a few decades earlier, his South American discoveries might have been more botanical curiosities than important advances, but their coinciding with the heyday of hybridization meant that many of them found their way into the mainstream. Resistance to at least sixteen diseases has been bred into modern tomatoes from Rick's South American discoveries, the result being that nearly every modern hybrid owes some of its DNA—and its success—to Charley Rick.

This golden age of hybridization brought tomatoes into the space age, as reflected in names like Jet Star and Supersonic. New hybrids, arriving almost too fast to keep track of, boasted improved disease resistance, earlier ripening, larger fruits, or brighter color. And because marketers knew a good thing when they saw it, Big Boy was followed by Better Boy, Sunny Boy, Tough Boy, Big Girl, Early Girl, New Girl, Golden Girl, and Brandy Boy.

Personally, I'd like to see more varieties named after Mendel, Livingston, Shifriss, and Rick, because the modern tomato owes an enormous debt to each of these men. In fact, it is difficult to find a commercial tomato that was not influenced by all four of these pioneers.

Which is a problem.

Because whether these new tomatoes were bigger, rounder, smoother, redder, easier to grow, or more disease-resistant than their predecessors; whether they came from your garden or your grocery store, the new generation of hybrids had one trait in common, and it did not go unnoticed in the last quarter of the twentieth century.

Tomatoes were tasting worse, not better.

Eight

WHO KILLED THE TOMATO?

The Tomato We Love to Hate: The Florida Mature Green

"Who owns the red suitcase?"

That's the last thing I want to hear at an airport security checkpoint. Particularly after a tiring week of touring Florida tomato farms, when I just want to get home and to bed. Once again—the previous time being when I was attempting to fly to France with a kilo of sourdough starter that bore an uncanny resemblance to a kilo of *plastique*—the TSA is standing between me and my plane.

This baggage must look equally explosive in the x-ray, so I preemptively explain, "They're tomatoes," as the agent unzips the bag.

He stares at them, confused. "You know, they're green."

And hard, which is fortunate, because a moment later, hastening to get to my gate, I snatch the suitcase without zipping it back up, sending all ten of them bouncing and careening across the floor of the Tampa International Airport like a sharply cracked rack of billiard balls.

"Oh, no, I'm so sorry!" a passenger says as she gingerly tiptoes through and around them in heels.

"Not to worry," I say. "They're Florida tomatoes. They've seen worse."

And I'm not kidding.

✱

It's hard to imagine a vegetable—or for that matter, *any* food—with a worse reputation than the Florida tomato, which for over half a century has been derided, demonized, and vilified. Yet, even while becoming the embodiment of tasteless and soulless factory food, "a general metaphor for our dissatisfaction," in the words of journalist Arthur Allen, the Florida tomato changed the way America eats. Fresh tomatoes were once an eagerly awaited seasonal—and local—treat to be enjoyed a precious few months out of the year, their first appearance at farm stands signifying for many the true beginning of summer. Except for the wealthiest Americans, who could afford to buy from (or owned) greenhouses, tomatoes in February were about as common as grapefruit in August.

Florida changed that, providing supermarkets with bins of cheap tomatoes from fall through early summer, putting a wedge of color into every restaurant salad, and abetting the phenomenal rise of what would become known as the fast-food restaurant. For all their success, however, I doubt you could find anyone who would own up to actually liking the damn things. Their bland taste and mealy texture are often compared to cardboard and Styrofoam. Americans invariably put tomatoes near the top (or rather the bottom) in food dissatisfaction surveys.

While eating *a billion pounds a year.*

How did we end up in such an odd place, where the most dis-liked vegetable in the country is also the most widely eaten? And how did they get to be so bad, so far removed from what toma-toes used to be? This is a mystery that's been nagging at me since my first three-pack of hard, cellophane-wrapped tomatoes, so I've come to Florida to find out who killed the tomato—and I'm not leaving until I've solved the crime.

The prime suspects—or at least their proxies—are in this very room with me, at the Immokalee, Florida, offices of Lipman Family Farms, the largest grower of field tomatoes in the United States. It feels like a live-action game of Clue, but instead of Colo-nel Mustard and Mrs. Peacock, our suspects are:

THE CEO: Kent Shoemaker, representing the factory farm, and all that implies, from pesticides to profits. Main reason to suspect him: He's invited me onto the premises.

THE FARMER: Toby Purse, chief farming officer, the man who grows and gasses the greenies. Former chief financial officer with a last name of *Purse*? Suspicious.

THE BREEDER: Mark Barineau, director of breeding and seed production. Says he wants to put flavor back into the tomato. A man with a guilty conscience?

Then there's the writer. I'm quite aware of being viewed with no small degree of suspicion myself, owing to what I call the "Estabrook effect." In 2009 *Gourmet* magazine ran an exposé by staff writer and editor Barry Estabrook (expanded upon two years later in his book *Tomatoland*) that brought widespread public attention to something that most of us had never given a moment's thought: how the tomato on our burger got there. And it turned out it wasn't a pretty picture. Abominable living conditions, low wages coupled with outright wage theft, beatings, and even literal enslavement (chains included) were among the routine abuses endured by the migrant workers around Immokalee, Florida, who at the time were harvesting up to 90 percent of all the tomatoes eaten in the US from December through May, including those that wound up on virtually every fast-food burger, taco, and salad in America.

Suddenly, all of us were complicit. Pulling up to the drive-thru window was tantamount to supporting twenty-first-century slavery. An advocacy group, the Coalition of Immokalee Workers (CIW), had been unsuccessfully pressing the growers for reforms since the 1990s, but the growers, family-run operations without stockholders or name recognition, proved to be immune to bad press and picketing. So, in 2001 the CIW tried a different tactic, taking the fight directly to the largest buyers of Immokalee tomatoes, companies who were acutely image-conscious—Taco Bell, Burger King, McDonald's, Wendy's, and Subway—demanding that they pay an extra penny a pound for tomatoes, with the extra cent going directly to the pickers as a bonus.

A penny a pound, which would add a crucial $60 to $100 a week to a picker's salary, while increasing the cost of a burger by less than *one-tenth of a cent*, was not even a rounding error to these hugely profitable corporations. Still, they refused to budge for years, washing their hands of the abuses and crimes taking place on the farms by claiming it wasn't their place to get involved in an "internal labor dispute." But the cumulative effects of a boycott of college campus Taco Bells and an unrelenting public relations campaign were taking their toll. The greatest damage, however, was self-inflicted.

From 2007 to 2008, someone using the internet handle "surfxaholic36" used various social media platforms to post frequent, furious, and serious allegations against the CIW. Following an article in the *Naples News* reporting on a visit to Immokalee by Vermont senator Bernie Sanders, surfxaholic36 commented, on the newspaper's website, "The CIW is an attack organization and will drive business out of Immokalee while they line their own pockets. They make money through donations by attacking... McDonald's and now Burger King to get money for there [*sic*] own organization. They are the lowest form of life...I will buy all the Whoppers I can, good going Burger King for uncovering these blood suckers."

This vitriolic attack, fed by a curious passion for Whoppers, piqued the interest of Amy Bennett Williams, a reporter for the Fort Myers *News-Press*, who was able to track down a phone number for surfxaholic36. Imagine Williams' surprise when a sweet, middle school–age girl answered the phone. *Oh, that wasn't me*, the girl insisted, denying any knowledge of the CIW. "That was my dad," she said, who used her social media accounts from time to time. Her dad happened to be Steven F. Grover, vice president of food safety, quality assurance, and regulatory affairs for Burger King. After this public relations disaster, Burger King, the other restaurants, and several major supermarket chains capitulated, with the notable exception of Wendy's, who instead just pulled out of Florida altogether.

"Dad" was invited to seek employment elsewhere.

The fast-food companies and supermarkets agreed not only to the small increase, but to the additional, more significant demand to purchase only from farms that signed on to CIW's Fair Food

Program, which guaranteed improved working conditions, fair treatment from management, and independent monitoring.

Finally, in 2010, a year after the *Gourmet* article, the farms and the Florida Tomato Growers Exchange, which controls everything red and round in Florida, gave in as well, and the agreement went into effect. The change was so dramatic that Immokalee is now held up as a national model of fair migrant farming practices, and in 2018 Estabrook felt compelled to publish an updated edition of *Tomatoland: How Modern Industrial Agriculture Destroyed Our Most Alluring Fruit* with a new, optimistic subtitle: *From Harvest of Shame to Harvest of Hope.*

A happy ending, but memories are famously long in the South, and tomato growers remain wary of another Northern writer coming down to write a book about their industry. Several turned me away before Kent Shoemaker agreed to my visit. After twenty-six years with the food service giant Sysco, Shoemaker, nearly six and a half feet of crisp jeans and button-down shirt, joined Lipman in 2011, the first "outsider" to serve as CEO at this family-owned enterprise. He didn't get much of a break-in period; his arrival coincided, he notes wryly, with the publication of *Tomatoland.*

Shoemaker, who says, "I eat tomatoes at every meal," has arranged two days of interviews and tours for me, promising unfettered access to Lipman's growing, picking, packing, and breeding operations—if, that is, I don't get thrown out first by asking the tough questions necessary to solve a crime. But everyone here seems in a rather good mood, relaxed and joshing around, and I'll soon learn why.

With self-preservation in mind, I've lined up a few flattering opening questions to soften them up a bit before I come in with the zingers—variations of *Why are your tomatoes so lousy?* I've yet to open my mouth when Shoemaker preempts my agenda, tossing me directly into the belly of the beast before I've had a chance to feed it.

"Maybe where you might want to start, as kind of the theme of Florida tomatoes, people regularly say to me, 'Why can't I get a tomato in February that tastes like my grandma's used to in August?'"

No, that is definitely *not* where I want to start; rather, that is where I want to finish, but ten seconds into the interview it's clear that when it comes to controlling a meeting, I am no match for the CEO of a multimillion-dollar company. I keep my mouth shut and start scribbling as Shoemaker answers his own question.

"Well, we have to get the tomato from Immokalee, Florida, to St. Louis in February. And your grandma's tomato wouldn't make it. Because it was a full red, vine-ripened tomato that just wouldn't hold up. So we have bred high-lycopene flavor"— lycopene being that carotenoid that gives tomatoes their red color—"into a tomato that has the ability to be picked, handled, and sent all over the country and be able to still be consumed. So that's always the challenge. You have to make choices."

"Be able to still be consumed" is not exactly a glowing endorsement for a food. When Burger King scrapped their slogan of forty years, "Have it your way," it wasn't for "Able to be consumed"—but Shoemaker has set the theme for my visit: challenges and choices. Although some of the challenges are a direct result of choices made over a century ago, when the seeds of this crime were planted.

✷

Tomatoes have been grown commercially in Florida since the Civil War, with the first farms hugging its east and west coasts for their protection from killing frosts. By the 1870s, tomatoes were being grown on Sanibel Island (before the farmland was replanted with condominiums) and shipped to Key West to be loaded onto boats bound for New York and Boston. The five most commonly grown tomato types in the state were Acme, Stone, Favorite, Perfection, and Beauty—all Alexander Livingston varieties.

Complaints about Florida tomatoes are as old as the Florida tomato, with a 1920 USDA bulletin noting, "In spite of the fact that thousands of cars of Florida tomatoes are shipped to the North each year, the quality . . . is admittedly inferior." Some found them "pink and hollow," likely because, facing a long journey on hot railroad cars, the tomatoes were of necessity picked well before they were ripe. Just how early the fruits should be harvested was a point of contention even in 1888, with one grower recommending they be picked "at the time when they are just ready to show color but do not yet begin to show it," reminding me of the directions I once saw on a bag of popcorn to "remove from heat just before the last kernel pops."

Following the Second World War, the development of the federal highway system, notably I-95, which runs from southern Florida to Maine, made long-distance trucking of fresh vegetables feasible. By the 1960s just about every supermarket and corner grocery in America was selling Florida tomatoes from October to June, often three or four to a cellophane-wrapped paper pack, perfectly uniform, blemish-free . . . and tasteless.

Where had the tomato's flavor gone?

⊛

Exhibit 1: Your Honor, this tomato is green!

Kent Shoemaker, in speaking of the challenges of shipping tomatoes across the country, had said, "You have to make choices."
The most consequential of those choices—the defining characteristic of Florida tomatoes—is to pick the fruits at what the industry
calls the "mature green" stage and ripen them with a gas. To anyone not in the Florida tomato business, "mature green tomato"
sounds like an oxymoron on a par with "well-done steak tartare."
But here in tomatoland, it is not only a growing strategy; it's a
belief system.

What does "mature green" mean? Chris Campbell, the farm
manager of Lipman's Naples farm, takes me into the field the next
day to show me. Tall, lean, and rural-friendly, Campbell reminds
me of the television farmers I grew up with on children's pro-
gramming in the late 1950s, when Florida tomatoes were just hitting their stride. Slicing into a hard, green tomato that, were it in
my garden, I wouldn't even be *thinking* about picking for another
couple of weeks, Campbell probes one of the locules (the squishy
part of a ripe tomato that contains the seeds) with the tip of his
knife. "You see how this is starting to become a gel, and the seeds
are darkening. So, we would say this is ready to be picked."

There may be a bit of gel inside, but like everything else it
is bright green, Irish springtime green, Kermit the Frog green.
"If that's a ripe tomato," I ask, "what does an *unripe* tomato look
like?"

Campbell cuts open a smaller fruit from higher up on the

plant to show me. But that one is also mature. As is the next one he selects. Apparently, even for an expert, the only way to tell a mature green from an immature green is to destroy the tomato. On the third try he gets what he is after, a tomato whose locules are still solid, with whitish seeds.

How, then, do the pickers know which ones to select? Some farms rig a horizontal string across the rows, with everything below the string—the older tomatoes—eligible to be harvested, but here the workers judge by size, using an apparently memorized template that Campbell carries in his truck. Once a crop has a sufficient percentage of tomatoes that have reached the mature green stage (meaning that a certain percentage is still immature), everything larger than about a tennis ball, specifically, 2⁹⁄₃₂ of an inch in diameter, is picked. In theory.

And weather permitting.

Despite a forecast of clear skies, an intermittent light drizzle blowing in from the Gulf is threatening today's harvest. Wet fruits can result in postharvest disease and other packaging issues, so the decision about whether to harvest today is crucial—not only to the company, but to the hundreds of workers who have been bused an hour and a half from Immokalee for the day.

As Campbell drives me out in his pickup truck through nearly five thousand acres of tomatoes, his phone never stops ringing with reports from the field. On a farm this vast, it can be dry in one part and raining in another.

We pull up near a crew harvesting tomatoes, silently working down the rows as a truck follows. I focus on the picker nearest me. Like most of the others, he is a Mexican migrant admitted on an H-2A temporary agricultural worker visa. Squatting in front of a tomato plant, a large plastic bucket clasped between his thighs, he strips the green fruits off their vines, his hands moving so rapidly that he looks like a six-armed Hindu god. In just seconds he has stripped the plant bare, except for a few tomatoes too small—or too ripe—to be picked. He hops quickly to the next plant, two feet away, stripping that one until his bucket is full.

Hefting the bucket onto his shoulder, he walks quickly to the truck and heaves the thirty-two-pound load up to a dumper, who throws the tomatoes into a thousand-pound bin and returns the bucket with a receipt, redeemable for 60 cents. The worker pockets the token and quickly returns to the next plant in his row. The entire cycle, from picking to dumping to returning, has taken him just ninety seconds.

Pick, dump, and repeat. Pick, dump, and repeat. It is a mesmerizing sight, two dozen human worker bees fanning out from the truck, returning moments later laden with food for the hive, depositing it, and rushing out for more, hours upon hours of

Tomato harvesters in Florida filling a truck with mature green tomatoes. (Jan Halaska / Alamy Stock Photo.)

activity. The men are generally short, and the tomato plants tall, so my view is of disembodied heads and buckets brimming with green tomatoes floating between the rows, a pastoral canvas worthy of Brueghel the Elder.

Whatever romanticism the scene evokes fades quickly when Campbell hands me a bucket and a pair of nitrile gloves. Squatting in front of a plant, I immediately screw up. "You have to remove the stem," he points out. A tomato bearing a stem is like a drunken sailor swinging a cutlass on a crowded ship; a single errant stem can inflict fatal wounds on countless other fruits. Unlike the jointless tomatoes that dominate the fields of processing tomatoes in California, these tomatoes break off at the weak spot in the pedicel. It takes me a few seconds to twist off each little stub, which can be quite resilient (remember, these are *green* tomatoes), but a seasoned worker removes it with a magician's sleight of hand, brushing the stem against his pants leg in one smooth, nearly invisible motion as he moves the tomato from plant to bucket. "Unskilled labor"? Hardly.

I'm also too deliberative, examining each tomato for proper size before I pick it. That's partly due to lack of experience, but I notice that the workers, paid by the bucket, are far less fussy, stripping a plant in the time it would take me to examine it. My goal had been to fill a bucket, but less than a third of the way, my titanium hip suggests that we call it a day, and my back doesn't disagree. This is a young man's game, a hard one at that. Yet for those who can handle the physical demands, it can be decent money. During the first and second harvests, when tomatoes are plentiful and buckets are filled the fastest, pickers average 30 to 33 buckets per hour. This translates to hourly earnings of $18 to $20 before the penny-a-pound bonus. This is close to what they'd make in a full day spent harvesting tomatoes in Mexico, which

has been steadily eating away at the Florida industry since the passage of NAFTA in 1994 (the US now imports more than twice as
many tomatoes from Mexico as it grows in Florida).

This by no means implies that these young men have landed a
cushy job. And there are days, like today, when the workers will
make little more than Florida's minimum agricultural wage of
$11.29 an hour. Because it has started to drizzle again.

"Do you mind if we make a detour?" Campbell asks as he continues to take phone calls about every three minutes.

Of course not. I apologize for being here on such a hectic day.

"Nah," he replies with a good-natured laugh. "This is pretty
normal." We drive to check the conditions of another sector. The
foliage on the tomato plants is wet but has so far kept the fruits
under its canopy dry. These can still be picked if the rain stops,
but it's maddeningly erratic. Campbell decides to halt picking for
a half hour while the weather decides what it wants to do.

What Campbell wants to do is get these tomatoes off the vine.
Rain has kept him from picking for the past two days, and some
of the tomatoes are starting to ripen. Which, remember, in the
topsy-turvy world of Florida tomatoes, is a bad thing.

Of more urgency is that, owing to poor weather and disease in Mexico, the price of Florida tomatoes is high—$25 per
twenty-five-pound box, a dollar a pound—which likely explains
the good cheer back in Immokalee. Tomato prices can fluctuate
wildly, even from day to day. In recent years they've been as low
as $5 a box, a price at which a crop will get plowed under, as it
costs more than that to harvest and ship them. So everyone wants
to get these tomatoes to market, and now.

Even if that means pushing the definition of "mature green"
just a bit. "Right now, the money's good," Campbell volunteers,
"so you might pick them just on the border. They're still going to

red up—ripen—in the gas room." Into the bucket they go. In a few hours they'll be in Immokalee.

Toby Purse, who joined Lipman Family Farms twenty years ago, served as its CFO—chief financial officer—before taking on the broader role of chief farming officer ("so they didn't have to print up new business cards," he jokes), a role that not only got him out from behind a desk, but put him in charge of the day-to-day operations. Purse takes me into the packing facility adjacent to Lipman's offices so that I can follow my tomatoes on their next steps to market, and, if you'll pardon another board-game reference, this looks and feels remarkably like a life-sized version of Chutes and Ladders. The first chute delivers the tomatoes from the truck into the facility, a thousand pounds at a time.

Now, you would think that dumping a thousand pounds of tomatoes from a truck would be detrimental, especially to the unfortunate souls who wind up on the bottom. Nope. No fruit is harmed in the making of this scene as they are dumped and swept into a chlorinated pool for disinfection. Emerging after a single lap via a ladder at the other end, they're dropped onto a conveyer belt, where they're bounced around *on purpose* to help them dry and to knock off any errant stems. They are then run under an optical sorter, which uses sophisticated high-speed optical analysis to kick anything too large, too small, too red, or too blemished down a chute.

Those that "pass" continue onto another belt lined with hair-netted women who pull out any imperfect tomatoes that the sorter missed, a job that requires concentration and dexterity. The fruits that make the grade—about 75 percent of what came off the vines—get sorted and packed into twenty-five-pound boxes.

Purse is ready to move on, but I am absolutely mesmerized by the sorter, which kicks out the tomatoes flying under it like a soccer goalie on steroids. First developed in Michigan in the 1930s for the bean industry, optical sorters, which today rely on a combination of cameras, lasers, and software algorithms, are used widely in applications ranging from coffee bean inspection to separating your recycling.

Shoemaker had said that Grandma's vine-ripened tomatoes would never make it to St. Louis. The truth is, thrown from buckets, dumped from trucks, bounced around on rollers, and tossed into crates, they wouldn't have made it out of Immokalee. Watching how these tomatoes are handled, I realize that it's a bit of a misrepresentation to say that the industry wants to pick the tomatoes green. They want to pick them *hard* because the entire business model of selling Florida tomatoes depends on being able to toss them around like softballs at a company picnic, and, unfortunately for the consumer, green goes hand in hand with hard.

Just why do they have to be treated so roughly? The answer is flying past my eyes: volume. The Naples farm alone, just one of several Lipman Florida locations, can produce up to two million pounds of tomatoes—fifty large truckloads—in a single day. At this scale, to handle each tomato even half as gingerly as I handle those from my garden would require the entire population of Immokalee.

About three-quarters of Florida tomatoes end up going to the food service industry: fast-food joints, food wholesalers like Sysco, and restaurants large and small. To sell them in such enormous volume—and *cheaply*, which I'll soon learn is paramount—you must be able to move them around with front-end loaders, not gloved hands.

Purse takes me to the last phase of the packing operation, the holding room, where boxes of tomatoes, ready for shipping, are stacked on pallets. But I realize there's something I haven't yet seen. I knew it: They're hiding the most controversial part of the process.

"When do they get the gas?" I ask.

"They're getting it right now."

I'm standing here breathing ethylene?! Purse registers the alarm in my eyes—or maybe my voice, as I may have blurted that private thought out loud. "It's quite safe. We use a concentration of only 100 to 150 parts per million."

Ethylene, a hydrocarbon used primarily in the manufacture of plastic (polyethylene), and—ahem, this seems appropriate—Styrofoam, is less safe in higher concentrations. In fact, right into the 1950s, when the tomatoes were gassed with pure ethylene from a hose stuck into a hole in the wall, the charred debris of ripening sheds and roasted green tomatoes—the result of a spark or an errant cigarette—was not an uncommon sight.

The use of ethylene began as an accident when nineteenth-century farmers started heating their ripening sheds with kerosene lamps to accelerate the process. It wasn't until 1924 that R. J. Harvey, a scientist at the University of Minnesota, discovered that the heat wasn't ripening the tomatoes, but rather the ethylene by-product of combustion. And the modern Florida tomato industry was born.

The industry insists that there is nothing unnatural about this process, that ethylene, an important hormone that regulates not only ripening, but the opening of flowers and the shedding of leaves, is a naturally occurring compound synthesized by the plants themselves. And that much is true. Although these tomatoes, having been picked at such an early stage that the genetic ripening switch has not yet been turned on, will never develop sufficient ethylene to ripen on their own, so they're given this dose of it in the ripening room.

"How long will they stay here?" I ask Purse.

"One to nine days."

Why such variation? Partly it depends on the preference of the buyer and how far they're going. But once again, the market rules: If the price is low, Purse will have the temperature turned down and hold them in anticipation of a better price. Not today.

"You heard Kent say that tomatoes are $25," he explains. "We want to get them out of here."

The buyers—the food service industry and supermarkets—won't know the difference and won't care. As long as they're red, everyone (except the consumer) is happy. But I wonder what is really happening in this room. Are these tomatoes actually ripening, or merely changing color?

Later I would put this question to my expert witness in the case of Who Killed the Tomato: Sam Hutton, an associate professor and director of the tomato breeding program at the University of Florida's Gulf Coast Research and Education Center (GCREC), which sits on a 475-acre campus southeast of Tampa.

A young, bearded professor with a doctorate in horticulture, Hutton doesn't have an issue with ethylene per se, provided the tomatoes are truly picked at the mature green stage. The real problem, as he sees it, is less with the theory than with the execution. Many tomatoes are picked too immature. Not only is it difficult for a picker to distinguish a mature from an immature green, but if the goal is filling a thirty-two-pound bucket in sixty seconds flat, he can afford neither the time nor the interest to care.

Understandably, his concern is putting food in his family's stomach, not the quality of your January BLT.

Compounding this, I suggest to Hutton, are the market factors that I saw at work in Naples and Immokalee. "Yep. Prices are good, rain is in the forecast, so they're going to fill the boxes up, even if they're immature," he agrees, slicing open a young green tomato from his research farm behind the classrooms. "So, they're picking things like this. I don't think it matters how pretty this thing looks after you gas it; that's never going to taste good." And this brings us to one of the weirdest contradictions surrounding the Florida tomato business.

"Now, as a consumer," Hutton says, "I would think I'm going to get better quality from a $25-a-box tomato than from a $6 box." Certainly, that would be true with a steak. But for tomatoes "it's just the opposite." When prices are high, they're picked too early, gassed too little, and rushed to market before the price falls. In other words, *the more expensive the tomatoes in your store, the worse they're likely to be.* Keep that in mind next time you buy a tomato.

The prevalence of immature greens may in part explain the unpredictability of Florida tomatoes in the supermarket, where they run the gamut from merely insipid to inedible. Studies have found that a full third of Florida tomatoes are picked as hopelessly immature as the one Hutton is holding, and just 15 percent—less than 1 in 6—are harvested at the ideal stage.

But let's look at the best-case scenario, when tomatoes are picked at the truly mature green stage. Hutton picks one off a plant and slices it open. "That's a mature green," he says. "You see, it's got some pink inside. That tomato has gotten almost everything it's going to get from the plant. They'll gas it up to turn it red faster, but that's a ripe tomato."

Really? Once it leaves the ripening room, will it truly have the flavor of a fully vine-ripened, deep crimson, just-picked-for-dinner tomato? His answer surprises me. "I don't know that you would find a difference." Then his brows knit, and he takes another moment before concluding, "I'm going to say... perhaps. There's been a couple of studies done, but there's not a lot of impact on us," meaning Florida tomato growers. That's because the industry can't pick and ship fully ripe tomatoes in twenty-five-pound boxes around the country. They couldn't do it in 1888, and they can't do it today.

One of those studies Hutton alluded to was conducted at the University of Florida in Gainesville. Measuring flavor by relying on both a panel of tasters and chemical analysis of the compounds most responsible for flavor, the researchers found that the less mature the tomato (determined by how many days of gas it needs to turn red), the fewer flavor compounds were present. As for subjective taste, the panelists noted "reduced aroma, flavor and sweetness, increased sourness and green/grassy notes" among the mature green tomatoes when compared to the vine-ripened fruits.

Unfortunately, they did not include *immature* green tomatoes in their analyses.

Well, I've seen enough. Later, back at my hotel, I'm reflecting on what I've learned. Having seen tomatoes picked greener than cucumbers, tossed around like baseballs, and rushed to market, I'm ready to deliver my verdict in the case of Who Killed the Tomato. No surprise, it's what everyone has always said: Florida tomatoes are tasteless and mealy because they're picked unripe and gassed to give them some color. Congratulations, Sherlock!

I kick off my shoes, grab a bottle of wine from the minibar, and take a bite of a *naturally* red tomato, picked at the peak of ripeness, that I'd found left behind on the vine (as are all ripe tomatoes) in Naples.

As *Mad* magazine used to say, *Blecch!* I expected so much better, but now I understand Sam Hutton's contention, hard to swallow at the time, that a gassed mature green tomato was as flavorful as vine-ripened. In Florida, it seems, that might be the case. This tastes like a typical Florida winter tomato, slightly better than a mature green, perhaps, but not by much, and maybe not at all. I push it aside and take a swig of wine from the bottle, my appetite gone. I was ready to close the case, but if a vine-ripened fruit is this lousy, then the green tomato is a red herring. And that can only mean one thing.

The murderer is still out there somewhere.

🍅

Next Suspect: I Call the Breeder to the Stand

When Kent Shoemaker declared, "We have bred...a tomato that has the ability to be picked, handled, and sent all over the country," I wondered if he had inadvertently fingered the perpetrator. So, I've driven with Toby Purse out to Lipman's research laboratory in Estero to question Mark Barineau, Lipman's chief breeder.

If Burpee's Simon Crawford is the archetypical British "to-mah-to" breeder, Barineau is his American counterpart—a large, mustachioed man who speaks with a soft Louisiana accent as smooth as aged bourbon. Barineau's path to breeding was hoed early. "I came from a farming family in Louisiana. We lived next door to a professional horticulturist/breeder, who trained me in all facets of horticulture, from eight years of age," which is when Barineau planted his first garden, consisting of three tomato plants.

"Then I worked for the tomato breeder at LSU while working on my BS and MS degrees." After earning a doctorate in horticultural science, he honed his skills at Seminis, a large commercial seed developer, and Syngenta, an agricultural technology provider, before arriving at Lipman Family Farms in 2001. He has developed, he says, seventy-five commercial hybrids over his career. Like both Shoemaker and Purse, who did stints with Big Four accounting firms before settling into Lipman, working for a family-run company instead of a multinational seems to suit his low-key nature. And, speaking of family, no sooner are the introductions out of the way when poor Grandma has been dragged back into this again.

"Grandma's Brandywine doesn't taste like Grandma's Brandywine," Barineau says. "It's a perception and a stereotype."

Perhaps. "But no one expects a Florida winter tomato to taste like Grandma's," I object. "They're more often compared to Styrofoam. Why can't you breed a tomato with at least *some* flavor?"

If someone compared *my* tomatoes to Styrofoam, I might have leapt out of the chair and gone for his throat, but Barineau replies, without a trace of anger, "That's just nature. Part of the Styrofoam problem is that we've had to make them firmer so that they can hold up and not explode in the field."

Or out of the field. In fact, the university laboratories who participated in developing the commercial tomatoes of the last century were instructed to literally think of the tomato *as a projectile*. Apparently, they listened. In 1977, *New Yorker* writer Thomas Whiteside measured a Florida tomato against federal safety standards—not food, but *automobile*—and found that the tomato exceeded by more than two and a half times the minimum impact requirement of your car's bumper.

Having established the importance of durability, I ask Barineau and Purse what else is important. "Price," Purse says, is at the top of the buyers' list. "Then, oh yeah, it's price, *and then it's price*, and then you get to color and size and locules, internal color, how they cut, shrink," meaning not "shrinkage," but the industry term for produce than cannot be sold because of damage or degradation. "Retail hates shrink," he adds.

With large buyers who will and do buy tomatoes from the cheapest source, price holds enormous sway in the Florida tomato market to a degree that even seems to frustrate Purse. The pressures exerted by cost are felt everywhere, from the indiscriminate harvesting (growers cannot afford to send the pickers out into the fields four or five times to carefully pick tomatoes at the perfect stage) to breeding. Tomatoes are bred not only to be durable, but high-yielding, because the most direct way to keep costs low and profits high is to get more tomatoes from each plant. The major costs of farming—land, fertilizer, water, pesticides, and labor— are essentially the same whether each plant produces ten pounds of tomatoes or twenty. But the plants that yield twenty pounds through breeding nearly double the farmer's net income. I'll learn later why this seemingly reasonable goal of high yield, one shared by every backyard gardener, has been so detrimental to the tomato.

I've noticed that flavor didn't make Purse's list of buyer requirements, which of course I can't help but point out. "Isn't the fundamental problem with Florida tomatoes the fact that your largest buyers—the fast-food restaurants—don't care about tomato flavor? No one is deciding whether to go to Burger King or Wendy's tonight based on who has the better tomato."

Barineau and Purse disagree that taste is irrelevant to the fast-food industry; however, they do concede that it's not near the top of the list. For most of their fast-food customers, Barineau says, the tomato "is an ingredient. Just one of many ingredients." A cog in the machine. But why, I ask again, can't this cog have just a *little* flavor?

"No one will say, 'I don't want flavor,'" Barineau replies. "As a breeder—and I've been in this game thirty-two years—I want that flavor all day long. I want to be the guy who makes tomatoes so desirable that it will not seem unusual to eat them for breakfast on cereals, in yogurt, and on ice cream. But there are physical and chemical laws that work against accumulating some of these high-flavor components. If you increase sugars, you immediately decrease size, you immediately decrease yields. There are real trade-offs that come with that in a commercial setting. High sugars and particularly lycopene—high color—come with negative genetic baggage. They lead to breakdown."

This is because sugars and lycopene are as attractive to bacteria and fungi as they are to you and me. Furthermore, Barineau adds, high sugars will increase what's called the osmotic potential, drawing in water and swelling the fruit, leading to splitting on the vine and increased shrink.

Barineau's argument, essentially, is that high flavor is *biologically incompatible* with the other properties required in a commercial tomato. But that's a corporate line, and a little too convenient, so for a second opinion I go back to academia, the University of Florida's Sam Hutton. After all, it was Hutton's predecessor and mentor at the research center, Harry Klee, who came up with the briefly celebrated Tasti-Lee, a hybrid that was strikingly red inside and out and packed more flavor than anything else grown in Florida. Seemingly poised to change the way Americans buy

tomatoes at the supermarket, it was, Hutton says, sunk by a combination of marketing and licensing blunders, its small size, and
the fact that it was just middling when picked green.

Why, I ask Hutton, couldn't breeders simply start with a good-
tasting heirloom and breed disease resistance and high yield into
it? "There's a lot of things associated with flavor that are negatively
associated with some of these other characteristics that you go
for," he explains, confirming what Barineau had told me. "Take
yield, for example. Yield is negatively correlated with sugars."

It is sugar more than anything that makes for a flavorful
tomato. But sugars are a by-product of photosynthesis, and there
is only so much to go around. The more fruits on the plant—that
is, the higher the yield—the less sugar is available for each tomato.
"That's just plant physiology," Hutton explains.

But, I point out, those lower-yielding plants would have tastier
tomatoes. Hutton agrees. "And are they going to sell for a higher
price?" he asks rhetorically, the answer obvious. The American
tomato market is, as Toby Purse said, so price-driven that previous attempts to market a premium tomato—including the Tasti-
Lee—have been resoundingly unsuccessful.

Purse had earlier enumerated the traits that the *buyers* want,
but that's only half the story. Hutton starts listing the litany of
traits that Florida *growers* demand: fruit size and shape, plant habit,
smoothness, and resistance to disease, cracking, and blossom end
scar. Last but not least, they have to "gas up" well after being
picked green.

"You're talking dozens and dozens of genes affecting all these
traits." As you breed for them, "you're moving away from the
heirloom type of those genes and toward the cultivated tomato
type of those genes."

The "heirloom type" tomatoes he's referring to are generally indeterminate varieties, such as those tall San Marzanos staked to tree limbs. Florida growers, like their Italian and Californian counterparts who grow processing tomatoes, stopped using indeterminate varieties in the 1950s. Hutton explains why: "You need taller stakes, more labor; you have to keep tying them; as the plants get bigger you've got to come in with big clippers and snip the tops off them to keep them from falling over and blowing over and stuff like that. It's just a hassle." As it is, Lipman's Naples farm alone uses some thirty-one thousand miles of twine—enough to circle the earth and add a transatlantic bow—to tie up each crop of bushy determinate tomatoes.

Plus, Hutton adds, determinate plants bear fruit over a period of just a couple of weeks. An indeterminate plant, one that grows and produces for months, creates months of additional labor, watering, and spraying until you've gotten all the crop off.

"Makes sense," I say. "But can't you get a good tomato off either?"

"You *can*, but let me show you something," Hutton says, snipping off a vine from one of his determinate plants. "There's a leaf, then another leaf, and then a flower cluster." He moves down the vine. "Again, leaf, leaf, flower. Always two leaves, then a flower cluster."

We walk down the row. "Here's an *in*determinate tomato." He starts counting. "Leaf, leaf, *leaf*, flower cluster." Three leaves for each flower cluster. So indeterminate tomatoes, impractical for commercial growers, have 50 percent more leaves than determinates, which means 50 percent more photosynthesis, which means more flavor. And not only do determinates have fewer leaves, but the commercial varieties have been bred for high yield, further stretching a photosynthetic factory already running full tilt.

For the twenty-first-century tomato breeder, handcuffed by

having to produce determinate plants teeming with large, inde-
structible, disease-resistant fruits, the goal of returning some flavor would seem nearly hopeless. Yet neither Hutton nor Barineau
are giving up on what Toby Purse calls the holy grail, a tasty
tomato that can be picked early. In one of Hutton's test plots, I ate
one of the finest plum tomatoes I've ever tasted, although it came
off a bush too small to be of interest to commercial growers.

For his part, Barineau looks at one hundred thousand tomato
plants a year. And he, like other breeders, is hoping to find clues
to finding the grail in the genes of ancient tomato ancestors still
to be discovered by the disciples of Charley Rick, who continue to
comb the mountains of Peru for fresh germplasm. Barineau is
optimistic. "I like to think I'm the guy who's going to bring flavor
back to the tomato," he says. Of course, implicit in that phrasing
is the admission that someone previously *removed* the flavor. The
generations of modern breeders who've created a profitable but
tasteless tomato that, in one consumer satisfaction survey, finished
twenty-ninth (out of twenty-nine vegetables) sure look guilty.

But I'm not leaping to any premature conclusions this time. I
have one more suspect to visit.

I Love the Smell of Pic-Clor in the Morning

In my current postapocalyptic setting, I would not be the least bit
surprised should Mad Max come roaring past, demonic pursuers
hot on his heels. Turning slowly in a full circle, I can see nothing
but dirty gray sand and desolation in every direction. *The only*

thing that would complete this movie-set dystopia, I find myself thinking, *is a smoldering fire.* And on cue (swear to God), there it is, a sinister curl of dark smoke, the remnants of last season's broken tomato stakes and discarded string, corkscrewing skyward like a serpent.

Sam Hutton has taken me to a tomato field being prepared for planting. He might've prepared *me* first. In my native Hudson Valley, there are few things as beautiful as a newly plowed field, freshly furrowed, the rich brown, sweet-smelling soil full of promise and life. This field, a huge expanse of sandy trenches clinging to last season's wizened, dead plants, tomatoes rotting on the ground, has the vibe of a World War I battlefield the morning after.

Trench warfare? After the groomers and fumigators come in, this eerie scene will be transformed into a freshly planted tomato field. (Photo by the author.)

This land is dead now, and becoming deader by the minute, as the fumigator works its way toward us. Yet life once thrived here and will thrive here again. In just three months this will be a verdant tomato field indistinguishable from the one I visited near Naples yesterday, a killing field turned paradise.

The one part I do recognize from Naples is the sand, although it is far more striking when it's this barren. To visualize a Florida tomato field, the first thing you need to do is clear your head of any images the word *field* brings to mind. This is no "field of dreams"; it is a field of sand, dreaming of an ocean. A small, completely intact shell picked from the sand at my feet is proof that this tomato farm in Duette, Florida, twenty-five miles from the Gulf of Mexico, was underwater in the recent geological past. Given the way things are heating up, it seems destined to end up there again.

The sand here is the same stuff found on the nearby barrier beaches, fine and moist, ideal for building sandcastles, which is an apt way to describe what is happening now, and at a dizzying pace. Indeed, my Mad Max metaphor nearly comes to life as motorized contraptions—souped-up, tricked-out tractors—whiz past, leveling, fluffing up, fertilizing, fumigating, and trenching. But the maddest machine of all is the one that actually builds the sandcastles. This tractor gathers up, compacts, fumigates, and grooms the moist sand into flawless trapezoidal beds, a little wider at the base than at the top, creating two-foot-wide and one-foot-high raised beds hundreds of feet long, in rows five feet apart. Following that, the whole thing is wrapped up—literally—with a tractor that shrink-wraps each bed in polyethylene. (Yes, *that* ethylene.)

The plastic mulch keeps weeds out and fumigant and fertilizer in. Forty percent of Florida's cropland is sheeted in this single-use

A sandy Florida tomato field being groomed and plastic-wrapped for planting. (Photo by the author.)

polyethylene, leaving behind twenty-five million pounds of waste every year. As I wander over for a closer look at one of the freshly wrapped beds, the crew chief warns, "Don't sit down." I figure he doesn't want me messing them up, so I take a reassuring step back. "Because, whoo!" he continues.

Whoo?

"You'll get blisters."

Right through the plastic? Holy smokes! I take *ten* steps back, and only then do I notice that most of the workers are wearing bandannas over their faces, and a woman just a few feet away is planting a sign bearing—I kid you not—a skull and crossbones. After we leave today, no one will be allowed back for fourteen days.

The fumigant varies, but the one being used here is Pic-Clor 60. Injected under pressure, the liquid vaporizes into a gas in the sand, permeating the beds and killing soil pathogens, weeds— anything in its path. Preemptive fumigation is all but mandatory in large-scale Florida farming because the ground here never freezes sufficiently to kill off nematodes and the other nasties lurking below. Thus, each growing cycle begins with obliterating every living thing, friend or foe, in the sand, leaving a lifeless, sterile medium.

This is not the end of the battle, merely the first offensive. The plants will need additional applications of pesticides and fungicides, delivered by land and air, to combat the twenty-seven insect species and twenty-nine diseases known to attack Florida's most lucrative vegetable crop. Large-scale pest control is a given with Big Ag, but nowhere is that truer than in Florida, where an acre of tomatoes gets hit with five to six times as much fungicide and pesticide as an acre of California tomatoes.

This acre also needs a lot more fertilizer than its West Coast cousin. Beach sand is, unsurprisingly, totally devoid of nutrients. After the fumigant has worked its deadly charms, what's left behind is essentially a sterile growing medium. All of the nitrogen, phosphorus, potassium, and anything else that a plant needs to survive, much less thrive, must be supplied. Some granular fertilizer has been mixed into the beds, but the main supply is a powerful mixture injected by twin hoses a few inches from the edge of each bed. Were the young plants to come in contact with it, their roots would fatally burn, but over the coming months the fertilizer will leach slowly into the sand as the plant's spreading roots reach out toward it, drawing in the nutrients throughout the growing season.

Another challenge is water, which explains the newly carved

V-shaped trenches running between the beds, as well as the network of canals crisscrossing the fields. Florida seems to have either too much or too little water. And when it rains here, there is no place for the water to go; just a foot or two beneath the sand lies an impermeable layer of "hardpan," a limestone and clay shelf that holds water nearly as well as your bathtub. So, every farm has pumps at the ready to move standing water into drainage canals after a heavy rain.

Yet this hardpan layer can also be used to advantage. While half the farms in Florida (including Lipman's) have switched to drip irrigation—perforated tape that runs down each tomato row, providing a trickle of moisture that can cut water consumption by 70 percent—the other half still use the original system of flooding the trenches to irrigate the tomatoes from beneath. Were it not for the hardpan, water would simply seep down into the sand like a receding wave vanishing on a beach.

This, then, is a Florida tomato farm. Even if you started with the best varieties and let the fruits ripen just a bit more, I wonder if you could ever grow a tasty tomato under these conditions, which also include, during the winter months, a lack of sunlight. Yes, even the famous sunshine that lends the state its nickname might be overrated. I was surprised to find myself getting out of bed in pitch darkness every morning, the sun not rising until well after 7:00 a.m. In December these tomatoes see barely ten and a half hours of daylight, while by contrast a New Jersey tomato in July basks in nearly fifteen hours of photosynthesizing sunlight, a difference of more than 40 percent.

In Campania I'd heard much about the rich, volcanic soil, pure water, and gentle sea breezes—the *terroir*—that make the San Marzano unique. I shudder to even apply that word to this barren scene, more evocative of terror than terroir. But on the other hand, if ever a food reflected its terroir, I suppose it would be the Florida tomato, as much a product of its environment as a San Marzano.

Maybe, then, what killed the Florida tomato is its terroir. In other words, Florida.

I Have Met the Enemy, and...

With my bouncing airport tomatoes mocking me with one final insult—"Ha-ha, I'm tougher than you are!"—it seems I'm to leave Florida without having satisfactorily solved the crime. Even with more conspirators than the Lincoln assassination, I've not been able to uncover one predominant factor to pin this on, that elusive smoking gun.

Maybe that's because it's in my hands. For while on my knees, gathering up the spilled tomatoes, I find myself looking up at the body scanner. There, on the screen, is the anonymous stick-figure image of the last person to have passed through. It stops me dead in my tracks.

The murderer, arms raised above his head in the universal pose of, yes—surrender! The villain is just a few feet away. And a thousand miles away. Who killed the tomato? *We the consumer.* By dropping them into our carts, no matter how tasteless, by demanding tomatoes twelve months of the year, by eating fast food in ever-growing amounts, by accepting mediocrity—we allowed this to happen.

Tomato companies in Florida aren't here to save the world or satisfy the tastes of tomato gourmands. They're here to operate a profitable business. If they can best do that by picking green tomatoes from poisoned sand and gassing them, that's what they're going to do. If the market ever demands they raise tasty vine-ripe tomatoes grown in actual soil, wrapped in foam sleeves and delivered by next-day air, they'll do that instead. But as long as price is the first, second, and third consideration, don't expect Florida tomatoes to change anytime soon.

There is a silver lining to the dark clouds gathering over Florida as I board my flight. In scraping the bottom of the hardpan to produce what is quite possibly the worst tomato since Cortés, the Florida tomato industry also left a national tomato landscape so utterly barren that it planted the seeds of a revolution.

Florida may have killed the tomato, but it couldn't destroy the memories of a few stubborn souls who never forgot what Grandma's tomato—not so easily dismissed as "a perception and a stereotype"—really tasted like, and who were determined to resurrect it from its sandy grave.

Nine

ATTACK OF THE HEIRLOOM TOMATOES

The Brandywine: A Star Heirloom Takes on a Half Century of Tomato Mediocrity

A revolt against the tomato, hybridized, gassed, and commodified almost beyond recognition, was inevitable. But who suspected that the vegetables themselves would lead it? Yet this is exactly what happened when, in 1978, angry tomatoes bent on revenge descended upon us.

On drive-in movie screens, that is.

Described by its publicist as "a musical comedy horror story about hybrid tomatoes that terrorize a community," the ultra-low-budget ($90,000) *Attack of the Killer Tomatoes* became an instant cult classic, cementing the tomato's place in American pop culture, spawning three sequels (including one starring a young George Clooney) and a cartoon series, while launching the career of—well, no one. In fact, the actors were just happy to get out of the production alive. Shooting nearly started and ended on the same day when a spectacular helicopter crash nearly beheaded half the cast.

In the script, the helicopter was supposed to have been piloted by a tomato. It might as well have been, because the human pilot, while attempting to land in a field near two actors playing detectives, allowed the tail rotor to dip, striking the ground and sending the chopper spinning wildly out of control, like a rotating guillotine, until it flipped over and went up in flames. All in all, a spectacle worthy of a big-budget Sylvester Stallone action movie.

With the cameras continuing to roll, the actors, ever the consummate professionals, did some quick improvisation while crawling away from the smoldering wreckage that destroyed the rented $60,000 aircraft. Their witty repartee included:

Detective 1: "The pilot's still in there!"

Detective 2: "Forget about the pilot."

In fact, the pilot was pulled to safety by the director and survived with only minor injuries, which seems remarkable if you've seen the footage. And you can. It appears in the first five minutes of the movie. Just promise you'll come back when you're done.

Attack of the Killer Tomatoes was filmed in 1977, the same year the *New Yorker* published a lengthy piece by Thomas Whiteside that confirmed for a lot of Americans what they had been suspecting for some time: Tomatoes weren't what they used to be. That something had happened to the tomato was evident even on the set of the movie: The propman had to parboil the tomatoes in order to make them splat, not bounce, when thrown.

A poster for the 1978 movie Attack of the Killer Tomatoes, *which remains a cult favorite almost a half century after its release. (Copyright KTE Inc. 1977.)*

Whiteside was far from alone. A few years earlier, *New York Times* food editor Craig Claiborne had labeled grocery store tomatoes "tasteless, hideous, and repulsive"; and the dean of American cookery, James Beard, devoted a full section to "The Decline and Fall of the Tomato" in his 1974 classic, *Beard on Food*, calling tomatoes "a total gastronomic loss." Supermarket tomatoes bore the brunt of the growing number of complaints, but anyone who'd been eating tomatoes for a lifetime knew that they weren't as flavorful as those of yore, whether they came from Florida, a local farm stand, or even your own backyard. What had happened? Here again, *Attack of the Killer Tomatoes* provides a clue when a government scientist sheepishly admits, "All we wanted was a healthier, bigger tomato." Unfortunately, real-life scientists had succeeded.

The names of some of them should, unless you've skipped a chapter or two, be familiar. Beginning with Alexander Livingston in the late 1800s, the work of geneticists and breeders such as Burpee's Oved Shifriss and UC Davis' Charley Rick—not to mention the ultra-engineering of the Florida tomato—had made the tomato redder, rounder, hardier, disease-resistant, more productive, and easier to grow. But these improvements came at the heavy cost of flavor and variety.

Yet it was a seemingly innocent trait, one that had crept into virtually every tomato hybrid in America, that was perhaps the most insidious of all, because its subtle but damaging effect wasn't even recognized until recently.

If you've ever wondered why supermarket tomatoes are almost too uniformly red, an even scarlet color from top to bottom, it's because they carry a mutation, discovered nearly a century ago, that causes the entire tomato to ripen all at once, rather than from the blossom end (bottom) up, often leaving a ring of green or white near the stem. Beginning in the 1950s, breeders seized upon this fortuitous mutation, breeding it into virtually every hybrid tomato on the market. After all, why not?

The "why not" didn't become apparent until 2012, when a research team led by Ann Powell, a plant scientist at UC Davis, discovered that the even-ripening mutation has an unfortunate side effect: It prevents the fruit from synthesizing its own sugars and flavor compounds. To be sure, most of these important taste components are manufactured in the photosynthetic factory of the plant's leaves, but up to 20 percent are produced in the tomato itself. *Unless it has this even-ripening gene.* So right out of the gate, before breeding for disease resistance or anything else, tomatoes have been robbed of a fifth of their flavor, owing to the presence of this gene.

Which brings us to genes.

When reduced to its essence, hybridization is the act of combining the genetic pools of separate populations, creating a new organism with traits of each. And, as we've seen, it's a pretty chancy act at that. It may take years or decades to achieve the desired result; indeed, you may never get there at all. Unless, that is, you take a more targeted approach to combining the gene pools of two tomato varieties. Why spend all those years playing Gregor Mendel, crossing thousands upon thousands of plants— with about the same success rate as flinging rotten tomatoes against a wall until you get a splat that resembles the *Mona Lisa*— when modern technology allows you to take the gene responsible for the specific trait you want and simply splice it into the target tomato?

Ask a certain extinct biotechnology company. It turns out, there *is* a killer tomato in our story. It's "The Tomato That Ate Calgene."

The 1980s saw landmark advances in the science of genetic engineering, and while still costly and experimental, its potential use in agriculture seemed limitless. World hunger could be vanquished by taking, say, the gene from a strain of wheat found to have drought tolerance (but was otherwise poor and low-yielding) and inserting that gene into a high-yielding strain. Malnutrition could be addressed by inserting the gene that synthesizes vitamin A into rice grown in impoverished, vitamin-deficient parts of the world.

Because genes are made up of DNA, and DNA is just sequences of four chemicals—arranged in that double helix you never really understood in high school, but don't worry about that now—there's nothing to distinguish, at a molecular level, a cow gene from a rice gene. So there's no reason why the gene you're inserting into wheat or rice needs to come from another strain of that plant. It could come from anything: bacteria, a carrot, or even a flounder. Which, we'll see shortly, is not merely hypothetical.

Surely, even knowing next to nothing about agriculture, you could conjure up a few exciting ways to genetically combine plants that would be beneficial to humankind. Go ahead, set aside any opinions you may have about the politics, science, or safety of genetically modified organisms, and take a moment to think about how genetically modified foods could make the world a better, kinder place.

I'm going to bet that *a tomato that rots more slowly on your windowsill* didn't come to mind. Yet this was the first—and I mean the world's very first—genetically modified food. How and why this happened provides one of the strangest chapters in the history of the tomato.

Among the Americans who agreed with Claiborne and Beard on the sorry state of supermarket tomatoes was a group of scientists at Calgene, a biotechnology start-up founded in 1980 by some University of California at Davis alums. They had some big ideas they believed could be achieved with a genetic snip here and a splice there, including healthier canola oil and denim-colored cotton (no dying required!). As luck would have it, though, their imaginations were captured, then held hostage, by the gene recently found to be responsible for making ripe tomatoes turn soft and shrivel.

This softening, a phenomenon all too familiar to anyone who's kept a tomato in the kitchen for more than a few days, is caused by a protein called *polygalacturonase*, or just (thank goodness) PG, that breaks down the pectin in the fruit. (The lack of pectin in overripe tomatoes was, remember, why Heinz insisted on using only the freshest tomatoes in his ketchup, which relied on pectin's preservative properties.) Calgene researchers discovered that if they cloned the gene responsible for producing PG, made a kind of mirror image of it, and inserted it back into the tomato, this so-called antisense gene would cancel out the PG gene, thus slowing the softening and rotting of harvested tomatoes by a week or so.

While of obvious (if slightly frivolous) benefit to the consumer, shelf life wasn't the only thing Calgene executives were excited about. They reasoned that if antisensing the PG gene slowed the softening of harvested tomatoes, it should also slow the softening of tomatoes still on the vine, meaning they could be left to ripen a few more days, yet still survive the rough handling that industrial tomatoes endure, all without the tomato's archenemy: refrigeration.

This extra time on the vine, so the thinking went, would give Calgene's tomatoes more flavor than Florida's mature green tomatoes, admittedly not a high bar to clear. Dubbing it the Flavr Savr, they predicted that their premium, branded tomato, short on vowels but high on flavor and shelf life, would fetch a price two to three times that of the generic supermarket variety, securing a nice slice of the $4 billion fresh tomato market.

Now, you'd think that an upstart research laboratory whose expertise was in genetic engineering might develop and license this technology to established tomato growers and be happy to collect royalties for the next couple of decades, but they were so seduced by their own press releases that they wanted the whole tomato. "Everybody is going to get rich," Calgene CEO Roger Salquist predicted six months before the tomato's release. So, this biotech start-up created within its walls a tomato start-up, a farm-to-store growing, distribution, and sales division they named Calgene Fresh. Never mind that the researchers were, by their own admission, "just a bunch of gene jockeys, not tomato farmers," or that the theory crucial to their business model—that silencing the PG gene would allow them to handle their vine-ripened tomatoes like green tomatoes—had yet to be tested in the field.

Details, details...Time was of the essence. They knew they weren't the only ones in town looking at controlling the PG gene. So, in their race to market, Calgene went all in, ramping up on R and D, building automated tomato sorting and packing facilities, and burning through tons of cash.

They also went to the Food and Drug Administration for an advisory opinion. In 1990 the FDA didn't yet have a policy on the regulation of genetically modified foods (because there weren't any). Calgene justifiably felt that getting the FDA seal of approval on the world's first GMO food was virtually mandatory, as much from a public relations as a legal standpoint. The regulatory process, however, would prove more difficult than the science.

In fact, the science—gene-splicing (or recombinant DNA)

technology—was by then pretty well established. To get the anti-sense gene into a tomato plant, Calgene scientists made use of *Agrobacterium tumefaciens*, a common soil bacterium that causes crown gall tumors, those hard, woody masses commonly seen on tree bark. Because the bacterium attacks an organism by inserting a small piece of its DNA into the host, scientists can take advantage of this genetic transfer ability by replacing the bacterial gene that causes the gall with the gene they want to transfer—in this case the antisensed PG gene—and soaking the tomato tissue in a solution of this modified bacterium.

The tomatoes don't always drink up the genetic soup, however, so you need a way to know which of your hundreds of tomato cuttings successfully incorporated the antisense gene before you invest months into nurturing them. Thus Calgene added another gene to ride shotgun alongside the PG gene: a "selectable marker gene" that made the Flavr Savr resistant to kanamycin, an antibiotic. With this gene on board, the scientists could simply grow the tomatoes in a medium containing this toxic antibiotic, and, conveniently, only those cuttings that had taken up the coupled antisensed and antibiotic genes would survive.

Hello! Did someone say antibiotic-resistant tomatoes? You can see where this is going. This technique of using kanamycin-resistant *A. tumefaciens* was commonplace in the laboratory, but of course not yet in any foods, although the candidates were starting to line up like peas in a pod. Calgene reasoned that even before getting the green light on PG-neutered tomatoes they had to first convince the FDA that this small piece of antibiotic DNA inserted into every tomato wasn't going to compromise the future effectiveness of antibiotic drug treatment for humans. Calgene tried to downplay the risks in their FDA submission, but the FDA kept coming back for more safety information, and more experimentation, meaning more time and money.

Meanwhile, the gene-jockeys-turned-tomato-farmers had been trying to find just the right tomato variety in which to insert their Flavr Savr gene.

They picked the wrong one.

The tomato that was unnaturally selected was a variety called Pacific, a lackluster tomato whose main asset was the lack of patents or other intellectual property rights that accompany newer varieties. That it bruised easily and didn't travel well became apparent to Calgene only when the inaugural shipment of Flavr Savr tomatoes arrived in a tractor trailer from Mexico for their midnight debut at Calgene Fresh headquarters, with company brass on hand for a big celebration.

With great anticipation the doors of the truck were flung open—to tons of tomato pulp and juice. The twenty-five-pound boxes of soft tomatoes had collapsed onto one another. The tomatoes were crushed, the shipment a total loss. One executive stood in shock, muttering, "It's over, it's over," while the director of finance rolled up his sleeves, got a shovel, and started cleaning up the mess.

The Pacific cultivar wasn't the only problem. The seductive theory, never proved in the field, that silencing the PG gene would keep vine-ripe tomatoes firm enough to be handled like unripe, green tomatoes, was as rotten as the tomatoes in the truck. That meant Calgene would have to abandon its costly, just-purchased automated processing equipment and carefully (and expensively) sort and pack tomatoes by hand.

The Flavr Savr tomato was eating Calgene alive, gobbling up as much as $43 million a year in tomato-red ink. And while the

FDA process dragged on into its second, then third year, interest in—and concern about—GMO foods was starting to build, much to Calgene's surprise and bewilderment. *Who could be against a better tomato?* they wondered. Jeremy Rifkin, for one.

Rifkin was an economist and social activist who'd previously made some waves at the two hundredth anniversary of the Boston Tea Party by dumping empty oil barrels into Boston Harbor to protest Big Oil. He had been warning of the dangers of biotechnology almost since it had been given a name, using lawsuits, congressional testimony, television appearances, and speeches and books to garner influence and publicity. His 1977 book, *Who Should Play God?*, warned in apocalyptic terms about the dangers of messing around with genes in the laboratory. The arguments and risks were hypothetical back then, but now, with an actual product on the horizon, Rifkin declared war on the Flavr Savr, pledging to fight it with every weapon that his Pure Food Campaign (the name perhaps intentionally recalling the Pure Food Movement of the late 1800s) could muster.

He had his Pure Food followers picket theaters showing the 1993 blockbuster *Jurassic Park* in one hundred cities across America, handing out flyers featuring a dinosaur pushing a grocery basket labeled "Bio-tech Frankenfoods." Six months later, Rifkin turned his attention to the Campbell Soup Company, which had been financing Calgene's research to the tune of a million dollars a year, with the potential of millions more if Campbell used the technology in their processed products. Campbell's interest was to control pectin decay in tomatoes on their way into the company's sauces and soups, although they were also flirting with the idea of getting into the fresh tomato market. That all went down the drain after Rifkin threatened a boycott of the company. Campbell's, with a hundred-year reputation built on wholesomeness, had no trouble choosing sides in this battle. They not only broke with Calgene, but also publicly pledged that they would *never* use GMO foods in their iconic products, one of the first American companies to do so.

The trouble was only beginning. An anti-GMO *New York Times* op-ed, bearing the alarming title "Tomatoes May Be Dangerous to Your Health," must have landed like a bombshell at Calgene. Of more lasting damage was a supporting letter to the editor a week later that coined the term *Frankenfood*, a word that language maven William Safire admiringly called "the hottest combining form in populist suspicion of science." Speaking of bombshells, even the Unabomber—Ted Kaczynski, the domestic terrorist who killed three people and injured twenty-three others in a nationwide bombing campaign directed against those he believed to be promoting technology—got into the act, using Calgene's return address on the manifesto he mailed to the *Times*.

Incredibly, *more* bad news followed. A competitor, DNA Plant Technology, announced that they were experimenting with inserting an "antifreeze" gene from an arctic flounder with the goal of producing a tomato that could withstand frost. Instead of taking the heat off Calgene, this far more sinister-sounding "fish tomato" became conflated with the Flavr Savr, as well as spoiling appetites for GMO tomatoes harvested from any sea.

Finally, on May 18, 1994, nearly five years after beginning a regulatory process that hadn't been required, short on cash, and with tomatoes rotting in the field, salvation in the form of FDA approval for the world's first genetically modified food arrived. Three days later the first shipments hit the market. It was too little, too late. Within three years the Flavr Savr tomato, having been nurtured with $200 million, had vanished without a trace. As had Calgene.

What happened is probably not what you think. Rifkin not-withstanding, it wasn't public opinion against genetically modified tomatoes (the anti-GMO movement wouldn't gain momentum for another few years). It wasn't bad press (Tom Brokaw, Connie Chung, and countless local newscasters swooned over the wonder of these genetically modified tomatoes, often expressing surprise that *it looks like a regular tomato!*). And it wasn't the flavor (they were nothing special, but they were better than the competition). In fact, they sold quite well to a public eager if not desperate for a better supermarket tomato.

Then what slew the Flavr Savr? Certainly, the fact that Calgene was spending $10 a pound to produce tomatoes that sold for $2 a pound was not a sustainable business model. A hurricane in Florida that carried an entire crop into the Atlantic didn't help, nor did Calgene's inexperience as tomato farmers and distributors, nor did the fact that Mexican growers had started shipping new, non-GMO vine-ripened varieties with improved shelf life. All of those factors contributed, but what really killed the Flavr Savr was that the company was simply exhausted and broke and was never going to regain solvency with a boutique tomato.

Calgene's stock plunged from $25 to $4 a share, and in 1996 the agrochemical giant Monsanto bought the company on the cheap—lock, stock, and patents—and shut down the tomato business for good. As now ex-CEO Roger Salquist said, in a line that could've come right out of *Attack of the Killer Tomatoes*, "The biggest mistake was we tried to make it too big, too fast."

Such was the bad taste that the Flavr Savr left behind, that twenty-five years later there is not a single GMO tomato on the market, which doesn't prevent the appearance of "Non-GMO" stickers on supermarket tomatoes. Every farmer, reseller, and breeder I met during the course of my research emphasized, always without prompting, that they were not breeding, growing, or selling genetically modified tomatoes.

Ironically, the Flavr Savr blazed the regulatory trail for the avalanche of GMO foods to follow. Open your cupboard, and almost everything in there—canola oil, cereal, cornmeal, soy milk, baby formula, soda, snack bars, cookies, and anything sweetened with corn syrup or sugar beets—has a genetically modified ingredient. But not for the idealistic reasons that motivated Calgene, such as the promise of a tastier tomato or healthier oil. After the Flavr Savr flopped, GMO went in quite a different direction: While Calgene's products were developed for the benefit of the consumer, nearly all GMO crops today are engineered to benefit the *producer*.

By far the most successful of these, found in 95 percent of the soybeans and 70 percent of the corn and cotton grown in the United States, carries the trademarked term *Roundup Ready*. First introduced in 1996, these crops have a patented gene that provides immunity to the widely used herbicide, allowing Roundup to be used with abandon, and relieving farmers of the expense of tilling or mechanically pulling weeds. The practice has become quite controversial in recent years, with the appearance of Roundup-resistant "superweeds" and reports of non-Hodgkin's lymphoma among farmworkers who have been exposed to the herbicide, but it's proving hard to coax the genie back into the bottle.

The manufacturer of these genetically modified seeds? The same as the manufacturer of Roundup.

Monsanto.

⊛

Hybridized, commoditized, and Frankensteined. The last decades of the twentieth century had been particularly cruel to the tomato. Yet far from the supermarket aisles and biotech laboratories a loosely organized underground movement of hobbyist gardeners, refusing to accept the miserable status quo, were quietly trading stories, tasting notes, and, most importantly, seeds. The revolution had begun.

It is difficult to pinpoint exactly when the heirloom tomato movement began. A search of newspaper archives for "heirloom tomato" turns up the occasional reference starting in the early 1990s, but it's not until 1997 that the phrase starts appearing with any frequency, steadily increasing into the first decade of this century. Yet hobbyist gardeners had been growing forgotten tomatoes under the radar since at least the 1970s, facilitated by the sprouting of organizations like the Seed Savers Exchange, or SSE.

The SSE was founded in 1975 after a couple of idealistic Missouri homesteaders still in their twenties, Diane Ott Whealy and Kent Whealy, found themselves in sole possession of the seeds of two plants—a tomato and a morning glory—brought over by Diane's Bavarian ancestors in 1884. When Diane's grandparents died shortly after gifting her some seeds of each, Diane realized that if she didn't grow (and even better, distribute) these varieties—family heirlooms as prized as antique silverware or china—they would be lost, forever.

This, Diane writes in her memoir, *Gathering*, started the Whealys thinking about the larger problem of vanishing cultivars:

> We started to speculate about other gardeners who were keeping seed brought to this country when their families

immigrated. We knew that seeds used for favorite foods back home—reminders of the old country—were hidden away in personal belongings like apron pockets and ferried across the ocean...and passed down through generations.

Surely, the Whealys figured, there had to be other people interested in preserving these "heirlooms" (defined loosely as being at least fifty years old and open pollinated, although some reserve the term for varieties that were present before the era of hybridization—that is, pre-1950). Today Kent might've posted on Reddit or found a Facebook group, but in 1975 he sought out other like-minded individuals by publishing letters in a handful of national gardening magazines such as *Mother Earth News*. Several readers responded, offering their own heirloom seeds for exchange. As word spread, more offers arrived in the mail, and before long the Whealys had assembled a six-page typed list (available to anyone who sent a self-addressed envelope and a quarter) with the names and addresses of seed traders either willing to share or seeking seeds. This put the SSE at the hub of an informal network of heirloom plant enthusiasts.

The 25 cents requested to cover expenses was revealing; the young couple was just barely scraping by. Kent, although holding a degree in journalism, worked a series of odd jobs (the closest he got to journalism was working a printing press, which would later come in handy), while Diane was raising their young family. Their house, near Princeton, Missouri, was constructed on a remote fifty-acre farm over a period of two years, using old telephone poles and stones culled from the property. Because no bank would grant a loan to an underemployed journalist and a self-described "vegetarian, hippie, yoga-practicing homesteader," much of the construction was done by family and friends. Diane planted a large orchard and garden that she hoped would help feed her family.

In 1981, with plastic sheeting serving as the windows in their unfinished home, the Whealys held their first annual "campout weekend," so that the savers, a geographically diverse group who knew one another only through correspondence, could meet. A dozen showed up that first year, pitching tents or living in campers on the Whealy farm. By the third year, the gathering had grown to fifty, exhausting the cistern, and the guests passed the hat to collect $30 for a water delivery.

As membership in the exchange grew, the mailbox filled with letters like this one, from Edward Lowden, a ninety-one-year-old from Ontario:

> Mr. Topp tomato, a very valuable tomato...with frost-resistant genes, has been lost...around 1917-1921...It has valuable characteristics, that surpassed anything I have ever seen in other tomatoes...but its most valuable characteristic was its ability to withstand light frost in the fall that ruined other tomatoes...I would give anything to secure that one...Maybe someone somewhere knows of it.

No word as to whether this wonderful-sounding tomato, frost-resistant without the help of a flounder gene, ever turned up. But for every seed seeker, there was a gardener eager to share. One of the six original members of the SSE, Lina Sisco, sent a package of beans from Winona, Missouri, with the following note:

> I have been gardening for more years than I like to think about and I do love to raise all kinds of stuff... The Bird Egg

beans have been in my family for many, many years, as my grandmother brought them to Missouri...They are all free to you. Hope you have good luck with them.

Sisco died the following spring, but by then the Whealys and two other savers had started growing her Bird Eggs, rescuing these lovely speckled beans from extinction.

Kent and Diane noticed that more than a few of the letters carried a similar, worrisome theme: *My seed catalog has stopped carrying this variety. Does anyone have any?* The seed industry was seeing rapid consolidation in the 1970s and 1980s (from 1970 to 1987, for example, Burpee ownership transferred from the Burpee family to first General Foods, then to the global aerospace and transportation conglomerate ITT, then to the investment firm McKinsey, before being rescued by seedsman George Ball in 1991), and the new corporate entities weren't willing to carry seeds that didn't sell well, whatever their qualities. Kent sounded the alarm in 1981, warning that "far from being obsolete or inferior, the varieties being dropped today are literally the cream of our vegetable crops...But they are being allowed to die out."

This sharp loss of biodiversity, alarming to gardeners and agricultural scientists alike, was the primary motivation of many seed savers, who saw themselves as custodians of the earth, literally "savers of seed." But many saw something more concerning— even sinister—happening in the seed business. Open-pollinated varieties were being replaced by hybrids. "If I buy a pack of standard tomato seeds," Kent told *Mother Earth News* in 1981, "I can save my own seeds from then on...and never have to order that particular vegetable from the supplier again. But if I want to keep planting a hybrid vegetable, I must go back to the company every spring for more seeds. So, as more and more of the hybrids push out the standard varieties, my choices become more and more limited...and I become more dependent on the seed companies."

Seed companies like Burpee, that is. It was the huge success of one hybrid in particular, the Big Boy tomato, that "reset the paradigm for tomato development," seed saver and self-proclaimed "tomato nut" Craig LeHoullier told me, propelling the other major seed companies to develop and sell hybrids of their own.

Like it or not, agribusiness now had growers firmly by the kernels, and the seed savers were ready to fight back. Seed exchanges large and small started sprouting up around the country, and garden magazines responded by publishing letters and seed-swap columns. In the early 1990s a new technology, an electronic mailing list called a "LISTSERV" (and, later, websites and internet bulletin boards) would exponentially expand the reach of the movement.

By then, hundreds of older, amateur-grown tomato varieties had surfaced, often with names and origin stories as colorful as their fruits: Green Zebra; Cream Sausage (a white, elongated tomato whose appearance sounds as unappealing as its name); and Radiator Charlie's Mortgage Lifter, a 1930s grapefruit-sized variety that was so popular that ol' Radiator Charlie (an auto mechanic whose name was not Charlie at all, but Marshall Cletis Byles) was able to pay off his mortgage with seed sales. But one rediscovered tomato stood out from the pack, so to speak. For many, the term *heirloom tomato* would become synonymous with this variety, the poster child of the heirloom tomato movement: the Brandywine.

As poster children go, it wasn't much to look at. Ungainly on the vine at about a pound, with a kind of sickly-looking pale skin that often cracked and turned leathery near the stem; a core that ran so deeply into the fruit that, after cutting it out, your first few slices were inevitably rings; and susceptible to wilt, blight, and rot, this late bloomer (ninety to one hundred days before you picked your first tomato) had one, and only one, thing going for it: It was scrumptious.

As in *revelation* scrumptious. Now *this*, you'd say, as juice dripped down your chin, is what tomatoes used to taste like. And you said that even if you'd never tasted yesterday's tomato, as if the flavors exploding in your mouth triggered a kind of genetic memory. LeHoullier, in *Epic Tomatoes*, writes, "After growing over a thousand different tomatoes over the years it is still Brandywine that I think of when I ponder the perfect tomato-eating experience . . . an unmatched succulent texture that melts in your mouth. The flavor enlivens the taste buds, with all the favorable components of the best tomatoes—tartness, sweetness, fullness, and complexity—in perfect balance."

Many agreed. *New York Times* garden columnist Anne Raver introduced the Brandywine to readers in 1995, and Martha Stewart declared its taste "the essence of summer."

It's not clear where the Brandywine originally came from. Its name would suggest the Brandywine Valley in southern Pennsylvania, and it's often described in seed catalogs as an Amish variety, but its origins have always been a little murky. The Seed Savers Exchange, which I suppose is as reliable a source as any for this kind of thing, attributes its reintroduction to the legendary Ohio seedsman Ben Quisenberry, then in his nineties, who said he received them from Dorris Sudduth Hill, who in turn said her family had been growing them in Tennessee for a hundred years. Thus, this Brandywine is often referred to as the *Sudduth strain*.

Strains (or variants), by which we mean a slight variation caused by mutation or cross-pollination, make things tricky when it comes to pinning paternity on heirlooms. The Brandywine is no exception because your Brandywine might not be the same cultivar as mine. Unlike hybrids, which are tightly controlled and sold by a handful of licensees, Brandywines have been preserved, distributed, and redistributed by any number of seed savers (and, more recently, seed companies), so there are several different strains out there. Plus, the occasional cross-pollination caused by a determined bee can change the genetic makeup without the grower realizing it. And to further blur things, several other tomatoes carry the Brandywine moniker. There's a Red Brandy-wine and a Yellow Brandywine, which, while fine tomatoes in themselves, are distinct from the Sudduth strain.

A Brandywine tomato makes an early appearance in the Johnson and Stokes 1890 seed catalog. (CC BY-SA 3.0.)

The Brandywine is easily identified by its uncommon "potato leaf" foliage. Tomatoes have perhaps the most recognizable leaves in the vegetable world, small and sharply serrated, but the Brandywine's leaves are large and smooth, with a single notch on each side near the base, closely resembling those of the potato. So much so that when growing potatoes in my garden for the first time, when the spuds leafed out, I momentarily wondered if some Brandywine seeds from last season's tomatoes had sprouted in the potato patch. I shouldn't have been so confused, though, since potatoes and tomatoes are cousins, members of the same genus (*Solanus*) of the nightshade family.

The implications of that relationship would become apparent in the summer of 2009, but for now, the late 1990s, abloom with heirlooms of all shapes, sizes, and colors, represented a true tomato renaissance in America. It was the 1830s all over again. The East Coast's doyenne of style, Martha Stewart, announced that she'd converted nearly her entire tomato patch to heirlooms, while the West Coast's farm-to-table tastemaker, Alice Waters, was featuring them on her Chez Panisse menus. From Los Angeles to East Hampton, no benefit worthy of the name would dare put out a spread that didn't include multiple varieties of colorful heirloom tomatoes. The farmers who'd started growing heirlooms could barely keep up with the demand.

How had heirloom tomatoes, just a few years earlier the exclusive purview of seed-trading garden geeks, helicoptered into the mainstream so quickly, and why did it happen in the last decade of the twentieth century? These are the kinds of questions that intrigue sociologists, leading the University of Wisconsin's Jennifer A. Jordan to wonder in a 2007 academic paper how it was that consumers suddenly started shelling out "$7 per pound for bug-eaten, calloused, mottled and splitting tomatoes that may or may not taste good."

Part of the answer, Jordan concluded, was that the tomato had achieved a certain status as not just a food, but as a *cultural object*, one that said something about its consumer. You felt virtuous about eating an heirloom tomato, with elements of both the old (its heritage) and the new (a stripy tomato!), and if you were tuned in to the social issues of biodiversity and agribusiness, you felt even better. Indeed, the heirloom tomato had become a status symbol, an indicator of wealth and taste. There was undeniably an element of snobbery in their consumption, both at the high-end restaurants that served them and the farmers' markets that sold them, set apart from the plebeians in a separate bin with a higher price tag.

In fact, those farmers' markets, which were expanding exponentially at precisely the same time as the heirlooms (from 1970 to 2009, the number of farmers' markets in New York State alone rose from a half dozen to more than four hundred), played a significant role in their popularization. The Slow Food and organic movements, both of which gained momentum in the 1990s, also nicely dovetailed with the heirlooms' ascent, making vine-ripened, organic heirloom tomatoes many a baby boomer's trifecta.

A 1997 *New York Times* article postulated that the heirloom gardening phenomenon was fueled by the abundant time, income, and sensibilities of that growing part of society dubbed the baby boomers. "[They] have more leisure time," one seed company owner was quoted as saying. "They have more sophisticated palates...I also think people are looking for something real, something that tells them about why we are on earth."

That apparently included, in addition to heirloom tomatoes, imported aged vinegars, artisanal cheeses, Napa Valley wines, and threads of saffron pricier than cocaine. Yet the wonderful thing about heirloom tomatoes, unique among the yuppie consumables of the '90s, is that you didn't have to be a member of the elite to possess them. Anyone could grow the same prestige tomato varieties as Martha Stewart, provided you had a few feet of yard to spare—or even a patio.

In 1997 I had more than a few feet of yard to spare. We'd purchased a dilapidated hundred-year-old house on three hilly acres and had converted one sunny slope to a large vegetable garden. Soon it was planted with more than two thousand square feet of heirloom tomatoes, heirloom strawberries, heirloom potatoes, heirloom squash, and heirloom apple trees. I never even considered any of the hybrid tomato "boys and girls," instead growing Brandywine and Cherokee Purple from seed, under four banks of fluorescent lights. I did feel good, as Jennifer Jordan suggests, about growing these older fruits and vegetables that connected me to the past. I loved the fact that not only were my Esopus Spitzenburg apples grown and favored by my boyhood idol Thomas Jefferson, but they were discovered in my very own Hudson Valley, near Esopus, New York.

I conveniently ignored the fact that my tree was dripping with more history than apples—easily done because the rough, thick-skinned Spitzenburgs were a challenge to the digestive system. I also tried to overlook the inconvenient truth that my Brandywine tomatoes, while undeniably delicious, were harder to raise than goldfish in the desert. Early blight yielded to verticillium wilt, which conceded to anthracnose fruit rot, which abdicated to—if any were left—late blight.

One thing I couldn't keep ignoring was my wallet. I seemed to be spending a fortune growing all these heirlooms. Wondering if I was getting less out of my garden than I was putting in, one late summer evening I sat down with the receipts to compute just how much I'd spent to grow each of the eighteen Brandywines I'd managed to salvage after deer, groundhogs, and disease had gotten the rest.

The answer became the title of my first book, *The $64 Tomato*.

The monetary stakes were much higher for those northeastern farmers who'd converted most of their tomato acreage to more lucrative heirloom varieties when, in 2009, late blight—the same disease responsible for the Irish potato famine of 1845 to 1849—destroyed some 75 percent of their heirloom crops (and 100 percent of mine). Encouraged by a cool, damp summer and possibly introduced by cheap seedlings that were bred in the South and sold in discount garden centers like Home Depot, Lowe's, and Walmart, the fungus spread on the wind like wildfire, infecting everything in its path, even tomatoes with some resistance. "I remember being shocked that late blight could overcome single resistance genes so quickly," Burpee breeder Simon Crawford had told me, calling it perhaps the biggest surprise of his long breeding career.

There are few effective chemical remedies for many of the diseases that plague tomatoes, and even fewer for organic growers like myself. To make matters worse, many of these bacteria and fungi live in the soil for years, making them extremely difficult to eradicate once they've arrived. Indeed, the best way to battle disease is to breed resistance into the tomatoes. In other words, *create a hybrid*.

There, I said it. But every self-respecting revolution needs a counterrevolution, and the heirloom tomato uprising was no exception. What *was* surprising was that the first countershot heard loudly round the world was fired by a former revolutionary, Dan Barber, the prominent New York haute-barnyard chef and restaurateur whose Blue Hill at Stone Barns $250 tasting menu often featured estate-grown heirloom cherry tomatoes on the vine, artistically woven across a miniature tabletop trellis. Barber was an early and vocal proponent of both the farm-to-table and heirloom trends, but in August 2009, reeling from a total loss of Stone Barns' tomato crop to late blight, he wrote a *New York Times* op-ed that resonated with farmers and chefs alike:

> To many advocates of sustainability, science...is considered suspect, a violation of the slow food aesthetic. It's a nostalgia I'm guilty of promoting as a chef when I celebrate only heirloom tomatoes on my menus. These venerable tomato varieties are indeed important to preserve, and they're often more flavorful than conventional varieties. But in our feverish pursuit of what's old, we can marginalize the development of what could be new.

Our feverish pursuit of what's old. This sentiment was echoed widely. A *Scientific American* article making "the case against heirloom tomatoes" characterized them as the vegetable equivalent of "the pug—that 'purebred' dog with the convoluted nose that snorts and hacks when it tries to catch a breath." Fewer stories were appearing about heirloom tomatoes and more about how a new generation of breeders was trying to return flavor to tomatoes through a more scientific approach to hybridization. They were taking advantage of technology that Oved Shifriss never had at his disposal, including the complete mapping of the tomato genome.

Undoubtedly part of this was merely heirloom-news fatigue, but after the novelty of growing heirlooms had passed, farmers had discovered the risks, and some gardeners (myself included) had grown weary of harvesting between zero and eighteen tomatoes over a two-month season. As Lipman's breeder, Mark Barineau, told me, "you can't taste a tomato that doesn't exist."

Heirloom tomatoes never caught on in the commercial tomato world, where they remain niche, representing just a tiny fraction of the tomatoes consumed in the country. Not necessarily because of disease susceptibility, but precisely *because* they're heirlooms— that is, they haven't been bred to perform as projectiles and thus don't travel or keep well. (You sometimes feel lucky if a Brandywine makes it from your garden to your table unscathed.)

Yet they've not gone away; if anything, heirlooms have become commodified over the past two decades, available today in mainstream seed catalogs and as seedlings at garden and home centers. My local grocery store always has a bin of anonymous (and awful) heirloom tomatoes from Mexican greenhouses. Heirlooms are still a staple of summer farmers' markets, although it seems that less emphasis is placed on specific varieties these days; apparently the "heirloom" label is sufficient to attract buyers with deeper pockets. Consequently, some are good; many are not.

But the heirloom tomato, rediscovered by backyard gardeners in backyard gardens, was never destined for large-scale farming, and to this day its cultural and culinary impact far exceeds its commercial clout. The heirloom revolution is maybe the most exciting thing to have happened to tomatoes in a century, proof that a handful of enthusiasts with no more technology than a postage stamp can shake up an industry.

More importantly, thanks to the seed savers' single-minded determination, millions of Americans tasted a real tomato *for the first time*, a tomato without the even-ripening gene, a tomato not artificially bred for travel, but naturally selected for flavor. And they are not likely to forget that taste. Some started visiting farmers' markets; others have, or will start, gardens of their own just to experience the joy of eating a freshly picked Brandywine, still warm from the sun.

In most of the country, though, by late September the sun is too low in the sky to ripen any more tomatoes, and even the indeterminate varieties are running out of steam, robbed of vitality by the short days and chilly nights, until the first hard frosts shiver the fruits and shrivel the vines. Quick, coax the last tomatoes into a little ripeness on your windowsill and enjoy one final taste of summer. For winter is coming.

Ten

WINTER IS COMING

Is the Northern Greenhouse Tomato a Harbinger of the Future or a Relic of an Already Unsustainable Past?

A bee buzzes by, oblivious to the snow falling above. Workers standing comfortably upright calmly snip off entire clusters of ripe tomatoes, laying them in a single layer in a shallow box as gently as if they were handling, well, tomatoes. Vines as thick as my thumb run horizontally, vineyard-style, along supporting wires for twenty, thirty, forty feet before turning skyward, reaching for the glass ceiling above. Outside it's freezing, but in here it's 72 degrees and dry, a perfect day for picking tomatoes. As tomorrow will be. And the day after that. *Toto, I have a feeling we're not in Florida anymore.*

Things that evoke a Canadian winter: Hockey. Skating. Curling. Hotel rooms carved from blocks of ice. Tomatoes.

Tomatoes? What are Canadian tomatoes doing in my supermarket in January? I first noticed them a couple of years ago, but these imports from our northern neighbor have been quietly sneaking up on us for the past decade, part of a billion-dollar indoor vegetable industry that, although it barely existed just a few years ago, now exceeds Canadian egg, potato, and durum wheat production. Every day some two hundred trucks loaded with tomatoes cross the border from Ontario into Michigan, moving tomatoes south—no doubt passing trucks driving north with Florida tomatoes. (One can only speculate about the new hybrid that might result from a head-on collision.)

Say what you will about Florida tomatoes; at least you can see the logic behind growing them in winter. The same with passive greenhouses that extend the season in sunny, warm climes. But Canada? Putting winter greenhouses in Canada seems to make about as much sense as building igloos in Mexico.

Approaching at dusk from Detroit, following the millions of watts of greenhouse lights that paint the sky an otherworldly shade of peach, I am drawn to Leamington, Ontario, like a moth to a flame. It's the dead of winter, but I find myself here because somehow, without anyone south of the border taking much notice or interest, the farmland that runs along the north shore of Lake Erie has become home to the greatest concentration of greenhouses in North America. And with some forty-eight hundred acres already under glass, it's growing larger by the day.

Everywhere you look, land is being cleared and leveled to become a new kind of farmland. Variously known as *protected agriculture*, *precision agriculture*, or *controlled environment*, these terms cumulatively reflect the activity happening within the transparent walls of these greenhouses, enormous structures of up to one hundred acres, not subject to the vagaries of climate or the whims of nature.

Because most of what is grown here winds up on American tables, the owners of these greenhouses have been expanding into the United States, supplying an ever-increasing proportion of our peppers, cucumbers, and, most recently, berries. But for the biggest of the greenhouse farmers, this quiet invasion began with— what else?—the quest for a tastier tomato.

Paul Mastronardi is a fourth-generation Leamington farmer whose family lays claim to the founding of Canada's modern greenhouse industry. Their story, in so many ways the typical immigrant success tale, began when Paul's great-grandfather Armando, a young, poor farmer, left his rural Italian village of Villa Canale in 1923, along with seven other *compagni*, a droplet in the wave of Italian migration that would swell the populations of not only eastern American cities, but of Montreal and Toronto as well.

The eight Italians made their way to Leamington, the southernmost point in Canada, where they found a thriving farming community blessed with good soil and mild winters, thanks to the presence of Lake Erie, the eleventh-largest body of fresh water on earth. A Heinz ketchup and pickle factory in town provided a reliable market for the farmers and steady jobs for the laborers. As word of the migrants' success reached families and friends back in Villa Canale, a full one-third of the old village emptied out, following the eight trailblazers to southwest Ontario.

Armando became a successful tomato farmer, as did his son, Umberto, who, during a trip to Holland in the early 1940s, saw sophisticated greenhouses growing tomatoes for much of the year, not just the few months typical of an Ontario farm. Beginning a close relationship with the Dutch that continues to this day, Umberto brought the technology home, his neighbors soon followed suit, and this unlikely town of Italians and Mennonites (who'd similarly emigrated from Russia at around the same time) was on its way to becoming a world greenhouse superpower.

"I never wanted to go into the family business," says Umberto's grandson Paul, forty-six, adding that he never really cared much for tomatoes either. But after majoring in math and physics in college, he told his father, who'd taken over the company from Umberto, that he'd return to the roost under one condition: that they would think big. Very big. By building not more greenhouses, but *larger* greenhouses. Size, he felt, was the key to profitability. So, at a time when the typical new greenhouse covered five acres, Paul, using Dutch technology and personnel, built the largest greenhouse in North America, a fifty-acre behemoth.

He filled it with tomatoes, to mixed results. Mastronardi, while visiting his customers, heard a refrain familiar to Florida growers: His tomatoes had no flavor. So he flew to Holland in search of a better tomato. At the Dutch seed giant Enza Zaden he found a variety, "this oddball size fruit that was the size of a golf ball. It tasted good, but it didn't fit any markets that are out there. It was just weird. But since it tasted outstanding, we said, 'Well, this is what people are looking for, something that tastes like the tomato of the past, that has flavor.' And you know, the good thing about greenhouses protecting the crop, you can grow varieties that are a little more finicky or aren't as hardy because they don't have to take on the elements. And so, we brought the variety over in '94 and started experimenting with it."

Test crops were successful, but Mastronardi needed a way to distinguish his new cultivar from all the other tomatoes out there. In a supermarket, after all, fresh tomatoes are anonymous, unlike canned tomatoes, which are, he realized, *branded*. So Mastronardi branded his golf ball–sized tomatoes with a catchy, Italian-sounding name suggesting friendship: Campari.

The diminutive, expensive Campari was a bust for several years, attracting more attention from lawyers for its namesake aperitif than from consumers. (Mastronardi successfully fended off a copyright lawsuit.) But watercooler talk kept it alive among tomato aficionados and when, somehow—Mastronardi swears to have been as surprised as anyone—a package of Campari tomatoes started showing up on HBO in the kitchen of Tony Soprano, a little puff of wind filled the Campari sails. The press got curious, foodies started gushing over it, and the Campari was on its way to success, despite its cost.

"I hear it's the most expensive tomato seed in the world," I say to Mastronardi.

"It's up there."

"Like, $150,000 a pound for seeds."

He won't say, of course, other than to point out, "I can tell you that if you walked out of here with a briefcase full of Campari seeds, it would be worth several hundred thousand dollars." In other words, Campari seeds are literally worth more—far more—than their weight in gold.

The idea of growing food in a protected environment is hardly new. In order to satisfy the emperor Tiberius' year-round craving for cucumbers (still among the most popular greenhouse crops), the ancient Romans grew the vines under cold frames—enclosures glazed with translucent gypsum.

Roman winters are cold, and these forerunners of the modern

greenhouse had to be wheeled indoors at night, limiting their size. The solution seems obvious, but the first written reference we have to a heated greenhouse is from Korea, around 1450. The heating system, called *ondol* and still found in Korean homes today, sounds remarkably modern, consisting of a thick masonry floor heated from below that retains heat long after everyone's gone to bed and the fires have died out. (The architect Frank Lloyd Wright stayed in an *ondol* home during a 1905 trip to Asia, after which he "invented" radiant floor heating, substituting hot water circulating through coils for the traditional underfloor roaring fire.)

Early greenhouses were limited in their size, and it wasn't until the Renaissance that glass technology evolved to the point where large, strong sheets of window glass could be manufactured. A good many went into the five-hundred-foot-long orangery at Versailles, which was constructed in 1684 to overwinter the more than one thousand citrus trees that line the château's formal gardens. Meaning that every fall, Louis XIV's gardeners had to lug each and every tree in its heavy oak and cast-iron planter (aspiring kings can buy replicas from the Versailles gift shop) from the gardens into the orangery, and then reverse the process in the spring.

The gardeners must have been wistfully thinking, *Well, this silly citrus fad will die out with the king, and these guys never last long.* Wistful, indeed. The Sun King ruled for 72 years and 110 days, a record still waiting to be broken. (Lookin' at you, Queen E.!)

The French did—briefly—get rid of their tyrannical kings, replacing them with tyrannical emperors, notably in the person of Napoléon Bonaparte. And it is a nephew of Napoléon's, Charles-Lucien Bonaparte, who is credited with inventing the modern greenhouse.

A prominent naturalist, ornithologist, zoologist, and (tricky for

a Bonaparte) fervent republican, Charles spent several years studying birds in the United States, discovering and cataloging more
than two hundred species and becoming, at just twenty-two years
of age, the most celebrated ornithologist of his day. (Bonaparte's
gull, a common West Coast gull with a distinctive black head,
was named after Charles-Lucien, not, as one might assume, his
more famous uncle.)

After leaving America, Charles settled in Rome, where he
published a book on the animals of Italy. This Frenchman with
the last name of "Bonaparte" even got himself elected to the
Roman Assembly, participating in the creation of the Roman
Republic in 1849. But Charles' democratic passions didn't sit well
with his family back in France, where his cousin Louis—that
would be Charles-Louis Napoléon Bonaparte, or Napoléon III—
had become the second Napoléon to claim the title of emperor.
After Charles joined the Italian side in an unsuccessful defense
against forty thousand French troops sent by his *cher cousin*, he had
to flee the country, winding up in Leiden, in southern Holland.
The eclectic Charles had by now moved from birds to botanicals,
and in Leiden he built what is generally considered the world's
first modern greenhouse in order to be able to grow and study his
medicinal plants year-round.

With flat land and a mild climate warmed by the same Gulf
Stream that protects Florida tomatoes from frosts, southern
Holland was, and is, an ideal location for greenhouses, but it
was another notorious tyrant a century later who was responsible for the advent of Holland's greenhouse industry. During
the last days of Nazi occupation, with food so scarce that some
resorted to digging up and eating tulip bulbs, twenty thousand
Dutch perished in the *Hongerwinter*, the famine of 1944–45. Following the war, the Dutch pledged they would never again allow

famine to sweep their land and started building greenhouses in earnest.

And I do mean "in earnest." Today fully 80 percent of Holland's agriculture takes place under glass. This tiny nation of only sixteen thousand square miles—just two-thirds the size of West Virginia—is the second-leading exporter of food globally, trailing only the United States, with their greenhouse industry raking in some $100 billion a year. They've achieved this remarkable accomplishment by developing the world's most advanced greenhouse technology—huge, controlled environments in which they optimize air and root temperatures, light, water, and nutrition. And by devoting a quarter of a percent of their tiny landmass to greenhouses. A quarter of a percent may not sound like much, but if the United States did the same, Connecticut, Delaware, and Rhode Island would *all* be under glass.

The greenhouses of Leamington, Ontario, are built on the Dutch model, using Dutch expertise, equipment, software, seeds, and personnel, and I'm eager to step inside. But first, Paul Mastronardi has two questions for me: "Have you been in a tomato field recently?" My gut tightens, for, of course, I have. "Did you wear those shoes or those pants in the field?" My gut tightens some more as I try to remember what I wore in Immokalee. I hope I haven't come hundreds of miles only to be turned away.

Greenhouse operators are always concerned about disease, but the precautions are heightened this winter because of fear of the tomato brown rugose fruit virus. In Florida I'd heard about rugose, which had been tearing through Mexican greenhouses, to the benefit of Florida producers.

For sure, disease is one of the inherent risks of greenhouse production. Growing indoors, it's easier to keep pests and pathogens out, but should they get in, it's like bringing a toddler with a runny nose into a nursery school. Hoping to keep rugose out of the United States, the USDA had recently announced heightened inspections for all vegetable imports, including those from Canada. In response, Ontario greenhouses have, I suppose sensibly, suspended access to visitors for fear of contamination. (In just another few weeks, a fear of "contamination" from a far more dangerous human virus, COVID-19, would close the Canadian border to Americans for the next year and a half.)

Fortunately, Mastronardi's showcase greenhouse, where the company brings prospective clients and the press, is not in Ontario, but across the border, in Coldwater, Michigan. Satisfied that I won't be patient zero of an outbreak that wipes out his hundred-million-dollar greenhouse, Mastronardi hands me a gauzy white jumpsuit with booties, gloves, and a hat to match. Two floppy ears short of looking like a giant white rabbit, I follow his footsteps through a puddle of sanitizer, rub my gloved hands with disinfectant from a wall dispenser, and I'm ready to enter one of North America's largest and most sophisticated indoor growing operations.

The size is almost hard to fathom. Imagine a greenhouse the size of a football field. Pretty impressive. Now add another seventy-five football fields, and you'll have an idea of the space I'm in, a glass-and-steel structure covering one hundred acres of land. A mile long, with a larger footprint than the Mall of America, it is like a skyscraper lying on its side that, were it to be tipped upright, would tower over *three* Empire State Buildings stacked end to end, with enough room left at the top for King Kong. The preferred method of getting around: bicycle.

In what might represent the future of farming, this lighted and heated greenhouse in Coldwater, Michigan, is more than a mile long. (Courtesy of Mastronardi Produce Limited.)

The greenhouse is partitioned into distinct growing areas, and the one I'm in has a pleasant, subtropical feel, neither terribly hot nor humid on this late January afternoon. The tall vines overhead are reminiscent of a botanical conservatory, except this conservatory houses only one species of plant: *Solanum lycopersicum*. Each of the thousands of tomato plants stretches to not the shoulder height typical of a field tomato, but up to seventy-five feet, their thick vines neatly bundled together like electrical cables and tied to horizontal wires before curving skyward, a reminder that the tomato is indeed vine. One almost expects Tarzan to come swinging by.

Heat from natural gas is supplied from hot water that circulates through twin pipes running down each row. There isn't enough sunlight in winter to supply the tomatoes' greedy needs (plants need fifty times more light for photosynthesis than humans require for vision), so supplemental light is provided by high-pressure sodium bulbs and LEDs powered by a diesel generator. The atmosphere in here is slightly artificial as well. Given the enclosed space, the plants would quickly exhaust all the available carbon dioxide, so enough CO_2 to make up the difference (plus some extra to goose up the photosynthesis) is captured from the generator's exhaust and pumped in.

This farm—and greenhouse operators do call these greenhouses "farms"—does have one thing in common with a Florida tomato field: There's not a tablespoon of soil to be found.

This is a hydroponic farm. The plants are grown in bags of inert ROCKWOOL, which Mastronardi describes as "basalt rock that you heat until it explodes, kind of like popcorn, into a fiberglass-looking material," through which runs a stream of nutrient-laden water. The water is filtered and recycled, so there is little waste or environmental runoff.

I think some bees have snuck in until I notice the cardboard hives mounted about eight feet high. Mastronardi explains their

Tomatoes stretch as far as the eye can see inside the Mastronardi greenhouse in Coldwater, Michigan. (Courtesy of Mastronardi Produce Limited.)

role. "There's no wind in here. As a boy, after school it was my job to go down the rows, shaking every plant" to coax the pollen to fall onto the stigma. No wonder he "never wanted to go into the family business."

Wasps and ladybugs are employed as well. Their salary: all you can eat. Modern greenhouses practice integrated pest management, or IPM, to control pests. Instead of drenching crops in the pesticides common to field tomatoes, greenhouse farmers introduce beneficial insects to eat the bad ones. As a ladybug lands on a leaf, Mastronardi notes, "Forget what you've heard about them being cute and gentle. They're vicious predators."

The system is so effective that unless things get out of control, which happens rarely, few or even no pesticides are used at all—certainly far less than on field tomatoes. Yet it's a complicated business and a delicate balance whenever you try to play Mother Nature. When Mastronardi experimented with converting all the lights to low-energy LED bulbs, the bees started falling out of their orbits. As for IPM, Mastronardi recalls, "Our wasp populations were so efficient at eradicating the whiteflies that they kept dying off [of hunger] and had to be replaced." The solution was to keep fewer wasps, tolerating a low, carefully monitored population of whiteflies—enough to make a meal, but not enough to significantly damage the crop.

Bumblebees, ladybugs, happy wasps, ripe tomatoes: Maybe it's the high CO_2 level talking, but as snow continues to fall outside, I find myself thinking, *Give me a Campari (the one in the bottle) and a lawn chair, and I could spend my winter vacation in here.* Although apparently this place can go from paradise to Pompeii in about the same amount of time, as happened in 2013 at a Backyard Farms greenhouse in Madison, Maine, when the owners had to destroy the village in order to save it. Unable to control a devastating whitefly infestation with wasps, the growers ended up having to rip out and destroy a half million tomato plants before sanitizing the greenhouse.

I don't see anything infesting these stunning, ripe fruits that are being harvested by just a handful of pickers. In a scene more evocative of a factory floor than a factory farm, the workers stand upright on hydraulic lifts similar to those used to load meal carts onto airplanes, allowing them to reach those tomatoes high above, never squatting, never stretching. Mounted on the rails that supply the greenhouse heat, these pipe trolleys, as they're called, roll quietly down each row of plants. The pickers work at a steady pace, but one that doesn't approach the furious stripping that I watched in Immokalee.

The harvesters, mostly Latinx immigrants, earn $15 an hour and, like their Immokalee counterparts, free housing, with an opportunity for productivity bonuses. But unlike in Florida, where pickers are paid from the tokens they stuff into their pockets, everything here is recorded electronically with RFID tracking tags.

The entire operation, it goes without saying, is computer-controlled, from anticipating orders eighteen months in the future to fine-tuning ventilation, water, and fertilizer. Within ten years, Mastronardi predicts, the harvesting will be computerized as well, done by robots that are sophisticated enough to recognize and gently pick ripe fruits without bruising them.

It's all quite impressive, antiseptic, and futuristic, yet the skeptic in me wonders how this operation can possibly compete in cost with field produce. After all, you can rent a tomato field in Ontario for just $500 an acre. The entry fee into the protected agriculture business, at least on this scale, is a cool hundred million. And that's just to build the greenhouse. Once in production, you've got the increased costs of heating, lighting, maintaining a hydroponic system, replacing your growing medium annually, labor (each and every seedling is manually grafted onto rootstock), greenhouse maintenance and repair, and higher wages than the typical farmworker earns. "What," I ask Mastronardi, "am I missing?"

Yield. Grown in a controlled environment enriched with CO_2, each seventy-five-foot plant can, depending upon the type of tomato, produce from ten to twenty times as much fruit as one grown in a field. Remember that whenever field tomato breeders try to increase yield, they sacrifice flavor, because, as the University of Florida's Sam Hutton pointed out, the same number of leaves is photosynthesizing sugars for an increased number of fruits. But in a greenhouse, where plants are the height of oak trees, and with indeterminate varieties providing a higher ratio of leaves to blossoms, there is plenty of photosynthesis to go around.

Not to mention the fact that, whereas a typical field tomato yields fruit for six to eight weeks, these plants will continue producing tomatoes for *forty*. While this hundred-acre greenhouse may seem puny by Florida standards, its productivity is equivalent to several thousand field acres, a good-sized farm. And his farm, Mastronardi points out, will never lose its crop to drought, floods, hail, or E. coli from the pig farm upstream. And if large buyers value one thing, it's supply-chain reliability.

"Seventy years ago," Mastronardi says, "when my great-grandfather and grandfather first started selling greenhouse tomatoes, retailers were like, 'Well, who's going to pay twice the price for a greenhouse tomato versus a field tomato,' because that's what it was back then. And today we are, I would say, within 15 percent of what it costs to grow a field tomato, and sometimes we can be cheaper than certain field tomato crops, depending on where they're grown in North America."

Perhaps there is no surer indicator of price parity than the fact that Wendy's now sources all of its tomatoes from greenhouses. They've spun it as a quality issue for the consumer, but it stems from their refusal to sign on to the Coalition of Immokalee Workers' Fair Food Program, effectively shutting them out of Florida.

Even if the tomatoes cost a bit more, consumers are willing to pay it, Mastronardi says, because greenhouse tomatoes are seen as a premium product. I ask how a greenhouse tomato, grown under artificial light and without soil, can be superior to a field tomato. "You can actually grow varieties for flavor," he says, "because we don't have to worry so much about ship ability or the hardiness of a variety." But still, these are *hydroponic* tomatoes, grown in fertilized water. How do you obtain the certain je ne sais quoi that you get from trace elements in soil, that terroir?

Mastronardi dismisses the importance of terroir as "ridiculous," maintaining that "the genetics of anything is what's going to give you the flavor and the profile of the tomato. It's about understanding what nutrients the plants need." In fact, his goal is to *eliminate* terroir, because he wants—and the consumer expects—a Campari tomato grown in a British Columbia greenhouse to taste exactly the same as one grown in Michigan. In that way, he says, his approach is not much different from that of some bottled water manufacturers. They start with tap water, remove all of the elements to get to a baseline of pure H_2O, then add back into the water the trace elements that give the final product its characteristic taste. "And it tastes the way you want it to taste, every single time," he says.

But we're not talking water here, I push back, citing about the only thing I know about wine, which is that sauvignon blanc and

Sancerre are made from the same grape from the same region in France, but on opposite sides of the Loire, where the soil is quite different, resulting in markedly different wines, even to a $12-a-bottle palate like mine.

"It's what's in that soil," Mastronardi says. "We put those trace elements into our fertilizer. That's part of the secret sauce. Give me a field tomato variety that tastes great, and we can put it in the greenhouse and make it better."

Indeed, while walking through the greenhouses, I've been sampling tomatoes, and while I'm not about to give up my summer tomato patch yet, these are not bad at all. In fact, some are very good, especially the smaller varieties, anywhere from grape size to Campari. The standard-size tomatoes grown for the mass market still taste like winter tomatoes, but you can judge for yourself. In much of the US, you won't have to look far for a greenhouse tomato, because the Canadian hothouse industry doesn't just want to be your off-season vegetable supplier, filling the void left when local farms are quiet, and providing an alternative to Florida; it wants to be your vegetable supplier, *period*. Twelve months of the year. And this growth is not limited to Canada. Greenhouse vegetable production is rising almost too fast to keep track of, on every continent. There are now twenty-three hundred hydroponic farms in the US alone.

Their increasing numbers include smaller "vertical farms" located near or in cities, sometimes in reclaimed warehouses or factories, rising several stories high instead of a hundred acres across. Owners of such operations claim that they can grow as much food on a single acre as a traditional farm grows on four hundred acres. Thus, it's increasingly likely that the lettuce, pepper, cucumber, or tomato you buy in a supermarket came from a greenhouse in the US, Canada, Mexico, or even Israel.

And now you can add berries to that list. Mastronardi has devoted two acres of the Coldwater greenhouse to test beds of new strawberry varieties, some of which were so tasty that they reminded me of homegrown. These not only could but *should* make bland Florida strawberries, raised in the same poisoned sand as Florida tomatoes, obsolete.

Home bakers who blanch at the cost of Madagascar vanilla will be heartened to learn that the Dutch are experimenting with a greenhouse variety. How far will we—can we—go with this? In what might well symbolize the coming greenhouse age, Anton Chekhov's play *The Cherry Orchard* ends to the heartbreaking sounds of an estate's prized cherry trees being chopped down to make way for villas. It's the kind of ending that usually brings out the Kleenex. But I know someone who isn't weeping. Because cherries are particularly sensitive to the vagaries of weather—a late rain leaves puddles in the divot near the stem, a strong wind bangs them together like a pair of dice hanging from a rearview mirror, and a late frost can destroy an entire crop—Paul Mastronardi's next big project may be a cherry orchard under glass. Chekhov's words could one day be Mastronardi's: "My God, my God, the cherry orchard's mine! Tell me I'm drunk, or mad, or dreaming."

What might seem revolutionary in America is already commonplace in Europe. Eighty-five percent of Holland's tomatoes come from greenhouses, some of these structures being half again as big as Mastronardi's Michigan leviathan, and other countries are chasing hard as the economics become more attractive. As impressive as Holland's technology is, most of Europe's tomatoes come not from these permanent, expensive, and sophisticated buildings, but from as low-tech a collection of greenhouses as you can imagine. An area near Almería, an outcropping on Spain's southern coast, has so much plastic strung up that its hundred square miles of wall-to-wall greenhouses have the distinction of being the world's most recognizable man-made structure from space.

With a warm, sunny climate, there's no need for supplemental heat or light. Instead, sheets of cheap, disposable polyethylene (in Europe called "polythene") attached to a ragtag assembly of metal frames and wooden supports keep the crops adequately warm during the winter months. That and cheap, disposable African labor have made this province Europe's Immokalee, supplying some 3.5 million pounds of tomatoes and other vegetables annually.

The waste from this disposable plastic on what some call the Costa del Polythene is an environmental nightmare, but the

The Costa del Polythene, the plastic greenhouses of Almería, Spain, photographed from the International Space Station. (Courtesy NASA/ JPL-Caltech.)

sheeting also seems to be helping the planet in an unexpected way. "Greenhouse effect" has a different meaning here, where the glacier-sized layer of plastic reflects sunlight back into the atmosphere, *cooling* the province by half a degree Fahrenheit per decade while the rest of Spain—and the world—is heating up like a Neapolitan pizza oven.

Lacking southern Spain's climate, the rest of the world is steadily moving toward the kind of indoor greenhouse technology practiced in Holland and Canada. Its proponents like to cite the advantages over field agriculture: 95 percent less pesticide use; 90 percent less water; minimal environmental impact; safer food production; insulation from floods, frosts, hail, and heat; and proximity to major population centers, meaning we can all "eat local."

So really, what's not to like?

Well...I hate to be a rotten you-know-what, but I did notice that it was bloody freezing outside while I was snacking on tomatoes inside a 72-degree greenhouse the size of a New England village. So, I do have to ask: What's the carbon footprint of a tomato grown in a heated, lighted Canadian greenhouse in January?

I'm not just being snarky. Scientists and consumers are increasingly looking at the greenhouse gases produced by agriculture, with beef production being the—no pun intended—prime target. A ruckus ensued in 2019 when Democrats were accused of wanting to rip the hamburgers from our very mouths after their Green New Deal cited the need to address agricultural greenhouse gases. In fact, the deal made no mention of either cows or beef; the controversy arose when a "clarifying" FAQ issued by the office of freshman congresswoman and resolution sponsor Alexandria Ocasio-Cortez referred glancingly to the methane from "farting cows."

Technically, "burping cows" is more accurate, but the truth is that agriculture is responsible for no less than a quarter of the world's greenhouse gas emissions, comparable to that emitted from all automobiles, buses, trains, and planes combined.

Even acknowledging that the bulk of agricultural emissions comes not from vegetables but from meat, poultry, and dairy production, this hardly seems the time to be increasing agriculture's share by *moving farming indoors*—responding to greenhouse gases by building more greenhouses. Yet this is exactly what's happening worldwide, and it's happening without any public or political discourse or policy guidance.

To determine the impact of this, it's necessary to do the math. That is, we need to calculate the carbon footprint of the vegetable that's leading this march, the greenhouse tomato. Defined as the pounds of carbon (or its equivalent greenhouse impact from another gas) produced per pound of food, arriving at this figure is as complex an endeavor as you might imagine. It's not just the carbon produced in growing the tomatoes; a complete life cycle assessment has to consider the greenhouse gases produced by everything from constructing the greenhouse to the fuel needed to operate it and the disposal of the waste it generates.

Confounding an attempt to arrive at a reliable figure is the fact that such critical variables as the greenhouse's latitude, outdoor temperature, fuel sources, and hours of sunlight vary from place to place. The climate around Leamington is relatively mild thanks to Lake Erie, but that Backyard Farms greenhouse in Madison, Maine, lies 130 miles *north* of Leamington. Winters are so dark there that the greenhouse's twenty thousand high-pressure sodium lights use as much electricity in thirty-two minutes as the average American household does in a year. Yet it comes from a hydroelectric plant, so, technically speaking, the lighting's footprint is negligible (although it's using clean energy that would otherwise be going into the grid).

Given the complexities and uncertainties, it's not surprising that various analyses have differing numbers. Generally speaking, though, tomatoes raised in a northern greenhouse carry a carbon footprint of roughly 3.0 to 3.5 pounds, with about two-thirds of that coming from heating the greenhouse (usually with natural gas). The rest of it is from lighting, construction, waste, packaging, and the production of the mineral wool growing media.

For comparison, a pound of apples has a footprint of a quarter-pound to a half-pound of carbon. Same for root vegetables. Beef's unsavory greenhouse gas reputation is well-deserved: If cows were a country, they would be the third-largest greenhouse gas emitter on the planet, with a pound of steak leaving a deep carbon footprint of about 26 pounds.

Okay, but we gotta eat. So, the real question is how greenhouse tomatoes compare to outdoor tomatoes, specifically their main competition, Florida tomatoes.

It turns out that a field-grown tomato's carbon footprint is only 0.25, most of it coming from fumigants and fertilizers that break down into nitrous oxide, a greenhouse gas three hundred times as potent as CO_2 emissions. With a quarter of a pound versus three pounds of carbon, greenhouses sound like a losing proposition for a warming planet.

But we're not done; we need to consider transportation. Unlike greenhouse crops, which are generally grown near population centers, tomatoes from southern Florida must be shipped around the country in refrigerated trucks, so surely the carbon generated from interstate travel is going to increase this figure.

It is, but not nearly as much as you might think, especially if you're one who thinks about "food miles." There may be some good reasons to be a locavore, but reducing one's carbon footprint is probably not one of them. It turns out it's not the *distance* your food travels to reach you that's important, it's *how it travels.* Land and sea transportation of most food contributes a surprisingly small amount to its carbon footprint. (Air freight, although rare, is another story altogether.)

Tomatoes shipped from Almería, at the very tip of southern Spain, to Vienna have just half the footprint of Viennese greenhouse tomatoes. And your friendly local farmer, driving a few hundred pounds of produce seventy-five miles to a Saturday morning farmers' market in her rickety utility truck, might well generate more carbon per pound of tomatoes than a Lipman Family Farms tractor trailer hauling fifteen tons of them a thousand miles.

The additional carbon from trucking Florida tomatoes to northern markets amounts to just another quarter-pound or less, depending on the distance, making the final carbon tally for Florida tomatoes about half a pound. That means typical greenhouse tomatoes have at least *six times* the carbon footprint of Florida field tomatoes. So, with more and more agriculture moving indoors, someone had better be asking the question: *Is the northern greenhouse a sustainable future or the relic of an already obsolete past?*

With the Dutch having started this whole thing and currently leading the world in both greenhouse technology and production, I put this question to Jasper Scholten. A life cycle assessment analyst, Scholten works for Blonk Consultants, a Dutch firm that specializes in environmental and sustainability issues within the international agricultural and food sector.

"It's not sustainable," he says flatly over a video link from his office in Holland. "Not the way it's being done now."

And the way it's being done now is pretty advanced, at least compared to the way North America does it. Most of the large Dutch greenhouses use CHP—combined heat and power—to generate heat and electricity at the same time, using about half the energy as when separately heating the greenhouse with natural gas and pulling electricity from the grid.

The principle behind CHP (in the US often called "cogeneration") is that generating electricity produces a lot of waste heat that normally just dissipates into the atmosphere. So, if you construct a CHP generator near your greenhouse, you can pretty much heat the tomatoes for free, while feeding the excess electricity back into the grid, for which the utility company pays you handsomely—at least in Holland, where a new CHP generator generally replaces an old carbon- and smog-spewing coal-fired plant. Everyone wins. At least until there are no coal-fueled power plants left to replace, an issue that Scholten acknowledges.

"What we are seeing in Holland," he says, "is a shift away from natural gas to renewable energy," namely geothermal, which is plentiful in the western part of the country. "But if you don't have that, I think greenhouses will be quite difficult from a sustainability point of view."

I wonder if the rest of my salad is about to become bitter as well. I've recently become hooked on another winter greenhouse crop, small heads of buttercrunch lettuce, with the roots still attached. Once a pricey exotic, they are now competitive with California lettuce. And, because the plant—yes, let's not forget that vegetables are plants—is still alive when it reaches my grocery cart, it is light-years (actually, about a week, which in lettuce age *is* light-years) ahead in freshness of the lettuce trucked in from the West.

I hate that they come in a plastic clamshell, but if you can get past that, it's a real treat to be able to enjoy a good salad on a cold night in February.

Or perhaps *was*. Given Scholten's discouraging outlook on greenhouse vegetables, I expect more heartburn when I call Neil Mattson, an associate professor at Cornell University who studies greenhouse environmental issues. But Mattson cheers me with his counterintuitive view, suggesting that the higher carbon footprint of greenhouse vegetables could be more than offset *if we just ate more of them*.

At first blush, it's a head-snapping notion, but, Mattson explains, vegetables—even from an inefficient greenhouse—have a lower carbon footprint than almost any animal protein. Replacing, say, a twelve-ounce steak dinner with a large greenhouse-grown salad, even one topped with a few slices of steak (or even better, chicken or beans), would result in a significant carbon reduction, as a bonus saving billions of dollars a year in health costs. So, if greenhouses grew produce of sufficient quality to induce us to eat more vegetables year-round, they could play a significant role in *reducing* greenhouse gases.

Additionally, Mattson points out, global warming is not the only environmental problem threatening our planet. In fact, it's not even the only effect of climate change. "We've seen years in California where there are mega-droughts and we may not be able to grow produce there if we wanted to."

Nine months after that conversation, Neil Mattson seems as much an oracle as a scientist, for as I write this, the Southwest is in the grips of a crisis that is being called a historic mega-drought, with 9 out of every 10 acres in Arizona—which, along with California, is the source of nearly all the lettuce farmed in the United States—under "severe drought." Lake Mead, the country's largest reservoir and once a reliable source of water in the Southwest, is looking like a drained bathtub (right down to the rings), having dropped to its lowest level since it was first filled in the 1930s. And it's barely June.

With agriculture accounting for between 70 and 90 percent of the world's fresh water use, and with critical aquifers rapidly becoming exhausted, water scarcity is emerging as a serious national and global issue. This makes a greenhouse, which uses 90 percent less water than a traditional farm, an attractive option. In fact, greenhouses are environmental boons by just about any measure other than energy, from pesticide use to the eutrophication of streams and waterways caused by fertilizer runoff. And, Mattson suggests, with farm labor becoming increasingly difficult to obtain, the robotic greenhouse may become a virtual necessity.

As for sustainability, the trick, Mattson and Scholten agree, is to be creative. Mastronardi Produce has built what they say is a fully carbon-neutral greenhouse in Sombra, Ontario. Adjacent to a fertilizer manufacturer, the greenhouse takes all the factory's excess steam for heat and its CO_2 emissions for the plants. Ontario is also experimenting with generating power from biofuels, specifically willow, a fast-growing tree that thrives in poor soils. In theory at least, biofuels are carbon recycling machines that, when burned as fuel, merely return to the atmosphere the carbon they've absorbed during their growth cycle.

England, which before Brexit imported virtually all of its tomatoes, has just built a pair of mega-greenhouses adjacent to wastewater processing facilities. Using waste heat from water treatment to warm the greenhouses, they are expected to supply 12 percent of the UK's tomatoes. And more energy- and photosynthetic-efficient lights are being developed all the time.

Sustainability aside, some see protected agriculture not as a

choice but as an imperative. With the global population expected
to grow by 20 percent, to ten billion, by 2050, it has been estimated that the world will have to produce as much food *in just the
next four decades* as it has grown in the past eight thousand years.
It's a formidable challenge. Hybridization has been tapped out,
having already increased yields of vegetables like corn and tomatoes by an order of magnitude. And turning forests into cultivated
fields is environmentally counterproductive, leaving one to wonder where this increased food supply is going to come from.

What's that sound I hear in the distance? Cherry trees being
chopped down to make room for buildings? "Tell me I'm drunk,
or mad, or dreaming."

I feel a little numb as I board my flight home from Michigan, my
suitcase again filled with tomatoes. I've spent over a year trying to
uncover the tomato's past, but in one day—literally the final day
of my quest—I've stumbled upon a totally unexpected glimpse of
its future. Feeling like Scrooge on Christmas Day, I try to process
the implications of what I've seen and what I've *foreseen*: a brave
new world in which not only tomatoes, but nearly everything in
our produce aisle, from subterranean onions to hanging fruits, is
grown indoors in precision microclimates, managed by comput-
ers, harvested by robots, and delivered in driverless trucks.

In this world, for the first time in the thirty-thousand-year
history of agriculture, societies don't need to be blessed with fertile soil and favorable weather to survive. On the other hand, the
entry fee to profitable farming, once open to anyone—including
a poor immigrant—with a strong back and a supportive family,
is $100 million. Crops are less subject to drought but are instead

dependent upon an increasingly stressed power grid. As white jumpsuits and hydraulic lifts displace blue jeans and a tractor, you might have to go back to McCormick's reaper to find an agricultural innovation as potentially disruptive to the status quo as the hundred-acre hydroponic greenhouse.

It feels like such a futuristic vision that I find myself half reluctant to commit it to paper. A reader would be justified to wonder if I've drunk the Mastronardi cherry Kool-Aid. Except that it's *not* a far-off dystopian future—certainly not in Holland. No, it's happening now, and the twin breadbaskets of Southern California and Florida are probably the main reason it's not yet happened to as great a degree in America. But with new mega-greenhouses and vertical farms popping up everywhere from Kentucky to Upstate New York, it seems to be on the way.

It's tempting to be alarmed, or at least uneasy, but if there is one constant to agriculture it's change, and without that change—mechanization, hybridization, preservation—it's unlikely that our modern society as we know it would exist, as all life, and thought, and innovation flow from nutrition. And if, as seems increasingly likely, within the next couple of decades the source of much of that nutrition comes from a greenhouse, it will have started with—no surprise—the tomato.

There is a nice symmetry here as the hydroponic greenhouse represents a homecoming of sorts. It seems fitting that the tomato, which began its domesticated life as a hydroponically grown vegetable, floating in an Aztec *chinampa*, should, more than five hundred years later, be leading a return to aquaculture as if it had been yearning for it all along, just biding its time.

And its time is now. Never has the tomato been more popular nor its prospects as bright. From its beginnings as a small, bitter berry in South America, the tomato might be considered the

Zelig of the vegetable world, present at so many important world events—witness to the overnight vaporization of an ancient and thriving civilization, victim of the excesses of the Renaissance, and revolutionizer of the diet of a new nation—you wonder how it could have been missed.

The tomato is now grown on every continent (Antarctica included) and, not to be constrained by something as trifling as earth's gravity, has secured passage on the first manned trip to Mars. Closer to home, farmers' markets are bursting with an abundance of new and old tomatoes not seen since market day in Tenochtitlán, while home gardeners, taking to their backyard and community gardens in ever-greater numbers, have an unprecedented variety of seeds to choose from, whether the latest hybrids or the century-old heirlooms that connect us to our ancestors, the land, and our history.

The single heirloom I've been growing this summer might better be called an antique. Collected in the wild in 1949 near Tenochtitlán and known only as "Accession LA0146," it has the deeply lobed fruits characteristic of the tomatoes cast into the cathedral doors in Pisa. This variety is nowhere near that old, but Roger Chetelat, who succeeded the legendary Charley Rick as director of the UC Davis Tomato Genetics Resource Center, has suggested that it might give me a rough approximation of what those early tomatoes were like.

Since March I've been nurturing these few precious seeds, starting them indoors under lights, moving them into larger containers when they outgrew their "incubators," then transplanting them in the garden, where a 10,000-volt electric fence keeps the groundhogs and deer at bay. With a gestation period equal to that of a goat, growing tomatoes is nothing if not an act of faith, but my patience is rewarded, and on this August afternoon, the first few are ripe.

I'm braced for a less-than-savory experience, given that this is neither a tomato prized for its flavor, nor one that has benefited from decades of human selection or breeding, at least not recently. Basically, it's a weed, and likely more suited for the ornamental use that sixteenth-century Italians relegated it to than to lunch. But duty calls. I need to know what this antique wild, ribbed tomato tastes like.

The answer is, *not bad*. It's no Brandywine, but I'm pleasantly surprised. There's none of the bitterness or acidity I'd expected. Rather, once you get past those deep furrows, this wild plant, neglected for who knows how many decades, looks and tastes like a modern tomato, an heirloom that would not be out of place at any farmers' market.

I slice it crossways, the lobes giving each slice the fanciful look of a gentle starburst.

Anne is hungry. "Let's make BLTs," she says. We do, and I swear I hear a soft moan escape from her after the first bite. We eat in silence, in reverence, in history.

Finally, I speak. "What do you think?" I ask, holding a tomato in the palm of my hand, feeling its weight, watching how the light plays on the crimson skin, the taste of the last bite still dancing on my tongue. "Does this thing have a future?"

ACKNOWLEDGMENTS

One of the rewards of writing a book that deals with farming and food is that the people who choose careers in those fields tend to be uncommonly warm, welcoming, and enthusiastic about their work. The fact that nearly the entirety of this book was researched and written during pandemic lockdowns, restrictions, and stress makes their generosity and assistance all the more remarkable.

For starters, I owe a big *grazie* to the *prefetto* of the province of Pisa for granting me access to the former de' Medici palace, a visit that would not have taken place without the determined efforts, emails, and phone calls made by Mark Carson-Selman in New York and Guiomar Parada in Italy. Likewise, thanks to Giulia Marinelli and Elena Hamisia for providing an off-hours visit to the Musei Pasta e Pomodoro. In Campania, I am grateful to Paolo Ruggiero, Nancy Gaudiello, and the ageless Vincenzo Zio for sharing the story of the San Marzano tomato. To give the historians their due, I am greatly indebted to David Gentilcore, whose book *Pomodoro!* is the definitive work on the history of the tomato in Italy; and to Zachary Nowak for the enlightening interview about the origins of the Margherita pizza.

In the US, thanks to Erin Monroe and Courtney Hebert at the Wadsworth Atheneum Museum of Art in Hartford, Connecticut; Curt Harker, Ronald Magill, and Rich Guido from the Salem

Country Historical Society; Dot Hall, formerly with the Campbell Soup Company; and Rutgers University's Thomas Orton and Alex DelCollo. For the early history of the tomato in America, from Colonel Johnson through the industrial tomato, I have benefited greatly from the extensive research done by historians John Hoenig and Andrew F. Smith, who have written excellent works on the history of the tomato in America.

At Burpee, I'm indebted to George Ball for sitting through an interview that ran well past its allotted time; and to Simon Crawford, first for his time (and patience) in educating me on the art and science of hybridization, and second, for suggesting and creating a living version of this book, a "Ten Tomatoes That Changed the World" exhibit for the 2021 Chelsea Garden Show in London. Thanks also to Emily L. Ruby, curator at the Senator John Heinz History Center, for providing information and archival photographs relating to Henry J. Heinz and the history of ketchup; and to authors Harold McGee and Craig LeHoullier for generously lending their time and valuable insights.

While Florida "mature green" tomatoes have often been vilified, I cannot say the same of the men and women responsible for growing them at Lipman Family Farms, all of whom were welcoming, candid, and generous in their time, information, and access. Thanks especially to Kent Shoemaker for allowing me full access to the operation, and to Toby Purse, Mark Barineau, and Chris Campbell for cheerfully putting up with several days of interviews, tours, and questions. Thanks also to Michael Schadler of the Florida Tomato Exchange for supplying background material on the Florida tomato industry.

Sam Hutton of the University of Florida Gulf Coast Research and Education Center not only served as a valuable resource and knowledge bank, but took a day out of his busy research and teaching schedule to take me to a sandy tomato field being prepared for planting.

Thanks to Neil Mattson of Cornell University and Jasper Scholten of Blonk Consultants for sharing their expertise on the sustainability of greenhouse vegetable growing; and to Roger Chetelat at the Tomato Genetics Resource Center at UC Davis for providing me with wild Mexican tomato seeds from their collection. In Canada, Joe Sbrocchi and Dean Taylor provided background information of the history of Leamington greenhouses and arranged my visit with Paul Mastronardi, who, like the Florida growers, was welcoming and generous with his time.

My research would have been far more difficult and even incomplete without the assistance of librarian Stuart Moss, who was able to provide me with every obscure journal article and book extract I requested—often within hours. Thanks also to Dan Skinner, Beatrice Ughi, Luca and Laura Martelli, and Nathan Kleinman for their contributions; and to my dear friend Jack Fuchs, for his insightful feedback on early sections of the manuscript.

I am deeply grateful to my terrific agents, Molly Friedrich and Heather Carr, for guiding me through the entire process, from proposal to publication to (literally, when I needed it the most) chicken soup, and for finding the perfect home for this book, Grand Central Publishing, as well as the perfect editor, Maddie Caldwell, whose probing curiosity and sharp editorial eye added immeasurably to the text, from the very first page to the last. Thanks as well to the entire team at Grand Central, including Tree Abraham for the brilliant jacket illustration; editorial assistant Jacqui Young for her expertise and assistance with the many images found within; Deborah Wiseman for her skilled copyediting; and, on the production and marketing side, the wonderful team of Carolyn Kurek, Roxanne Jones, and Amanda Pritzker.

I've reserved the final and greatest thanks for my remarkable wife, Anne Mullin, for cheerfully putting up with my writing another book—which this time meant being masked and dragged around Italy not once, but twice during a global pandemic, at a time when most other husbands were merely demanding that their wives eat another loaf of their sourdough.

Although I may have done that too.

SELECTED SOURCES

Alberts, Robert C. *The Good Provider: H.J. Heinz and His 57 Varieties*. Boston: Houghton Mifflin, 1973.

Allen, Arthur. *Ripe: The Search for the Perfect Tomato*. Berkeley: Counterpoint, 2010.

Brown, Martin, and Peter Philips, "Craft Labor and Mechanization in Nineteenth-Century American Canning." *Journal of Economic History* 46, no. 3 (1986): 743–56.

Dickie, John. *Delizia! The Epic History of the Italians and Their Food*. New York: Free Press, 2008.

Dienstag, Eleanor Foa. *In Good Company: 125 Years at the Heinz Table, 1869–1994*. New York: Warner, 1994.

Dunn, Daisy. *The Shadow of Vesuvius: A Life of Pliny*. New York: Liveright, 2019.

Estabrook, Barry. *Tomatoland: How Modern Industrial Agriculture Destroyed Our Most Alluring Fruit*. Kansas City: Andrews McMeel, 2011.

Gentilcore, David. *Pomodoro! A History of the Tomato in Italy*. New York: Columbia University Press, 2010.

Gladwell, Malcolm. "The Ketchup Conundrum." *New Yorker*, September 6, 2004.

Goldman, Amy. *The Heirloom Tomato: From Garden to Table; Recipes, Portraits, and History of the World's Most Beautiful Fruit*. New York: Bloomsbury, 2008.

Helstosky, Carol. *Pizza: A Global History*. London: Reaktion, 2008.

Hoenig, John. *Garden Variety: The American Tomato from Corporate to Heirloom*. New York: Columbia University Press, 2018.

Hyman, Clarissa. *Tomato: A Global History*. London: Reaktion, 2019.

Jordan, Jennifer A. *Edible Memory: The Lure of Heirloom Tomatoes and Other Forgotten Foods.* Chicago: Chicago University Press, 2015.

———. "The Heirloom Tomato as Cultural Object: Investigating Taste and Space." *Sociologia Ruralis* 47, no. 1 (2007): 20–41.

Kummer, Corby. "Pasta." *Atlantic,* July 1986.

LeHoullier, Craig. *Epic Tomatoes: How to Select and Grow the Best Varieties of All Time.* North Adams, MA: Storey, 2015.

Levine, Ed. *Pizza: A Slice of Heaven.* New York: Universe, 2005.

Long, Janet. "Tomatoes." In *The Cambridge World History of Food.* Cambridge: Cambridge University Press, 2000.

Martineau, Belinda. *First Fruit: The Creation of the Flavr Savr Tomato and the Birth of Genetically Engineered Food.* New York: McGraw Hill, 2001.

Mattozzi, Antonio. *Inventing the Pizzeria: A History of Pizza Making in Naples.* New York: Bloomsbury, 2009.

Miller, Henry I, and Gregory P. Conko. *The Frankenfood Myth: How Protest and Politics Threaten the Biotech Revolution.* Westport, CT: Praeger, 2004.

Mukherjee, Siddhartha. *The Gene: An Intimate History.* New York: Scribner, 2016.

Nowak, Zachary. "Folklore, Fakelore, History: Invented Tradition and the Origins of the Pizza Margherita." *Food, Culture & Society* 17, no. 1 (2014): 103–12.

Ott Whealy, Diane. *Gathering: Memoir of a Seed Saver.* Decorah, IA: Seed Savers Exchange, 2011.

Parasecoli, Fabio. *Al Dente: A History of Food in Italy.* London: Reaktion, 2014.

Prezzolini, Giuseppe. *Spaghetti Dinner.* Greenville, OH: Coachwhip, 2018.

Restall, Matthew. *When Montezuma Met Cortés: The True Story of the Meeting That Changed History.* New York: HarperCollins, 2018.

Rozin, Elisabeth. "Ketchup and the Collective Unconscious." *Journal of Gastronomy* 4, no. 2 (1988): 45–55.

Skrabec, Quentin R., Jr. *H.J. Heinz. A Biography.* Jefferson, NC: McFarland, 2009.

Smith, Andrew F. "The Making of Robert Gibbon Johnson and the Tomato." *New Jersey History* 108 (1990): 59–74.

———. *Pure Ketchup: A History of America's National Condiment.* Columbia: University of South Carolina Press, 1996.

————. *Souper Tomatoes: The Story of America's Favorite Food*. New Brunswick, NJ: Rutgers University Press, 2000.

————. *The Tomato in America: Early History, Culture, and Cookery*. Columbia: University of South Carolina Press, 1994.

Whealy, Kent, and Arllys Adelmann, eds. *Seed Savers Exchange: The First Ten Years*. Decorah, IA: Seed Saver Publications, 1986.

ABOUT THE AUTHOR

William Alexander is a *New York Times* bestselling author and the writer of three critically acclaimed books, including *The $64 Tomato: How One Man Nearly Lost His Sanity, Spent a Fortune, and Endured an Existential Crisis in the Quest for the Perfect Garden*. He's been featured on NPR's *Morning Edition* and *Weekend Edition*, and has written for the *New York Times*, the *LA Times*, *Saveur*, and others.